Peter Bazalgette was Chair of A... 2013 to 201... He also chaired th... Foundation. He was educated at ... law at Fitzwilliam College, Cambridge, but escaped the law to spend most of his career working in television. He devised some of the biggest entertainment shows in recent TV history such as *Ready Steady Cook* and *Changing Rooms*, and brought *Big Brother* to the UK. He now chairs ITV. His previous books include *Billion Dollar Game* and *The Food Revolution* (co-authored). In 2011 he was knighted for services to broadcasting.

THE EMPATHY INSTINCT

How to Create a
More Civil Society

Peter Bazalgette

JOHN MURRAY

First published in Great Britain in 2017 by John Murray (Publishers)
An Hachette UK Company

First published in paperback in 2017

2

© Peter Bazalgette 2017

A CIP catalogue record for this title is
available from the British Library

ISBN 978-1-47363-753-5
Ebook ISBN 978-1-47363-752-8

Typeset in Plantin Light by Palimpsest Book Production Limited,
Falkirk, Stirlingshire

Printed and bound by Clays Ltd, St Ives plc

John Murray policy is to use papers that are natural, renewable and
recyclable products and made from wood grown in sustainable forests.
The logging and manufacturing processes are expected to conform to
the environmental regulations of the country of origin.

John Murray (Publishers)
Carmelite House
50 Victoria Embankment
London EC4Y 0DZ

www.johnmurray.co.uk

To the Nobel Prize winners, Paul Lauterbur and Peter Mansfield, whose work on Magnetic Resonance Imaging opened our minds to the empathy instinct.

CONTENTS

INTRODUCTION

In 1973, the journal *Nature* made history by publishing the first Magnetic Resonance image. It was of two tiny tubes filled with water. By the mid-1970s, scientists were racing to capture objects of greater and greater complexity. Esteemed journals were soon peppered with cross-sections of a mouse, a finger, a lemon, a wrist and, finally, a human head. By the 1980s images could be produced and viewed within a fraction of a second, rather than hours. Soon it was possible to go beyond mere organs and tissues to detect specific areas of activity in the brain, by looking at the blood flow within them. Functional Magnetic Resonance Imaging (fMRI) had been born.[1] In the 1990s, fMRI sparked a revolution in brain mapping. The technology has not only changed how we understand our bodies, it's also given us profound insights into the human mind. The mapping of our emotions using functional brain imaging, now well under way and revealing more every year, is leading to startling discoveries that are changing our understanding of human nature itself.

One of the extraordinary discoveries has been how we connect with each other. Empathy is a wonderful quality nearly all of us share. It relies on many different circuits in the brain to fire and interact. How well these function explains why we get on and why we don't. If we made more of our capacity for empathy we'd all be optimistic about the future. Now we can understand what happens when it malfunctions, in the case of, say, people with autism or psychopathic tendencies. Whereas we used to believe our brain's physical development ended with childhood, we now realise it continues growing in adulthood, repairing circuits that didn't previously work. And we can see that, at home, at work and at play, it's possible to enhance our interactions with others, to everyone's benefit. This is the empathy instinct.

But it's something I stumbled on entirely by accident. In 2014 I was asked by the then British Prime Minister to sit on a Holocaust Commission and consider how we might educate future generations about this after the last survivors, primary witnesses to what had happened, were no longer with us. I was then invited to chair a Foundation to implement the Commission's ideas about commemoration and education. I thought I knew about the Holocaust. But meeting the survivors and visiting the sites of the concentration camps in central Europe I came to realise how little I knew. I started to ask about how and why, for large sections of the population, mid-twentieth-century Germany became a society without empathy. I discovered historians who argue that the answers lie in their scholarly analysis of politics and economics. But I saw that this is not enough. We also need an anthropological understanding of this darkest period in Europe's past. And a study of the people reveals the fundamental importance of empathy to human society. It's the glue that binds us together in functioning and beneficial families, communities and countries.

In 2013 I became Chair of Arts Council England, the

body charged with investing public money into arts and culture. In an era of austerity, with government funding being cut, we set out to articulate the strongest possible case for arts monies being preserved. This is when we started talking about 'empathetic citizens'. The insight was that arts and culture, at their core a telling of stories about the human condition, rely on and feed our basic instinct for empathy. And as a television producer before that I had seen programmes, both drama and factual, have a profound influence on us when they connected with our emotions. I now realised that we had, without fully understanding it, been relying on empathy to power our entertainments. And that the popular arts were powering our empathy in return. I also discovered that I was by no means early or alone in considering this peculiar human capability. This is what President Barack Obama said in 2006:

> If we hope to meet the moral test of our times . . . then I think we're going to have to talk more about The Empathy Deficit. The ability to put ourselves in somebody else's shoes, to see the world through somebody else's eyes . . .[2]

For Obama empathy is the power to understand others, to enter imaginatively into their thoughts and feelings. It is a fundamental human attribute, without which mutually co-operative societies cannot function. But we're also, by nature, tribal. We're inclined to care for those in our group and act with hostility towards others outside it. And this is only one of the reasons for a deficit. As the world's population expands, consuming the planet's finite resources, as people haunted by poverty and war are on the move and as digital and transport infrastructures infinitely complicate our social interactions, we find our patience and our sympathy constantly challenged. Even modern societies with their tradition of state welfare discover that demand for these services is endless, while tax revenues are not.

We are just at the dawn of what will be the digital millennium. Its apostles point to the many advantages of this new era: instant contact, a cornucopia of information, new industries and economies. But with these blessings come darker things, challenges which we only dimly perceive and have not yet tackled. What is the limitless availability of loveless, hard-core porn on mobiles doing to the attitudes of thirteen-year-olds? Can we counter the radicalisation of solitary teenagers secluded in their bedrooms? How can we teach the vast social network of online scribblers and bloggers that their cyber-bullying wounds? Can we prevent politics and public discourse descending ever further into an angry, sometimes violent interchange? These are all new problems of empathy, to add to all the other human challenges that successful societies have always had to overcome. Why are we, by instinct, racist and how do we combat this? What are the solutions to cases of nurses and care workers who fail to look after their charges with decency? How do we turn serial offenders into good citizens and help them understand what they did to their victims? Can we nurture better parenting so that children understand what compassion is? Again, these are all issues of empathy, and how those who exercise it act as a result.

We have just emerged from the twentieth century which was dominated by three of the biggest monsters civilisation has ever been confronted with: Adolf Hitler, Mao Zedong and Joseph Stalin. Between them they killed more than a hundred million people. The novelist Julian Barnes muses on it in *A History of the World in 10½ Chapters*. He makes the distinction between tyrants and empathetic leaders:

> You can't love someone without imaginative sympathy, without beginning to see the world from another point of view. You can't be a good lover, a good artist or a good politician without this capacity . . . Show me the tyrants who have been great lovers.

Barnes uses the phrase 'imaginative sympathy' rather than 'empathy'. Many thinkers, in particular those writing before the turn of the twenty-first century, used 'sympathy' to mean what we now more commonly call 'empathy'. In this book I'll use 'sympathy' only in its sense of 'a feeling of compassion for the suffering of another'.[3] As for 'empathy', by that I mean something broader: 'the ability to understand and share in another person's feelings and experiences'.[4] Some psychologists add to this definition 'and respond in an appropriate way'. But, as we'll see, empathy does not *necessarily* lead to sympathy or compassionate action. So I'll try to consider them separately. Instinct, by the way, is defined as the way animals naturally behave, making complex and specific responses to outside stimuli – behaviour that's mediated by reactions below the conscious level.[5]

I'm not a scientist or a psychologist. My interest is in how what we've learnt about empathy in the past twenty-five years can be applied both at home and, more widely, as beneficial public policy. Evolutionary biologists and primatologists have worked out why we developed such a capacity of cooperation and they continue to yield profound insights from experiments with the likes of apes, dolphins and elephants. Neuroscientists, psychologists and geneticists now know which parts of the brain are specifically linked to empathy and compassion and are considering how we can enhance these abilities. Meanwhile arts and popular culture tell human stories, satisfying and honing our empathetic instinct.

As we'll discover, the word 'empathy' is much in use today but often without a precise understanding of what it is. Some distrust the idea. Some are even 'against empathy'. Although the detractors go too far, we should certainly not allow the idea to become some sort of lazy, unthinking cliché. Empathy on its own is not enough. How can it lead to compassionate action? How does it link to a code of ethics, a sense of fairness or reciprocity? We'll explore these ideas to show it really is possible to harness the positive power of empathy and improve our society. This book pulls together the latest thinking and new ideas, from scientists to social activists and from public servants to artists. It concludes with a Charter for Empathy where challenges such as religious conflict and racism, decent health and social care, effective and humane criminal justice and even artificial intelligence are addressed by this new thinking. It's a remarkably powerful idea when acted upon. We are already beginning to do just that. The empathy instinct is an idea whose time has come.

1

SOCIETIES WITHOUT
EMPATHY

Empathy is strongest in groups where people identify with
each other: family, friends, clubs, gangs, religions or races.
When empathy operates beyond those groups it's our most
civilising force. But, as a powerful bond within a tribe, it can
result in hostility towards outsiders and, at its most extreme,
it has engendered whole societies apparently without empathy.
As the primatologist Frans de Waal puts it:

> We've evolved to hate our enemies, to ignore people we
> barely know, and to distrust anybody who doesn't look like
> us. Even if we are largely cooperative within our communities,
> we become almost a different animal in our treatment of
> strangers.[1]

In the twentieth century, this negative aspect of a positive
instinct was exploited with dire consequences. I want to
explore what happened in 1930s Germany, in Armenia in
the early years of the century and in Rwanda towards the
end – three continents where a similar story played out and

empathy was largely abandoned, but where a few people showed they could still exercise the empathy instinct, even if it meant losing their lives.

THE NAZI HOLOCAUST

Ernst vom Rath was a German diplomat working at his country's embassy in Paris. On 7 November 1938 he was shot and fatally wounded by a young Jewish refugee protesting at his parents' expulsion from Hanover. In Berlin, Reinhard Heydrich, the ultimate head of the Gestapo, and other leading Nazis immediately unleashed a pogrom in which Jewish homes, businesses, schools, hospitals and synagogues were attacked, set on fire and destroyed. Heydrich sent a telegram to the Gestapo, the police and the fire departments permitting arson and destruction. The infamous event became known as 'Kristallnacht', the Night of Broken Glass. In addition to the hundred or more German Jews killed during forty-eight hours of extreme, state-endorsed violence, a much greater number were expelled from their jobs. Thirty thousand Jewish citizens were rounded up soon afterwards and sent to concentration camps, the first time they had been held in isolation, distinguished exclusively by ethnicity.

In January 1939 Adolf Hitler made a speech in the Reichstag in which he warned the powers of Europe that a war would mean 'the annihilation of German Jewry'. Fifteen years earlier he'd published *Mein Kampf* where, after quoting Schopenhauer approvingly about the Jew being 'the great master of lies', he wrote: 'the personification of the devil as the symbol of all evil assumes the living shape of the Jew'.[2]

And from 1933 onwards Joseph Goebbels had been using his Propaganda Ministry to control all media, in which he sowed extreme anti-Semitism. Jews were vermin, viruses, bloodsucking parasites, mongrels with poisonous blood. By this time the Nazis were also demonising the Roma people and homosexuals. But they reserved their most terrible ire for the Jews, who were simultaneously capitalists stealing the nation's wealth and Bolsheviks undermining capitalism. They were to blame for the Great Depression and the consequent poverty and unemployment of the Weimar Republic. At the 1935 Nazi Party Congress in Nuremberg Goebbels said: 'Bolshevism is the declaration of war by Jewish-led international sub-humans against culture itself.'

Here was a minority, seen as outsiders, excluded from a full role in society and thus active in commerce, who had been the subject of discrimination and previous pogroms. As we'll discover, these are common factors in nearly all genocides. But the political scientist Daniel Goldhagen makes an important distinction between the different emotions exploited in the pursuit of genocide. Groups are usually either dehumanised (made the target of moralised disgust), demonised (made the subject of moralised anger) or both.[3] In the Armenian massacre of 1915–17, the victims were labelled by the nationalists in government, the 'Young Turks', as disgusting vermin. By contrast, in the lead-up to the Srebrenica genocide of 1995, Bosnian Serbs had demonised Bosnian Muslims. In the wake of Yugoslavia's disintegration they wanted Muslims to be seen as political predators seeking control of Bosnia at the expense of other populations. They thus needed to be pre-emptively attacked. The Nazis left nothing to chance. They both demonised the Jews ('the personification of the devil') and dehumanised them ('bloodsuckers'). This, the most incendiary possible combination, was also the tactic of the Hutu leadership during the massacre of the Tutsis in Rwanda in 1994. The Harvard psychologist Steven Pinker argues that we are all susceptible to these categorisations: 'Eliminating the people [of a genocide] is enabled by nothing fancier in our psychology than the fact that human sympathy can be turned on or off depending on how another person is categorised.'[4] Heinrich Himmler, the head of the SS, wrote adoring letters to his wife, Marga, in which he matter-of-factly recorded that he was off to visit Auschwitz and rounded off with 'enjoy your days with our little daughter. Many warm greetings and kisses!'[5]

We'll look at the Armenian massacre shortly. But there were other critical differences between the Turks involved in it and the Nazis. The Turks had clear political as well as racial motivations, because their neighbours, the Russians, were using this minority as an excuse to invade. The German Jews were not allied to any foreign power in this way. The Nazis carefully developed a corrosive ideology over twenty years and promulgated it with modern media techniques. They then used the apparatus of the state in an attempt to wipe out an entire race across a whole continent and they invented a sophisticated bureaucracy and technology to prosecute it. These are the reasons why the Holocaust is unprecedented and different from other genocides, including the killings in Rwanda.

In November 1938, nine months before the outbreak of

war, the official SS newspaper, *Schwarze Korps*, referred to 'the actual and definitive end of Jewry in Germany, its total extermination'.[6]

The means by which this would be achieved was already in train. From July 1939 the T4 euthanasia programme was implemented in psychiatric institutions. Those deemed 'unfit for further existence' were either gassed or shot. By 1940, after the invasion of Poland, 5,000 patients a month were being murdered in the T4 units operating in both countries. And Jews in the occupied territories such as Poland, Czechoslovakia and the Ukraine were being rounded up and killed by SS divisions in arbitrary and opportunistic rampages. Then came the *Ermächtigung*, the infamous 'authorisation' by Marshal of the Reich Hermann Göring in July 1941:

> I hereby assign you [Reinhard Heydrich, head of the Gestapo and the SD] the task of making all the necessary organisational, practical and financial preparations in order to facilitate a total solution to the Jewish question in all the territories of Europe under German occupation.[7]

Nineteen-forty-one saw the establishment of ghettos into which Jews were herded, there to suffer unspeakable starvation and disease. Others were despatched to forced-labour camps. And in November the Germans built their first concentration camp specifically for the purpose of extermination. It was constructed at Bełżec near Lublin in Poland. Soon Auschwitz was also in operation, where the poison gas Zyklon B was in use from the beginning. This was a tipping point from appalling, widespread violence to state-sponsored extermination. As we know, with chilling simplicity the Nazis called it *Endlösung der Judenfrage*, or 'the Final Solution to the Jewish Question'.

On 20 January 1942, Heydrich called a meeting in a comfortable, bourgeois villa on the southern outskirts of Berlin. By now he was the Acting Protector of Bohemia/ Moravia, where he had been ruthlessly implementing the ghettos policy. This committee of Nazi bureaucrats, under Heydrich's chairmanship, coolly drew up a detailed plan for the mass extermination of Europe's Jewish population in concentration camps. It's now known as the Wannsee Conference and it formalised the Final Solution for Hermann Göring and Heinrich Himmler. In his book about the Second World War, *All Hell Let Loose*, Max Hastings records the terrible speed with which this plan was carried out. In mid-March 1942, almost three-quarters of those who perished in the Holocaust were still alive. Eleven months later, the same proportion were dead. When Heydrich was shot and killed in Prague a few months later, Himmler said in his eulogy: 'He was filled with an incorruptible sense of justice. Truthful and decent people could always rely on his chivalrous sentiment and humane understanding.'[8]

In 1933 Europe's Jews numbered nine million. By 1945 six million of them had died, some from disease and starvation but most murdered industrially by the Nazis and their collaborators. In all the territories the Nazis occupied lived citizens who enthusiastically took part in the attack on Europe's Jewry, or simply stood by. But there was a minority which showed a different side of human nature. We know of numerous acts of bravery in Germany itself, for which many lost their lives. We know about figures from elsewhere, such as Oskar Schindler and Nicholas Winton, who saved hundreds from the gas chambers. Consider the behaviour, though, of two Polish citizens among the few who did not collaborate or stand by. Anti-Semitism was as prevalent in Poland as it was in Germany. And in October 1941, the Nazis decreed that any Jew leaving the ghetto would be liable to the death penalty. They added that the same penalty applied to persons who sheltered such Jews. The fate of someone found hiding Jews was often also death at the hands of fellow Poles (even after the war had ended).

Josef Placzek was a builder near the village of Bobolice in southern Poland. He concealed Zissel Zborowski, her two sons and her daughter for twenty months in hiding places specially constructed in the attic and cellar. He would come in once a day to empty their chamber pots and give them any news. By doing this he was risking not only his life but those of his wife and daughter too. He had to feed this additional family of four, in times of great scarcity, throughout 1943 and up to August 1944. At that point a policeman tipped him off that rumours were spreading about his clandestine house guests. They moved on and so were not there when the house was searched a week later. The Zborowskis survived the war.[9]

Zofia Kossak had been a bestselling novelist before the war and the head of the Catholic Front for the Reborn Poland. If that sounds sinister, then you're right: she was a prominent anti-Semite who said the Jews were the enemies of Poland.

But she could not tolerate the savagery of the Nazis. In this battle for her soul, decency won out. She issued a public appeal in August 1942:

> The total number of Jews killed already exceeds a million, and the number enlarges with each passing day. Everyone dies. The wealthy and the impoverished, the elderly, women, men, youth, infants ... Who remains silent in the face of slaughter – becomes an enabler of the murderer. Who does not condemn – then consents.[10]

A month later Kossak set up Zegota, which is a Polish acronym standing for Council for Assistance to the Jews. Zegota would save thousands of Jewish children, spiriting them out of ghettos into orphanages, convents and private homes. Several of the members of Zegota were arrested, tortured and sent to Auschwitz, including Kossak herself. But, despite having both legs broken by her interrogators, she survived and never denounced her co-conspirators. The late historian Martin Gilbert paid tribute to all the individuals whose extraordinary bravery saved so many from the Holocaust. In his book *The Righteous*, he speculates on their motives:

> Dislike of Nazism and its racial doctrines; a refusal to succumb to them, a refusal to be bullied, even by superior force; an unwillingness to allow evil to triumph ... contempt for prejudice, a sense of decency: each played its part in making acts of rescue possible, even desirable.[11]

In the United Kingdom today survivors of the camps still tour schools to give their testimony to the next generation. They are mostly in their nineties now and many have already died. The former Prime Minister David Cameron set up a Commission in 2013 to recommend ways in which the Holocaust could be commemorated in the future, after the survivors are gone. The Commission, of which I was a member, recommended a new memorial in central London, renewed programmes of education and recording the testimony of these primary witnesses:

> In educating young people about the Holocaust, Britain reaffirms its commitment to stand up against prejudice and hatred in all its forms. The prize is empathetic citizens with tolerance for the beliefs and cultures of others. But eternal vigilance is needed to instil this in every generation.[12]

Among those nonagenarians bearing witness in 2016 for the first time was Sara Sonja Griffin, a Jewish toddler hidden in Haarlem during the Nazi occupation of the Netherlands. Her story includes a small act of mercy with a profound consequence. She survived the war and now has great-grandchildren:

> There was a time when we had been hiding in a house, where there were other Jewish people. There was a raid. I had been crying. People had been complaining that I was keeping them awake and so my mother had moved me into the loft space. They were all taken away. A German soldier came up the ladder and found me and my mother. She was trying to keep me quiet. He took me out of my mother's arms and shouted,

'All is clear up here!' He left me with my mother. I used to dream about him.[13]

———————————————— • • • ————————————————

Hitler, Stalin and Mao

In her family history *Wild Swans*, Jung Chang wrote the definitive account of destitution and persecution during Mao's Cultural Revolution from 1966 to 1976. When she was twelve my daughter read it. She asked *why* a 'great leader' would starve and torture his people. She couldn't comprehend the level of cruelty or see any possible logic to Mao's tyranny. When more than a hundred million were liquidated by the actions of Mao, Stalin and Hitler it does seem to make the question too vast, too terrible to answer satisfactorily.

But one answer is a psychological one: not only Mao, but also Hitler and Stalin, were classic psychopaths. As we'll see in Chapter 2, this meant they lacked crucial aspects of empathy. In his book *Zero Degrees of Empathy* (2011), the Cambridge psychologist Simon Baron-Cohen lists the signs indicating those with antisocial personality disorder, a proportion of whom are psychopaths:

- Failure to conform to social norms of lawfulness
- Deceitfulness
- Impulsivity or failure to plan ahead
- Irritability and aggression
- Reckless disregard for the safety of others or oneself
- Consistent irresponsibility
- Lack of remorse[14]

Had we the benefit of today's diagnostic tools, chiefly fMRI scanners, we might have seen some serious abnormalities in the three dictators' brain functions. Instead we rely on memoirs and historians. Mao's doctor and sole confidant described him as voracious for flattery, demanding of sexual servicing and devoid of warmth or compassion.[15]

In his monumental biography of Stalin, Simon Sebag Montefiore records how, during the inexplicable 'Great Terror', Stalin drove the massacre of thousands of innocent officials with chilling instructions. For instance, scrawling on a memo which survives, 'Shoot all 138 of them.'[16]

Hugh Trevor-Roper interviewed Hitler's architect, Albert Speer, in 1946, about how they had all been led to perdition by the Führer: 'he [Speer] could not withstand the mysterious intensity of those chill, glaucous eyes, the messianic egotism of that harsh, oracular voice'.[17]

Steven Pinker sums up these three men who plundered the twentieth century by observing they were ideologically driven and believed any means justified the end: 'Let these ingredients brew in the mind of a narcissist with a lack of empathy, a need for admiration, and fantasies of unlimited success, power, brilliance, and goodness, and the result can be a drive to implement a belief system that results in the deaths of millions.'[18]

●●●

THE ARMENIAN MASSACRE

Before the Holocaust there had been other mass racial murders (though they were not termed 'genocide' until 1944). In fact, human history is littered with the corpses of tribal exterminations.[19] Few were as terrible as that which befell the Armenian Christians of Anatolia in the early twentieth century. In February 1915, Dr Sakir, a member of the Ottoman Empire's Central Committee, returned to Istanbul from the Caucasus front where the Turks were fighting the Imperial Russian forces.[20] He reported the situation to two committee colleagues, Dr Nazim and Talaat Pasha, the Interior Minister. Sakir's particular concern was 'the enemy within' – the Christian Armenian population in Anatolia who were sympathetic to the Russians and, in some places, overtly supporting them. No paperwork exists to show what these three men concluded. We do know they gave orders for mass deportations of Armenians (enshrined in law by the Ottoman Council of Ministers in May 1915). Written deportation orders were sent to provincial governors and the task began almost immediately. Police with fixed bayonets drove families out of their houses. Muslims were then settled in vacated Armenian properties.

It's now widely accepted that these three 'Young Turks' also made the decision on that February day to go further and annihilate the Armenian population of two million. The Interior Ministry, carefully issuing oral orders only, instructed that the menfolk should be killed and the rest expelled. Armed gangs were recruited wherever those thuggish enough could be found, including from among convicted murderers in the prisons. Armenians were gassed, poisoned, crucified, burnt alive, as well as shot or starved. A district governor in Diyarbakır Province bravely asked for written confirmation of the mass-murder decree. He was recalled to Diyarbakır and assassinated en route.

In the city of Van, near the Russian front, 16,000 Muslims and 13,500 Armenians coexisted. The Armenians rose up to defend themselves and were shelled by the Turkish army, which set about massacring as many of them as it could. A Venezuelan mercenary serving the Ottomans later recalled the carnage. When he confronted an official and demanded the killing be stopped, he was told that the orders from the Governor of Van were to 'exterminate all Armenian males of twelve years of age and over'.

On the night of 23 April, back in the capital, the government arrested 240 of the leading Armenians. Only a few of these politicians, writers, clerics and teachers would survive. They joined a perilous forced march to desert settlements in Syria and Iraq, alongside those who'd not already been murdered in their towns and villages, that is, mostly the women and children. One of those arrested was a priest, Grigoris Balakian, who somehow managed to survive and who published his testimony after the war.[21] Armed gangs of bandits and local Kurdish villagers stripped them of their few remaining possessions. If they stopped walking they were shot, perhaps a more merciful fate than undergoing the multiple tortures of eye-gouging, genital mutilation and disembowelling along the way. Manuel Lerkyasharian was a nine-year-old boy accompanying his mother. Her feet swelled so much that she could not go on. She persuaded a relative to cast her into the Euphrates, which she preferred to the torture she'd otherwise receive from the Ottoman soldiers. Manuel witnessed his mother being carried off by the current. It is said that in places the Euphrates changed course, impeded by the weight of corpses.

By the autumn of 1915 word of this catastrophe was spreading far and wide. That year the *New York Times* published a total of 145 articles about the Armenian massacres. From then until the end of the war the newspaper regularly used phrases like 'organized by government' and 'systematic race extermination'.[22] But despite being reported contemporaneously, and notwithstanding the accounts published later, it is still known as the 'forgotten genocide'. In 2016 it remains a crime in Turkey to refer to the episode as 'genocide'. The Turkish government still argues that what happened was legitimate action against the state's enemies. Even in Britain today, in the niceties of Foreign Office argot, our diplomats are not permitted to use the 'g-word'. But the cold fact is that by 1922 only about 400,000 Armenians remained in the Ottoman Empire. Between 600,000 and 1.5 million had been expunged, with the most likely figure for the number of victims exceeding one million. Mass, state-sponsored killings do not occur spontaneously, without cause. What were the roots of the Armenian genocide?

The Armenians were Christians whose homelands had been absorbed into the Muslim Ottoman Empire in the fifteenth century. They were never given the same political and legal status as the Muslims and so concentrated on commerce, with many becoming wealthy merchants. They agitated for equality and, in the 1870s, were used as a pretext by Russia to annex Ottoman territory, for the Armenians' 'protection'. There had been bitter pogroms in the mid-1890s in which hundreds of thousands of Armenians died at the hands of the Turks. So they were outsiders, a minority, seen to be wealthy, the subject of discrimination and persecution in the past – this familiar pattern would, of course, give rise to further terrible events in the twentieth century. Whole communities switched off their empathy to do cruel things to their fellow citizens. Of those Turks who did experience a sense of empathy for the plight of the Armenians, most did nothing as a result. However, a few did act – no society was completely without compassion.

Mehmed Jelal was the distinguished Governor-General of Aleppo. He'd previously headed the empire's civil service college and three other provinces. He knew and respected many Armenians and regarded them as friends and not enemies. In 1915 he received the same orders to begin the persecution. At considerable personal risk he replied, 'Each human has the right to live.' In June 1915 he was removed by the government and sent in disgrace to another, less critical province, Konya. From there he wrote to the Central Committee, trying a more pragmatic argument:

The Armenian race constitutes a significant part of our country's population. Armenians hold a significant part of the general wealth and they run half the country's commercial activities. Trying to destroy them will cause damage to the country. If all our enemies sat down and thought for a month, they couldn't find a more damaging thing for us.[23]

He received no reply, so he went to Istanbul. There he thought he'd secured an agreement to stop deporting Armenians living in Konya. But on his return he found thousands more had been rounded up and assembled at the railway station to begin the exodus to Syria. He sent them back to their homes. A multitude came through the railhead from other regions on their way to exile. This he could not stop, but he managed to provide some refugee funding so as to alleviate their suffering. The local Armenians were never deported and he even managed to rescue and settle locally another 30,000 passing through. But he couldn't prevent this massive, state exercise in what we now call ethnic cleansing:

> In Konya, I was like a person sitting by the side of a river, with absolutely no way to save anyone. Blood was flowing in the river and thousands of innocent children, blameless old people, helpless women, and strong young men were carried down this river toward oblivion. Anyone I could save with my bare hands, I saved; the others, I suppose, were carried down the river, never to return.[24]

What does it take to stand up, almost alone, against the state? Why did Mehmed Jelal have such compassionate instincts for a different race and such a keen sense of justice? Where did his altruism spring from, how did he bring himself to recognise the suffering of the Armenians? Was it by imagining how *they* felt about the destruction of their lives? He demonstrated the power of empathy all the more vividly by acting at a moment when his fellow Turks had switched their own empathy instinct off.

Altruism

The debate about whether there's any such thing as a truly selfless act is ancient. In 1975 the psychologist Dennis Krebs took an important and somewhat diabolical step forward in the debate by constructing a special game of roulette. Players received money on even numbers and an electric shock on the odd squares. In fact, the apparatus was not electrified; the players merely acted as if they had been shocked. Krebs' focus was on the students he'd invited to watch the spectacle. He told some of them that the player they were watching was a fellow student with a similar personality, and others that he or she was an outsider with a different personality. Only when the spectators saw fellow students get shocked did their hearts pound and their sweat break out. They were even willing to suffer a shock themselves to save their co-students. This they would not do for the others. On the basis of his experiment, Krebs put forward the *empathy–altruism hypothesis*: that empathy induces altruism.

But it was still possible that the spectators had taken the shock for their fellows because it was a price worth paying for avoiding the even greater distress of watching the shock. Did their behaviour only *resemble* altruism? That's where Daniel Batson came in. In the 1980s he conducted similar experiments to Krebs'. The key difference was that some of the spectators had the option of leaving the building halfway through. Batson reasoned that if they did this it would prove that their primary motivation was to avoid distress. It turned out that when the spectators believed they had things in common with the person getting shocked, they were still willing to get shocked in their place. This was in keeping with the empathy–altruism hypothesis.[25]

Batson also recognises the importance of *moral motivation*, where we act in accordance with a fair and reasoned principle.[26] This allows those who do not identify with others also to show empathy, overriding their natural bias and promoting altruistic behaviour towards individuals and groups with whom they don't have much in common.

The psychiatrist Iain McGilchrist sees altruism as a 'necessary consequence of empathy' and a positive force which comes from more than mere reciprocation, a concern for one's friends and family or a desire for good reputation: 'It is mutuality not reciprocity, fellow feeling not calculation, which is both the motive and the reward for successful co-operation. And the outcome, in utilitarian terms, is not the important point: it is the process, the relationship, that matters.'[27]

He notes that the exercise of this 'mutuality' lights up parts of our brain associated with pleasure. Altruism may have its evolutionary roots in beneficially cooperative behaviour within a tribe. But, unmoored from this, the genuinely selfless act exists.

Pearl and Samuel Oliner conducted a landmark study of altruism in the 1980s. They investigated Germans who had helped rescue Jews during the Second World War. One of the strongest predictors of their heroic behaviour was having memories of growing up in a family that valued compassion. They concluded that children with parents who are compassionate tend to be more altruistic.[28]

— • • • —

THE RWANDAN GENOCIDE

In July 1993 a new radio station crackled into life in Rwanda. With its charismatic disc jockeys, Radio Télévision Libre des Mille Collines (RTLMC) attracted a devoted young audience. Amid the cool, contemporary music tracks they frequently heard other apparently mysterious messages: 'cut down the tall trees . . . clear the bush . . . finish the work'.[29] But everyone understood these sinister metaphors. The 'tall trees' were the minority Tutsis, generally greater in height than the majority Hutus. The population of this Central/Eastern African country was being treated to sustained and insidious incitement to kill the Tutsis (mark Goebbels' words in 1933: 'It would not have been possible for us to take power or to use it in the ways we have without the radio . . .').[30]

On 6 April 1994 the Rwandan President, a Hutu called Juvénal Habyarimana, died when his private aeroplane was shot down. It's never been established whether this was the work of Hutu militia or rebel Tutsis. But it proved to be the spark that ignited the volatile country. A small cabal of Hutus unleashed a terrible genocide. The inner circle included Habyarimana's wife Agathe and another Tutsi hater, Théonaste Bagosora. This murderous conspiracy was known as Akazu, or 'little house'.

The following day the moderate Prime Minister, who might have saved the fragile peace in the country, was hunted down and murdered. The army and paramilitaries set up roadblocks in the capital, Kigali, and other towns and a frenzied murder spree began – of Tutsis, of the other minority group, the Twa, and of any Hutus who got in the way. Before long RTLMC became more explicit: 'And you people . . . go out. You will see the [Tutsi rebels'] straw huts in the marsh . . . I think that those who have guns should immediately go to these [rebels], encircle them and kill them.'[31]

The extreme racism of the radio station helped attract violent recruits to paramilitaries like the Interahamwe – gangs of young men who then killed with their weapon of choice, the machete. For ninety days a Tutsi was murdered every ten seconds. So widespread and so intense was the pogrom that doctors killed their patients and pastors killed their flocks. Tutsi parishioners of the Seventh-Day Adventist Church in Mugonero wrote a letter to their pastor lamenting that they expected to be killed the following day. He swiftly replied that God had abandoned them and they should prepare to die. Before the end of the catastrophe 75 per cent of the Tutsis living in Rwanda were dead. It's probable that three-quarters of a million perished.

The Rwandan genocide conformed to several of the norms for these tragedies. The Tutsis were seen as richer and more successful than the Hutus. They amounted to a little over 10 per cent of the population. In colonial times, after the First World War, the Belgians had originally dubbed as Tutsis the taller, richer citizens who owned herds of cattle, and they claimed an ethnically superior, Ethiopian origin for them. After the Second World War the Hutu majority was increasingly seen as downtrodden at the expense of the Tutsi elite. As independence approached in 1962 the Belgians turned a blind eye to a number of pogroms carried out against the Tutsis by the Hutus. After independence, serial tribal violence continued. This resulted in one million

Tutsis going into exile in neighbouring countries. It was in Uganda that they developed the largest Tutsi rebel army, the Rwandan Patriotic Front (RPF). These troops invaded Rwanda in 1990, only to be driven back out. Earlier, in the 1950s, Tutsi loyalist rebels had referred to themselves as *inyenzi*, cockroaches (tough and able to creep out unexpectedly from anywhere). Thus they helped write the racist propaganda which would be used against their kind, along with other epithets we are familiar with: dirty, dishonest, traitorous, dangerous. A peace treaty in 1992 was only a sticking plaster over a running sore.

In the mayhem unleashed by the Akazu, the RPF took the opportunity to invade again. With political ambition they swept rapidly towards the capital. The RPF had little difficulty with the Hutu army, preoccupied as it was with genocide. They took Kigali on 4 July 1994. The genocide was then over, but the wells were poisoned with corpses and 100,000 households had children with no adults. There was a mental-health crisis among the survivors. And the arduous task of trying to reintegrate the two communities, while prosecuting the war criminals, had to begin. (For the story of how the radio then reversed into a medium for empathy, see Chapter 8.)

The active participation of doctors and priests is, perhaps, the single most shocking detail in a series of ghastly events. But, once again, there were Hutus whose empathy stretched beyond their own tribe. Baudouin Busunyu was an assistant priest whose superior backed the genocide and whose own father was a leader of the Interahamwe. He worked secretly with a network of other pastors, smuggling Tutsis across the border into the Democratic Republic of the Congo (DRC). He was harassed and beaten up but kept the operation going to the end of the genocide. He ended up in a Hutu refugee camp in the DRC and was murdered in 1997, probably by the Interahamwe, who controlled the camps.

Gabriel Mvunganyi was an elderly man living on the outskirts of Kigali. He was religious and a longstanding opponent of ethnic discrimination. He helped several Tutsis to evade capture. His house was frequently searched. Even during this time he successfully hid two Tutsi girls. But in May 1994, while he was out with his daughter, he was spotted and apprehended. He was physically humiliated and then shot.

Sula Karuhimbi was a widowed farmer and healer living in the Ntongwe commune in Gitarama. She hid Tutsis on her farm in agricultural buildings, feeding them with her own produce. Trigger-happy militias attempted to search her property on several occasions, but she rebuffed them, suggesting that she could command evil spirits to harm them. It's thought she saved seventeen Tutsis in all, and she survived the conflict.

In Rwanda today there's a genocide memorial day on 7 July, followed by a week's mourning. There are laws which prohibit discrimination on the basis of ethnicity, race or religion. It's important for a country's national days and laws to assert its community's values. But to tackle such deep-seated, visceral sentiments we all need to understand how fundamental tribalism is to our culture and psyche.

EMPATHY, TRIBALISM AND GROUP-THINK

I once disappointed (and possibly outraged) a very idealistic
Swede who had come to London to investigate how arts and
cultural projects can form a bridge between communities. I
told him that we're tribal by nature and that, left to our own
devices and prejudices, we instinctively prefer our own kind.
Why do we have such careful criteria and protocols for
professional job interviews? To correct this unconscious bias.
My view is that we should openly accept this trait, the better
to tackle it. In other words, admitting we're racist is the best
way to do something about it. My guest was adamant: our
natural state is one of being colour-blind, gender-blind, deaf
to different accents and so on. For him our anti-social behaviour was solely down to our upbringing and the societies
which nurture us. I countered by asking where these ungen-
erous, unempathetic traits came from in the first place. He
was not impressed. But I'm not budging: we *are* by nature
tribal. For the primatologist Frans de Waal, this has its origin
in necessity:

> As is true for many mammals, every human life cycle includes
> stages at which we either depend on others (when we are
> young, old or sick) or others depend on us (when we care
> for the young, old or sick). We very much rely on one another
> for survival.[32]

De Waal points to Charles Darwin, in *The Descent of Man*,
seeing this gregariousness as the origin of morality: 'Any
animal whatever, endowed with well-marked social instincts

. . . would inevitably acquire a moral sense or conscience, as soon as its intellectual powers had become as well developed, or nearly as well developed, as in man.'[33]

We may buy Darwin's argument as it relates to the promotion of empathetic behaviour towards those in our group – family, friend, co-religionist, work colleague, football fan of the same team or fellow countryman. But we should side with the philosopher John Stuart Mill when it comes to how we feel about others. In 1875, he wrote of 'sympathetic selfishness': '[sympathetic characters] may be very amiable and delightful to those with whom they sympathise, and grossly unjust and unfeeling to the rest of the world'.[34]

Jean Decety, a Chicago professor of psychology, has recently surveyed these in-group/out-group attitudes, assisted by the insights afforded by fMRI. His work owes much to that of Dennis Krebs before him. He based his 2015 paper 'Empathy, Justice, and Moral Behavior' on analysis of our brain activity when confronted with other people in distress:

> The neural response elicited by the perception of others in distress is either strengthened or weakened by interpersonal relationships, implicit attitudes and group preferences . . . notably . . . the response . . . to viewing others in pain decreased remarkably when participants viewed faces of racial out-group members relative to in-group members . . . Another study demonstrated that the failures of an in-group member are painful, whereas those of a rival out-group member give pleasure – a feeling that may motivate harming rivals.[35]

In a 2010 study, Decety asked participants in an MRI scanner to watch animations of hands and feet in painful contortions.[36] When the spectators imagined that the bodies belonged to loved ones, they reported more intense pain than when they imagined they were watching strangers. And the fMRI scans demonstrated this at the neural level.

It would appear that this prejudice in favour of our own kind is something baked into us. Martha Nussbaum is a professor of law and ethics, interested in the power of love and empathy in overcoming our baser instincts. She points to the findings of a psychologist who studies infants: 'Babies, like nonhuman animals, are biased toward their own kind. They prefer the faces of a racial type that is most familiar to those of unfamiliar races; they prefer speakers of their language to speakers of a foreign language.'[37]

And we take these preferences into our adult life: we unconsciously favour those with the same colour skin, those speaking the same language, even folk with the same accent. This is the raw material so skilfully manipulated by the Young Turks, the Nazis and the Hutu militias. Add a foe (external if you like, but internal is even more threatening), a sense of injustice and, if possible, alienation or full-blown disgust, and you have the conditions for genocide. Mass killings require this sort of general complicity by the population. The inspiration of the European Union after the Second World War (whatever we may feel about it today) was to obviate such conflict. Many of the nations in the EU – Holland, Denmark, Belgium – no longer sabre-rattle at their own citizens or seek dominion over other parts of the world.

But race is only one example of so-called *social dominance*

– that is, behaving in a tribal way. And we slip into and out of some of these groups very easily. A game of playground football is intense in its passion and comradeship but may be forgotten in minutes. The famous Stanford Prison Experiment (see below), in which 'guards' so mistreated 'prisoners' that the experiment had to be stopped early, showed how quickly we identify with 'our side'. And it can change quickly too. We shout and jeer with passion at the fans of another football club during a local derby. The following weekend we're united in loyalty as we support our national side. There's a famous ABC documentary from 1970 in which a class teacher takes no more than fifteen minutes to persuade her ten-year-olds to discriminate against those with brown eyes, through her propaganda that blue-eyed pupils are an obviously superior breed. The economist and philosopher Amartya Sen personally experienced the flexibility of our allegiances:

> Within-group solidarity can help to feed between-group discord. We may suddenly be informed that we are not just Rwandans but specifically Hutus ('we hate Tutsis'), or that we are not really mere Yugoslavs but actually Serbs ('we absolutely don't like Muslims'). From my own childhood memory of Hindu–Muslim riots in the 1940s, linked with the politics of partition, I recollect the speed with which the broad human beings of January were suddenly transformed into the ruthless Hindus and fierce Muslims of July.[38]

But Sen is a qualified optimist about our potential as humans. He argues that everybody belongs to multiple groups – based on citizenship, residence, gender, class, politics, profession, employment, food tastes, sports interests, music predilections – and that it's only over-narrow thinking about the choices we have that leads to violence. We can choose to adopt broader, more empathetic outlooks.

— • • • —

The Stanford Prison Experiment

Here's a university study that's often quoted, but what actually happened and how valid was it? In the summer of 1971 a small ad appeared in a local newspaper in Palo Alto, California: 'Male college students required for psychological study of prison life'. It was placed by Dr Philip Lombardo of nearby Stanford University. He wanted to conduct a two-week prisoners-and-warders experiment. Around a hundred students applied and, after those with criminal records, mental illness or histories of drug abuse had been eliminated, twenty-four were selected to take part with the promise of fifteen dollars a day. On the flip of a coin, twelve became 'warders' and twelve became 'prisoners'.

Lombardo kitted out 'cells' and established a pretty harsh regime for the prisoners from the start, including their being stripped, 'deloused' and then dressed in identical smocks with ID numbers rather than names. The guards, also in uniforms, were given dark glasses 'to prevent anyone from seeing their eyes or reading their emotions', as Lombardo put it. They soon split into two opposing groups with the prisoners resenting the regime and the guards allowed to create their own rules and methods for keeping order. These turned out to include projecting the fire extinguishers at the inmates, demanding punishment exercises such as push-ups, denial of proper toilet facilities and imposing solitary confinement. Several prisoners had to be released after emotional crises and one even went on hunger strike. After six days Lombardo felt obliged to call the experiment off, because of the extremes that the students were all experiencing.

In the years since then Lombardo has used the experiment to suggest how easily humans can slip into group-led anti-social behaviour and has lectured on prison reform. Critics of the experiment say Lombardo over-influenced the events by the way he set up the project and briefed the warders. Others have pointed to the way the participants self-selected themselves via the newspaper advertisement. A study in 2007 placed two similar small ads, one which mentioned 'prison' and one which didn't.[39] They found that those who applied to the former had on average higher levels of aggressiveness and narcissism, and lower levels of empathy and altruism. Perhaps another lesson of the Stanford Prison Experiment, then, is whether we should assess our prisoners and warders for emotional intellience.

— • • • —

There's plenty of evidence, from Stanford and elsewhere, that having made a choice and joined a group, we like to conform. First a benign example of this: American sociologists arranged an uncomfortably revealing wine tasting in which four wine samples were all from the same bottle, but one had been spiked with vinegar. They then included some stooges at the tasting who purported to be experts and extolled the refinement and general excellence of the spiked wine. Other members of the group went along with this, even though the sample was mouth-puckeringly sour. Later another stooge broke out of the consensus and declared that the vinegary sample sucked. At this point many of the tasters were prepared to acknowledge how disgusting it was in their private notes, but not in front of everyone else. In the public situation they were inclined to condemn this minority view. They felt most comfortable with the group-think, however far removed it was from their private perception.[40]

Now the malign example. The historian Christopher Browning investigated Reserve Police Battalion 101 – a unit of mostly middle-aged men from Hamburg which killed 40,000 Jews during the Holocaust. Their experience was well documented partly because many of them were put on trial in the 1960s and 1970s. In the summer of 1942 they were serving in Poland. They did not have the means to transport Jews to the camps and so were ordered to shoot them. Their battalion leader gave them a speech explaining that shooting women and children was justified not only because 'the Jews had brought the Americans into the war' but also because Allied bombing raids were killing German families in their own cities. The 500 members of the battalion were then asked if they wanted to be excused. Only twelve stepped down. The rest became willing executioners (it's been pointed out that there's not a single, documented case of any serious disciplinary consequences for German soldiers in the war who declined to murder civilians). As Browning puts it: 'These were not desk murderers who could take refuge in distance, routine and bureaucratic euphemisms that veiled the reality of mass murder. These men saw their victims face to face.'[41]

So why did they do it? They spoke of their initial physical revulsion at the gore, the screams, the raw feeling of killing at close quarters. But they soon rationalised it. They talked of not wanting to look like cowards, of believing it made no difference whether they participated or not because the Jews would die anyway. In this way they became increasingly efficient and callous. Steven Pinker uses this and other episodes to put a gloss on what empathy is and is not:

> People often feel distress at witnessing the suffering of another person . . . This is the reaction . . . that made the Nazi reservists nauseous when they first started shooting Jews at close range. As [this example makes] all too clear, distress at another's suffering is not the same as sympathetic concern with their well-being. Instead it can be an unwanted reaction which people may suppress, or an annoyance they may try to escape.[42]

How easy is it to get people to feel empathy and even compassion for those outside their own circle? It can be done and is, indeed, a key element of conflict resolution and restorative justice, as we'll see. Daniel Batson doesn't believe we can feel empathy for abstract concepts, like the world, the poor or the environment. But he argues it is possible to induce empathy for individuals, for members of out-groups, and in the process improve attitudes to the group as a whole. Jean Decety points to those individuals who helped the Jews during the Holocaust:

Involvement in rescue activity frequently began with concern for a specific individual or individuals for whom compassion was felt – often individuals known previously. This initial involvement subsequently led to further contact and rescue activity, and to a concern for justice that extended well beyond the bounds of the initial empathetic concern.[43]

Decety also tells the story of the Sinhalese and Tamils who took part in a four-day peace workshop in 2001, after years of civil war in Sri Lanka. A year later the Sinhalese continued to feel enhanced empathy and pro-social behaviour towards the Tamils, as did the Tamils towards the Sinhalese (see Chapter 7).

After the Second World War and the Nuremberg Trials the international crime of genocide was enshrined in a special UN Convention of 1948: 'to destroy, in whole or in part, a national, ethnical, racial or religious group'.

It's clearly beneficial to set down values which the world subscribes to and which might act as a deterrent. (The International Criminal Court in The Hague has tried, for instance, mass murderers from the conflict in former Yugoslavia.) But preventing conflict is even better than resolving it.

BAD DEEDS ARE NOW EXPLICABLE

How often have I heard a cleric intone from the pulpit about some murder or other man-made calamity, 'It was pure evil.' Today this seems rather an unthinking cliché. It comes from centuries of trying and failing to explain why we're capable of terrible deeds. Ideas like the devil come from the same place. You may have noticed that the word 'evil' has not appeared until now in this chapter. That's because using it in relation to the genocides of the twentieth century is not only lazy, it's also a counsel of despair. It suggests there is something inexplicable, about which we can do nothing. That won't do because science is now unlocking both the origins of our behaviour – good and bad – and the functions in our brain. We can begin to see why some criminal psychopaths do what they do.

Another response, which belies such hopeless over-simplification, is to recognise that the empathy instinct is an extraordinary force for good, if understood and then shrewdly deployed. Emile Bruneau is an American neuroscientist we'll meet later. He studies groups in conflict, such as the Israelis and Palestinians and the Roma gypsies and the 'white' Hungarians. He says that neuroscience has begun to identify the brain regions involved in empathising, but that it's early days:

> We still need to map a host of other empathy-related tasks – like judging the reasonableness of people's arguments and sympathising with their mental and emotional states – to specific brain regions. And then we need to figure out how these neural flashes translate into actual behaviour: Why does understanding what someone else feels not always translate to being concerned for their welfare? Why is empathising across groups so much more difficult?[44]

That's a perfect cue to look at what we do already know about the science of empathy. While religions have tended to fall back on 'evil', 'the devil' and 'original sin', we can do better. We're now unlocking our dark side, as well as our capacity for doing good.

2

THE SCIENCE OF
EMPATHY

There's been a revolution in our understanding of empathy in the last quarter-century, with scientific inquiry into this instinct gathering pace rapidly. In 1992, an Italian neuroscientist reported the discovery of 'mirror neurons' in the brains of macaque monkeys. These were areas which activated not only when a monkey reached for a raisin but also when it saw someone else, a human researcher, do so. Could this act of imagination be the source, or part of the source, of empathy? Inspired by these new discoveries an American neuroscientist, in 1994, published a book entitled *Descartes' Error*. He argued that the classic Cartesian idea of dualism, the separation of mind and body, was now dead. Could it be that the mind and body were one and the same thing?

In 1994 and 1996 a Dutch primatologist published pioneering books on chimpanzees. He observed in these colonies not only mimicry but signs of empathy and even apparent selflessness among primates, leading to the suggestion that the origins of 'humane' behaviour might actually predate the human species itself.

In 1994 an American psychologist made the first attempt at measuring emotional intelligence, now known as EQ. In addition, he published a radical study of identical twins which indicated that empathy, or a lack of it, can be inherited. In other words, here was evidence that genes play a part. Meanwhile, in the same year, a British psychologist used an fMRI scanner to identify a part of the brain which enables us to employ empathy; he would later draw together this and other regions into a map which he called the 'empathy circuit'. He now calls empathy 'the most valuable resource in our world'.[1]

This chapter explores the work of these pioneers and examines how rapidly it has developed over the past two decades. Evolutionary biologists, psychologists and neuroscientists in many countries are crystallising empathy – its origins, how it works and what happens when it fails.

--- • • • ---

Boys and Girls

Men and women have many more similarities than differences. But the empathy instinct is one distinction. In general, women are better at it. It's apparent even in babies. One of the early signs of emotional contagion, the first stirrings of empathy, is when a baby cries at the sound of another infant wailing. Typically, girls start doing this before boys.[2] Even in adulthood, a 2016 Italian study showed, women are a third more likely to yawn when they see someone else yawn – another well-known act of emotional contagion.[3] However, it appears that the older we get the more our levels of emotional intelligence converge, so the differences are starker in early life.[4]

In 2003 the psychologist Simon Baron-Cohen published *The Essential Difference: Men, Women and the Extreme Male Brain*. He argued that men are better at systematising ('Type S') and women are better at empathising ('Type E'). But he accepts that this is a generalisation because there are plenty of men who are more Type E and there are, of course, women who are more Type S.

Baron-Cohen says he was ready to write his book in the 1990s but felt that, if he had, the reaction might have been too hostile to the gender differences he had found. He and his team in Cambridge have carried out many experiments with children and adults, often using the latest brain-scanning technology, so they can track how we function in different situations. Here are some of his conclusions:

- One-day-old girls look at faces more than one-day-old boys
- Girls play less roughly and less self-centredly than boys
- Twelve-month-old girls show comforting behaviour to people who show distress, some time before boys do
- At the age of three girls perceive and understand the emotions of others better than boys are able to
- Women are better at judging emotions from facial expressions
- Women often value altruistic, reciprocal relationships, men tend to value power, politics and competition
- Men tend to show more physical aggression, women favour more indirect aggression such as verbal snipes (which requires better mind-reading skills).

I spoke to two women who both sit on the boards of FTSE 100 companies. Among their remarks were these: 'Gender balance on boards is critical . . . women are more collaborative . . . if you're low in ego men don't think you have a point of view . . . women are more likely to articulate the emotion in the room, which promotes more honesty . . . we let the air out of the male balloon . . . male drive and self-belief has a value so I prefer a gender mix'.

Both our political system and our judicial system are aggressively adversarial and they were designed by men. How different would they be had they been set up by women? Currently there are fewer women leading FTSE 100 companies than men in such positions called John.[5] How much more creative and dynamic would workplaces be if more women led them?

— • • • —

WHAT ANIMALS CAN TEACH US ABOUT OURSELVES

There was no sudden epiphany in the 1990s of course, with scientists in white coats emerging from labs shouting, 'We've discovered empathy, and it works!' For centuries, philosophers and scientists alike had been fascinated by our ability to function in societies, anticipating each other's needs. Charles Darwin, as ever, did some exciting original thinking about this, long before such ideas could be proved. He was intrigued by our propensity to place ourselves in other people's shoes: 'From the power of the imagination and of sympathy we put ourselves in the position of the sufferer.'[6] Darwin went on to argue that our sense of morality and altruism stems from this ability to sympathise and the need for it in functioning societies: 'The so-called moral sense is aboriginally derived from the social instincts, for both relate at first exclusively to the community.'[7]

Given these sentiments it might seem surprising that that great champion of Charles Darwin, Richard Dawkins, called his bestseller *The Selfish Gene*. Indeed, it was perhaps a regrettable title because it has led to a misunderstanding. Dawkins was arguing that genes seek the best chance of being replicated. They are, in that sense, selfish. But he was not actually suggesting that genes have emotions or psychological characteristics. Contrast that with people, sentient beings, who can certainly behave selfishly but are also programmed to be social animals. As Matt Ridley puts it, in *The Origins of Virtue*: 'Our minds have been built by selfish genes, but they have been built to be social, trustworthy and cooperative.'[8]

Darwin saw the origins of this instinct in animal behaviour, for instance observing how his family's pet dog licked their sick cat in sympathy every time it passed the cat's basket.[9] Some of the necessary elements of empathy began to emerge in the twentieth century in experiments with monkeys and apes, our nearest animal relations according to Darwin's theory of evolution (accepted by all but a few candidates for the Republican presidential nomination). A German psychologist in the 1920s showed how one monkey, seeing another climb to the top of a construction to retrieve a banana, would mimic its movements.[10] (This was an early pointer to mirror neurons and no surprise if you've ever, for instance, watched a coach shadow-boxing their fighter's bout from beside the ring.) Then in the early 1960s experiments at two American universities took the story further. One trained monkeys to press a lever to avoid receiving a mild electric shock. They then demonstrated how monkeys would also press the lever to prevent another monkey receiving a shock. This was a breakthrough which was taken further a couple of years later when it was discovered that the majority of monkeys would even refuse a food reward to press the lever if it meant preventing another monkey getting shocked.[11] Mimicry, sympathy, altruism: this begins to give us a breakdown of where empathy comes from and what it can lead to.

One of the world's leading primatologists, Frans de Waal, has now analysed and pulled together an anatomy of empathy based on his many years of observing monkeys and apes. His book is entitled *The Age of Empathy: Nature's Lessons for a Kinder Society*. First there is mimicry, which de Waal says not only allows us to identify with others, but strengthens the bond between us thereafter. He witnessed one of his chimpanzees, Mai, preparing to give birth by cupping her hand between her legs to catch the baby when it emerged. Another, older female, Atlanta, stood beside her with her hand cupped between her own legs, where it was redundant. She'd given birth in the past and was synchronising her behaviour based on that experience.[12] He then recalls how, when a mature male chimpanzee injured his fingers and leant on a bent wrist to walk, all the young males started to walk the same way.[13] De Waal also cites an American zoologist who saw a mother elephant perform a 'subtle trunk-and-foot dance', on the spot, as she watched her son chasing away a wildebeest.[14] This synchrony is reflected in mothers who clap with their toddlers and lovers who walk arm in arm: 'When I see synchrony and mimicry – whether it concerns yawning, laughing, dancing, or aping – I see social connection and bonding. I see an old herd instinct that has been taken up a notch.'[15]

Chimps, like humans, yawn when they see other chimps yawn, even if they're on videotape. And they laugh when other chimps chuckle. Why should that surprise us, when we invite live audiences to television comedies in order to make viewers laugh at home as well? This denotes a full-hearted sharing of the joke. Perhaps the most basic form of empathy is emotional contagion. A widely quoted example is how a baby will cry when it hears another baby bawling. It has been affected and prompted by the sound but has no sympathy, as such, for the other infant (as we said, girls are more prone to this than boys). It's essentially a self-centred response and is reflected across many species of mammal. Elephants affected by an alarmed or injured herd member will stretch their tails, flap their ears and, in more extreme cases, urinate or defecate.[16]

Chimps and humans both react to body language, tone of voice and facial expressions. It's fundamental to empathy that we have the ability to read these signals (later in this chapter we'll see what happens when people don't have it). And we need a sense of self, something I first realised at an early age when my elder brother had a book about dinosaurs which labelled them, in not terribly academic prose, 'so stupid that they were barely aware of their own existence'. It was the

American psychologist Gordon Gallup who first showed that apes, but not monkeys, were able to recognise themselves in mirrors. The classic test is to place a bit of rouge on their forehead and see if they react to it. De Waal wanted to see if elephants, another highly developed species, could pass the mirror test too. But it took some preparation since a standard looking glass would hardly measure up to the task. He rigged up a giant reflector at the Bronx Zoo in New York and, sure enough, the majority of the elephants marked with a white cross above their eyes were extremely curious about how they'd been gilded. Dolphins also pass the mirror test, as do most children by the age of two:

> What makes mirror tests exciting is what they tell us about how an individual positions itself in the world. A strong sense of self allows it to treat another's situation as separate from itself, such as when a child first drinks from a glass of water and then offers the same glass to her doll.[17]

The ultimate empathetic act is one of altruism, where a good deed is performed with no obvious reward. De Waal has a host of stories of monkeys and apes behaving selflessly: young chimpanzees fetching fruit or mouthfuls of water for old, arthritic members of the troop; an experienced chimp from the wild saving a former laboratory animal from a poisonous snake; and an adult ape drowning after wading into water to save an unrelated infant who had fallen in:

> Commitment to others, emotional sensitivity to their situation, and understanding what kind of help might be effective is

such a human combination that we often refer to it as being humane . . . yet our species is not the first or only one to help others insightfully.[18]

It turns out that chimpanzees also have a sense of reciprocity and fairness. De Waal and his team analysed 7,000 approaches made by a chimp without food to a chimp who was eating. They found that successful petitions were likely to be between animals where an earlier favour, such as grooming, had been performed by the petitioner. Between chimps who were really close friends grooming was so commonplace it didn't make much difference. But with a pair, Socko and May, who were mere acquaintances, Socko's morning grooming was rewarded by a succulent branch in the afternoon.[19] Another time de Waal tested capuchin monkeys on their apparent jealousy when they saw other members of the troop get better rewards. They taught a pair of capuchins to trade pebbles with a researcher for slices of cucumber. This they were enthusiastic about. Then, while they continued to supply one with cucumber, they started to give the other juicy, highly prized grapes. The monkey which was being discriminated against not only lost interest in the cucumber but soon began angrily to throw the pebbles out of the test chamber.[20] This shows that the pursuit of empathy is not some sort of lazy, hippy philosophy which opens us up to being uncritical or easily exploited. Other impulses, such as a sense of fairness, balance the practice of empathy.

De Waal believes that the empathy instinct started millions of years ago. It began with motor mimicry and emotional contagion, which we share with many other mammals. The evolution of our ancestors' brains added new layers of subtlety and sophistication, until we could not only feel what others feel but understand their perspectives enough to comprehend what their needs might be. He likens it to a Russian doll with emotional contagion at the centre, concern for others at the intermediate stage, and the ability to form a perspective and target help as the outer, more recent shell.[21] Interestingly it's been shown that baboons are capable only of emotional contagion, whereas chimps have the full empathy equipment.[22] But even when we place our capacity for empathy in its proper evolutionary continuum, we can recognise many things that distinguish human behaviour from that of other mammals. Our facility for complex language, for example, opens up seemingly limitless avenues for perspective-taking. And de Waal suggests that language itself may have developed from our desire not just to communicate but also to empathise effectively.[23]

· · ·

Sharing the Joke

Think of a crowd of people all laughing at the routine of a stand-up comedian. Or consider a national television audience of more than twenty million united in mirth at the BBC's Morecambe and Wise Christmas Specials in the days of truly mass television audiences. Before that radio comedy was recognised as crucial to maintaining national morale in the Second World War. Beyond the individual appreciation of a joke is the shared experience. It's a form of social bonding – we often look sideways at our companions to spread the contagion. You can sometimes see laughter ripple across a group, just as we've all been willing conspirators in communal giggling fits in the classroom. If we share a joke we're making some sort of empathetic connection. But what are the origins of laughter?

According to two Spanish neuroscientists, reported in the *MIT Technology Review*, the answer lies in the 'social brain hypothesis'. This holds that the human brain grew and evolved so that it could cope with the social demands of living in larger groups. Language skills developed to enable the quicker establishment of bonds with larger numbers of people. A conversation between, say, ten people would have greatly improved group dynamics. Pedro Marijuan and Jorge Navarro argue that laughter is an extension of this process, allowing participation and bonding in even bigger groups. Their theory is that the way we chuckle, chortle, smile or smirk is behaviour that evolved for this socially valuable purpose.[24]

As with much of the empathy instinct, the origins of the behaviour can be found among primates. Experiments tickling bonobos and orang-utans have found that they too indulge in what sounds like laughter, but it isn't identical to the human variety. There are as yet no primate stand-ups. Yet if you search on YouTube for 'Orangutan Finds Magic Trick Hilarious', you'll see a primate apparently crack up when shown a conjuring trick by its handler. I defy you not to laugh out loud.

• • •

WHAT THE HUMAN BRAIN TELLS US ABOUT EMPATHY

Occasionally individuals unwittingly achieve immortality, long after their deaths, by virtue of their significance to medical science. Mary Mallon died in the 1930s but is still written about and studied as 'Typhoid Mary' because she was forced to spend nearly three decades in isolation after causing numerous outbreaks of typhoid (despite never showing symptoms of the disease herself).[25] Henrietta Lacks died of cancer in 1951 but she lives on because doctors managed to grow cells from her tumour into a successful culture.[26] If empathy has a poster child it is Phineas Gage, a construction foreman on the American railroad in the mid-nineteenth century.

On 13 September 1848 Gage was overseeing the use of gunpowder to blast rock out of the course of a new railroad in Vermont. He used his own straight metallic pole, known as a tamping rod, to compact the charge and explosives in a hole. The rod accidentally sparked against a rock, igniting the explosives and driving the rod past his lower jaw and up through his skull, entering the left side of his brain, exiting at the top. Astonishingly, within minutes of this excruciating injury he was speaking and even walked to an oxcart to be taken to a doctor. The rod was removed and he was bandaged up, suffering considerable blood loss and then infection. He became delirious but still seemed to recognise his relatives. Within a couple of months he was walking about and able to return to the family home. His mother said his memory was impaired a little but that he was able to help on their farm as he regained his strength. He also experienced a significant personality change, to the extent that his employers would not take him back. He was said to have become profane, capricious and lacking in deference towards his fellows. This gave rise to an unsympathetic limerick:

> *A moral man, Phineas Gage,*
> *Tamping powder down holes for his wage,*
> *Blew his special-made probe,*
> *Through his left frontal lobe,*
> *Now he drinks, swears, and flies in a rage.*

He lived for another twelve years and found employment both as a public spectacle at P. T. Barnum's American Museum in New York and, later, as a stagecoach driver in Chile. His case has been reported, misreported, embellished and twisted to fit all sorts of cockermaimy theories, particularly that of phrenology, which was all the rage in his lifetime. It's not clear how dramatically his personality changed, but the reports imply that he found it more difficult to relate to others after the accident. Modern neuro-imaging techniques applied to models of his skull and his actual skull suggest that the fateful course of the tamping rod damaged two important parts of his brain which both govern behaviour: the *ventromedial prefrontal cortex* and the *orbitofrontal cortex*. Both, as we'll see, play an important part in the empathy circuit. Some of the modern work on Gage's cranium was carried out by the American neuroscientist Antonio Damasio, the man who wrote *Descartes' Error*, debunking the classic idea of the mind and the body as two separate entities.[27]

Some forty years after Gage's death, a German philosopher, Theodore Lipps, laid the foundations for much of the work that would take place in the twentieth century. He wondered why we feel nervous when we watch a tightrope walker, and proposed that we vicariously share the risk the performer is taking; we imagine being on the rope too. (Adam Smith wrote about the same phenomenon in his 1759 book *The Theory of Moral Sentiments*.)[28] Lipps called this *Einfühlung*, whose literal meaning is 'feeling into'. He later suggested 'empatheia' as an Ancient Greek equivalent, meaning 'experiencing strong emotion or passion', and for English-speaking psychologists this became 'empathy'. Lipps also described our ability to think ourselves into the actions of another as an 'instinct'.[29] Thus he supplied the entire title of this book. Like his fellow German who later observed one monkey mimicking another, Lipps had anticipated emotional contagion. These speculations are now being corroborated by modern science.

When the Italian neuroscientist Giacomo Rizzolatti first noted how the same area of his macaque monkeys' brains lit up whether they were reaching for a much desired raisin or watching someone else make the same action, he failed to get the research published.[30] The scientific journals told him that the phenomenon he had dubbed mirror neurons wasn't of sufficient interest. Back at the University of Parma he was undaunted, continuing to work on scanning the brains of monkeys and persisting in his quest for publication. He believed he had discovered something extraordinary, something which challenged the classic understanding that perception leads to cognition and then to movement. Here was evidence of neurons which sensed and moved *at the same time*. In 1992 the findings were published in the journal *Experimental Brain Research* and far from being ignored he now found he was being fêted, at times alarmingly. Mirror neurons were not only erroneously hailed as the source of all empathy, in that special world of tabloid fantasy (home to magic diets and miracle cures). All sorts of other claims were made, including that mirror neurons dictate which movies become hits. As a result, a writer for *Psychology Today* dubbed mirror neurons 'the most hyped concept in neuroscience'.[31] It is now thought that mirror neurons probably exist in different parts of the brain, perform different functions and are only one element of the empathy circuit. But they're an important element. As Rizzolatti puts it, they help us 'to match the movements we observe to the movements we ourselves can perform, and so to appreciate their meaning'.[32]

A simple example occurred at a supper party I was at while writing this book. By chance there was someone sitting opposite me from my publishers, John Murray. So we got to talking about empathy and as we did I moved a dish of gratinated potatoes slightly to my right. I might have been about to offer them to a fellow diner or I might merely have decided to rearrange the table setting. But actually my intention was more self-interested: to get access to a platter of delicious-looking Italian roast pork beyond. The guest on my left saw my arm go out to the potatoes and instantly and correctly divined my motive, picking up the pork to offer it to me. Her mirror neurons were in excellent shape and she proved a highly empathetic person with the most solicitous manners. We all enjoyed the spontaneous demonstration of the empathy instinct and I enjoyed a large helping of pork. So there is some truth in this bolder claim from Rizzolatti, so long as we think of mirror neurons in context and not isolation: 'The mirror neuron system is indispensable to that sharing of experience which is at the root of our capacity to act as individuals but also as members of society.'[33]

And the psychiatrist and expert in neuro-imaging Iain McGilchrist (see below for his celebrated work on the left and right brains) agrees with this assessment: 'Mirror neurons are a means of understanding another's intentions . . . and are not just about copying actions. They form part of our capacity to understand others and empathise with them.'[34]

While Rizolatti has exploited brain imaging to elucidate the empathy circuit in monkeys, the work of Simon Baron-Cohen in Cambridge has been helping to do the same in humans. He has spent decades investigating people who lack different elements of the empathy instinct. His book *Zero Degrees of Empathy* puts forward the idea that while some empathy deficits are only negative (think of psychopaths), others can be positive (for example, people on the autistic spectrum who are extraordinarily good systematisers). He summarises what we know so far about how the brain engenders empathy. He explains that the consensus among scientists has been that there are ten brain regions involved in the empathy circuit. But he adds this disclaimer: 'More await discovery.' Indeed, one new region has since been identified, as we shall see.

With his pioneering use of fMRI technology, Baron-Cohen

has investigated some of the most important regions. The *amygdala* is involved in regulating emotional learning and reading emotional expressions. The *anterior cingulate cortex* is activated both when we experience pain and when we observe someone else in pain. The *anterior insula* is also involved in experiencing one's own and another's pain. But perhaps the most crucial empathy region is the *medial prefrontal cortex*, almost certainly where Phineas Gage's trauma occurred. It is a 'hub' for social information processing, modulating our awareness of both our own and other people's thoughts and feelings. It helps us 'mark' emotional experiences so as to give us short cuts to actions that are positive and rewarding. Patients with damage to the ventro-medial part of the medial prefrontal cortex – the section closely associated with self-awareness – have trouble learning from previous emotional experiences or making decisions. Essentially they see equal merit in every course of action. Such patients also show less of a change in their heart rate when they look at distressing images (something that's true of psychopaths as well).[35] And there's the *temporoparietal junction*, which plays a central role in judging someone else's intentions and beliefs.

It is notable how so many of these key regions are involved in the experiencing and understanding of *both* self and other. We need to understand ourselves before we can empathise with others. This insight is endorsed by child development specialists as well as by psychiatrists.

In 1994, Baron-Cohen identified another region of the empathy circuit – the *orbitofrontal cortex*. This is activated when we're asked to consider how our mind functions, and if damaged it reduces social judgement and inhibition (as it seems Phineas Gage and his friends found out).

And in 2013, Tania Singer and colleagues at the Max Planck Institute in Germany hit on another piece of the jigsaw. The *right supramarginal gyrus* helps us to separate our own feelings about a situation from those of the subject of our empathy. Without it, we would project our own experiences and feelings on to the subject.[36] In other words we have a strong tendency to make sense of the world through our own feelings and opinions, and the right supramarginal gyrus helps us escape this egoism.

If you'd like to know about the remaining brain regions in the empathy circuit, you won't find a better introduction than Simon Baron-Cohen's excellent book.[37]

— • • • —

Right Brain/Left Brain

You often hear people speak of emotional right-brain types, and rational left-brain folk. There's some truth in this division but the reality is more complex (and fascinating). Iain McGilchrist has helpfully summarised his view in his book *The Master and His Emissary*.[38] As we'll see, this relates to empathy, though several of the key circuits are situated in both hemispheres. In broad terms, circuits of the left hemisphere are more particular – abstracting, rationalising and controlling, all from what it knows. The right gives us more of our emotional understanding and mediates our social behaviour. It governs our self-awareness and identification with others. If the right predominates, we're likely to be more favourably disposed to others and more readily swayed by their opinions. The right has a broader focus, is alert to context and novelty, to the metaphorical and implicit.

Faces
The right leads on reading emotions because it processes the upper half of someone else's face, including the revealing eyes. The left scrutinises the lower half and receives fewer, blunter clues from such things as the position of the mouth.

Emotions
Most of these are processed by the right, not just through facial clues but also the voice. The exception is that the left seems to be in charge of anger and aggression.

Language
This is mostly processed on the left, but smiling and laughter come from the right.

Pain
Personal pain activates both hemispheres, but someone else's pain is processed only on the right.

Music and poetry
These are delivered by the right hemisphere, not just because of their inherent emotion but because of their allusiveness.

People with autism often have a malfunction of the right brain. Along with people who've suffered a stroke there, they tend to experience a diminished capacity for empathy. If the right and left brains were people, you might think you'd know whom you'd rather have at a party. But, of course, in reality we need the resources of both hemispheres to function fully as human beings.

———————————— • • • ————————————

Despite these apparently specific functions the truth is that even discrete brain regions, which serve basic emotions like happiness or sadness, have not yet been definitively identified. But we're learning more about how our brains legislate for our emotions all the time, thanks to advanced neuro-imaging. For instance, *spindle neurons* have been found in three of the brain's regions. They appear to allow rapid communication across the brain, processing the information necessary for social behaviour, such as self-awareness. An American professor of neuroscience has called spindle neurons, 'air traffic controllers for emotion'. Unsurprisingly they have also been found in apes, dolphins, whales and elephants.[39]

One of these three areas, the *anterior cingulate cortex*, seems to host extreme emotions, such as anger and lust, but also love. It activates, for instance, when a mother hears her baby cry. The signal activating the anterior cingulate comes from the amygdala and this introduces yet another critical element of the empathy instinct: hormones. This is because the amygdala cannot send the appropriate signal unless it is itself activated by *oxytocin*, described by Steven Pinker as 'hormonal plumbing'. He goes on to say:

Its original evolutionary function was to turn on the components of motherhood, including giving birth, nursing, and nurturing the young. But the ability of the hormone to reduce the fear of closeness to other creatures lent itself over the course of evolutionary history to being co-opted to supporting other forms of affiliation. They include sexual arousal, heterosexual bonding in monogamous species, marital and companionate love, and sympathy and trust among nonrelatives. For these reasons, oxytocin is sometimes called the cuddle hormone.[40]

Pinker relates that behavioural economists have experimented with giving a nasal spray of oxytocin to players of games based on trust. Participants were told that they could give their own money to a 'trustee' who would invest it for them. Half were given real oxytocin and they handed rather more of their savings to a perfect stranger than the other half, who'd been given a placebo. So those inhaling the real stuff didn't start cuddling, but they did become demonstrably more trusting. There is no record, though, of oxytocin being pumped into auction rooms or jewellers to loosen us up as shoppers.

Simon Baron-Cohen has asked subjects lying in an fMRI scanner to look at photographs of other people's eyes and judge their emotional state. He watched as the amygdala clearly activated. Looking at the eyes of others is a critical part of being able to understand their emotions. Baron-Cohen cites the work done by Antonio Damasio and his wife Hanna on a celebrated patient, S.M., whose amygdala was known to be damaged. She had difficulty looking into other people's eyes and as a result found it difficult to read their emotions.[41]

Just to underline how we're only beginning our exploration

of the brain, and how extraordinary our future discoveries will be, consider these more recent neuro-imaging revelations. A Japanese team have announced that they can identify when someone sleeping is dreaming about specific objects like a house, a clock or a husband.[42] Another project has found that they could correctly identify when a journalist was thinking about and visualising a skyscraper and when a strawberry.[43] When it comes to feelings fMRI researchers have proved that emotions, simulated by actors, can be distinguished by brain pattern: anger, happiness, sadness, fear, pride, shame were all seen to have distinct neural signatures. But the easiest and clearest to identify was lust.[44]

We've seen how empathy's roots lie in our evolutionary past. We've outlined the empathy equipment human beings have, how wonderfully resourceful and complex it is and how its functions are even now still revealing themselves to scientists. Now, before we explore the two crucial and interlinked parts of empathetic behaviour, let's meet an unusual person.

EMPATHY DEFINED: WHAT HAPPENS WHEN IT WORKS, AND WHEN IT DOESN'T

In 1988 I produced a human-interest TV series for BBC1 called *People*. Of the fifty stories presented during the run, by far the most successful and memorable was a film made about a ten-year-old called Derek Paravicini. He'd been born three and a half months prematurely and the oxygen therapy given to him had rendered this tiny infant not only blind but also, as soon became apparent, severely autistic. His family were well-to-do (he's related to both Somerset Maugham and the Duchess of Cornwall) and he had a nanny. She decided she should sing to this uncommunicative baby, which he appeared to love. Then a redundant keyboard was brought down from the attic and the child, from the age of two, as one of his teachers puts it, 'outplayed most adults'. There's an electrifying old cassette tape recording of him at the age of four playing the Percy Grainger-arranged 'Country Gardens', but not as Grainger would have recognised it. Derek slides effortlessly between the folksy, the baroque and even boogie-woogie. We filmed him in his class at the blind school accompanying them singing the sentimental but touching 1985 US charity single 'We Are the World'. The report ended with him playing the haunting refrain solo, hunched over the keyboard. Shortly afterwards he performed at the Barbican in London and now, as an adult, is much fêted as a performer in person and online. This has included his being featured in that ultimate internet accolade, a TED Talk, with his teacher and guide Alex Ockelford.[45]

Music, for most of us, goes straight to the heart, evoking emotion in a strange alchemy we find hard to explain. Derek has an extraordinary ability to systematise music, and this clearly gives him pleasure in the execution. But how exactly and to what extent it affects him is very hard to say, due to his severe autism. He has legal guardians and needs constant care. He finds it very difficult to understand other people's feelings (this going beyond his inability to see and read their faces), and to act appropriately as a result. He has serious impairment of both aspects of empathy which most of us take for granted: emotional and cognitive. We'll look at those more closely, after a short diversion into autism.

● ● ●

Autism

Autism is diagnosed, says our leading expert Simon Baron-Cohen, when a person shows abnormalities in social development and communication, and displays unusually strong obsessional interests from an early age. The word autism derives from the Greek *auto*, meaning 'self', on account of the self-obsession of people with the condition. In the first half of the twentieth century many of these children, more often boys than girls, were considered schizophrenic. Then in 1938 the Viennese psychologist Hans Asperger managed to distinguish be-tween schizophrenia and autism. While Asperger spoke of 'autistic psychopaths', the American psychiatrist Leo Kanner was the first to refer to 'early infantile autism', in 1943.[46]

It's now estimated that one in a hundred adults is on the autistic spectrum, ranging from severe autism to higher-functioning conditions such as Asperger's Syndrome (and debates continue as to whether too many children are now diagnosed as Asperger's).[47] Baron-Cohen's work shows how they all display under-activity in the parts of the brain associated with empathy. They have difficulty working out what others feel or think. There has been a sea change in our attitude to those with autism, now that we understand the condition better. In part this is thanks to films such as *Rain Man* and books such as *The Curious Incident of the Dog in the Night-Time*. And in part it comes from a wider understanding that all of us have greater or lesser degrees of emotional intelligence (EQ).

It would appear that the origins of autism can be genetic and are certainly congenital. Myths still abound in relation to autism with quacks claiming they can cure the condition with diets or, most wickedly, that vaccination causes it. What Baron-Cohen and others have shown is that, now that the condition is understood, strategies for teaching autistic children to relate to others and thus function socially can be successful. One programme, pioneered at the Autism Research Centre in Cambridge, is getting children on the spectrum to watch videos of actors expressing different emotions. The children practise labelling the emotions. Doing so for two hours a week for ten weeks can lead to big improvements in their understanding of others' emotions.[48]

Kanner's very first diagnosis in 1943 – 'Case No. 1' – was Donald Grey Triplett. As a young boy he never met his mother's smile, never answered her, but repeated 'chrysanthemum' metronomically, and sang Christmas carols in perfect pitch. He has recently been traced: at the time of writing he's eighty-two, plays golf, travels abroad and is a much loved character in his community. He made it. But many don't: a Swedish study demonstrates that people with autism die, on average, much younger than the rest of us.[49]

• • •

We've tended to divide empathy into the *emotional* and *cognitive*. Emotional (or 'affective') empathy is all about *experiencing* the feelings of someone else. It includes *body mapping*, such as when a very young baby sticks out its tongue in response to an adult's doing so (primates do this too). Closely related to body mapping is *emotional contagion*. We considered the example of a baby crying when it hears another doing so, and we've all laughed when others do (unless, of course, we have severe autism). When Theodore Lipps felt apprehensive about a tightrope walker, it was down to emotional contagion. When we start to care about another person's state, emotional empathy has become sympathy. Psychologists sometimes also refer to this as *empathetic concern*. How useless would it be if a mother merely cried when her daughter was distressed? The point about sympathy is that it can lead to compassionate action – putting a soothing arm round the daughter's shoulders – although it doesn't necessarily do so. The example of seeing a homeless man begging on the street is sometimes given. Your distress at the sight might overpower your sympathy, leading you to walk past him instead of approaching and lending a sympathetic ear. In both cases you've displayed emotional empathy, but in only one have you acted compassionately as a result.

Alternatively you may feel nothing at the sight of the homeless man, or look away before you're affected. Psychologists call this *disconnection* and some argue that it's so important that it should be treated as a third component of empathy. You might disconnect for purposes of self-protection against distress, pain and other extreme emotions.[50] If you felt genuine and profound empathy for every single, struggling person you'd fail to function normally any more. Instead, when for example we watch the news, we go through a process of 'hardening our hearts', often simply to avoid emotional exhaustion. Disconnection is primarily, therefore, a defensive mechanism. As we'll see, these experiences are particularly relevant to those working in health and social care. But it also explains how people we may regard as good or generous are capable of mean behaviour. Empathy can be switched on and off.

Cognitive empathy is a more 'thinking' connection with another. It is our attempt to *understand* the emotions and thoughts of others. While we share contagion and concern with many other mammals, there are few clear examples of cognitive empathy outside the human race. It may be inextricably linked to the evolutionarily older parts of our brain function, but cognitive empathy also relies on parts which recent evolution has changed greatly. It is essentially a feat of imagination by which we think about and come to understand the feelings of another person. It can be broken down into two overlapping activities: *mind-reading* (or *theory of mind*), by which we discern what someone is thinking or feeling from their expression, behaviour or predicament; and *perspective-taking*, when we imagine what the world looks or feels like from someone else's point of view. From these, of course, could flow empathetic concern. But not always. Psychopaths, for example, often have acute cognitive empathy, understanding others only too well, and yet cannot sympathise with them. Those of us who are good at perspective-taking tend also to be adept at giving helpful directions, because we can envisage what it's like for a person taking a route for the first time. We've all been given what seem like duff directions, from time to time, now you know why.

It's useful to understand these key elements of empathy but important to remember that, for most of us, they work constantly together in a complex neurological interplay. We can empathise, for example, with a distressed person who is not right in front of us. So if you were listening to someone on the radio relating how they'd lost a loved one, cognitive perspective-taking might trigger your own feeling of sadness. But emotional contagion from the speaker's doleful voice could be equally responsible for your shoulders drooping or mouth quivering. Another example would be a story like Anne Frank's. Of course we *cognitively* understand her experience of persecution. But we also bring our own *emotional* experience to bear on the story, perhaps unconsciously influenced by how we felt when isolated or bullied as a child. Yet if we'd heard stories about the Holocaust several days running we might still be capable of *disconnecting* from their essential tragedy.

THE LIMITS OF EMPATHY

We tend to be good at empathy, at instinctively combining its different elements, if we're also self-aware and have a keen sense of how others perceive us. Not long ago I was at a small conference for business people and politicians about leadership. We had a guest speaker who began his address by telling us what position he occupied on the *Sunday Times* Rich List. He intended honestly to convey his hard-won success, but we perceived him as bragging and insensitive. If there were an Olympic medal for low self-awareness, he'd have won gold. He also claimed to have an empathetic relationship with his senior colleagues. I doubt it.

While human beings display different capacities for empathy, we've seen we can all switch it off from time to time. *Schadenfreude* is one of those idiosyncratic German portmanteau words meaning 'to delight in others' misfortune'. We may feel the subject of our delight has done us a wrong in the past, we may be jealous of their success or we may merely enjoy seeing someone boastful or pompous taken down a peg or two. In a Japanese study subjects were put in an fMRI scanner and asked to imagine themselves as an unsuccessful type who's normally out of luck (the sort of person we may refer to, rather unkindly, as a 'plonker'). They were asked to suppose they were meeting a number of more successful school contemporaries at a reunion, including a conspicuously rich peer for whom everything has gone right. When they were then told that this *Wunderkind* had suffered a series of terrible misfortunes the scans showed their striatum lighting up strongly. The striatum is a part of our brain that's all about 'wanting' and 'liking', sometimes referred to as part of the 'reward circuit'. In the study the results were identical for men and women.[51] One check on this uncharitable instinct is our capacity for empathy, or more specifically, the sympathy and compassion it can engender.

Jean Decety of Chicago University has made a study of empathy and its absence. In one project he took teenagers who had a history of being involved in fights. They were scanned while watching film of people being injured, either by accident or deliberately. When witnessing the deliberate cruelty, they demonstrated markedly higher activity than is normal in both their amygdala and their reward circuit (the ventral striatum). And they showed no activity in the parts of the empathy circuit like the temporoparietal junction, which is normally involved in understanding intentions when making moral judgements, or in parts which govern the pain matrix (active both when we experience pain and when we observe others in pain). Simon Baron-Cohen remarks that such young people actually enjoy seeing others suffer and that a proportion of them will grow up to be psychopaths. Some will also become sadists.[52] If you indulge in occasional *Schadenfreude* that does not make you a sadist. But you could call *Schadenfreude* the first step on the road to sadism.

The American psychology professor Abigail Marsh has found that our ability to be afraid is also an indicator of empathetic ability. She observes that even before young children have developed theory of mind and the ability to take the perspective of other people, they'll help someone else who is afraid. This is because their amygdala is already operating to help them feel fear, and this also gives them an early ability to identify another's fear. In a study Marsh created a fictional character called Katie Banks and audio-recorded her tale of woe: a terrible car accident, the death of both her parents and her struggle to raise her younger brothers and sisters. Those taking part in the study were separately given facial-recognition tests to see how well they perceived fear in human faces. Those who did so most easily were also the participants who were very affected by Katie's testimony and pledged the most help to her. Logically but somewhat counter-intuitively Marsh suggests fear might be 'the only neurocognitive requirement for generating sympathetic concern'.[53]

Psychopaths have been shown to experience difficulty in recognising fearful expressions. And in fMRI scans they are seen to have dysfunctional amygdalae.[54] Contrast this with people on the autistic spectrum. They have problems with mind-reading. But, far from doing horrible things to others, they often have a keen (even pedantic) sense of fairness and justice. And Simon Baron-Cohen says he's known many people with Asperger's Syndrome care for large collections of stray dogs and cats because they feel sorry for them. Psychopaths, on the other hand, may be great at the cognitive stuff but can use their perceptiveness against others. They might go as far as meting out pain to their victims, having no sense of pity for them. Here's Iago, Shakespeare's very own psychopathic 'hellish villain':

> *not I for love and duty*
> *But seeming so, for my peculiar end . . .*[55]

We saw in Chapter 1 how empathy for our own family, friends or social group can be mirrored by hostility towards others. Another difficulty with empathy is the challenge of extending it to large groups of people, devoid of particular human characteristics we can lock on to. We tend to respond to individual stories we can identify with, better than we do to the plight of many. So we are shocked and moved by the pictures of a dead toddler on a Greek beach, a victim of the Syrian exodus. But we find it much more difficult to empathise with the entire Syrian population. 'When one man dies it's a tragedy, but when a million die it's a statistic,' a chilling aphorism often attributed to Stalin, echoes this.[56] Attempting to identify with a population could lead to feelings of power-lessness or mental exhaustion. This has been called empathetic burn-out. Steven Pinker points to the need for a commitment to moral codes in order for the world to act: 'Empathy, like love, is in fact not all you need.'[57]

Several writers on empathy point out that Christianity reflects the journey mankind has been on. The Old Testament tells us to love our neighbours while the New Testament attempts to widen that, perhaps against our instincts, to love our enemies. This is reflected, too, in Buddhism whose followers are warned against 'sentimental compassion' (which we can take to be empathy) because it's too exhausting. What's recommended is 'great compas-sion' – love for others without sentimental attachment or distress.[58] We may share the opinions of Pinker and Batson, and the doctrines of Christians and Buddhists, that we need moral codes and sets of values. But positively functioning empathy and an understanding of it are also prerequisites of civilisation. We can agree with Charles Darwin that one leads to the other, and today's scientific discoveries are backing him up.

EARLY THINKING ABOUT EMPATHY

Writers and philosophers have always been intrigued by our ability to cooperate in functioning societies. We've seen Darwin speculate about imagination, empathy and our social instincts. Adam Smith and then Theodore Lipps wanted to know why a tightrope walker excites fear in us as we watch. Now primatologists, geneticists, neuroscientists and clinical psychologists (all with a good deal of help from the fMRI scanner) are assembling the proof for the hypotheses of those who went before them. And it's extraordinary how close the great thinkers of the last three centuries got to the truth about empathy. Again and again philosophers and artists explored and investigated why and how we get on with each other in societies.

John Stuart Mill, the British philosopher and empiricist, advocated a 'Religion of Humanity' in order to direct people's emotions for the benefit of society. For him, altruism must first be recognised as pure before it can be cultivated. He derided a Christian view which saw the ultimate motivation for helping others as being to gain a ticket to heaven. Instead, Mill's Religion of Humanity would 'carr[y] the thoughts and feelings out of self, and fix them on an unselfish object, loved and pursued as an end for its own sake'.[59]

Another philosopher, Ludwig Wittgenstein, then defined what today we'd call cognitive empathy:

> We see emotion. We do not see facial contortions and make an inference that he is feeling joy, grief, boredom. We describe a face *immediately* as sad, radiant, bored, even when we are unable to give any other description of the features.[60]

Shakespeare, in his Sonnet 23, wrote that 'to hear with eyes belongs to love's fine wit'. While Walt Whitman, the nineteenth-century American poet and humanist, described beautifully the difference between theory of mind and emotional empathy, though he didn't employ those terms: 'I do not ask the wounded person how he feels. I myself become the wounded person.'[61] A century before him Adam Smith had spoken of our ability to 'chang[e] places in fancy with the sufferer'.[62] Smith also contemplated the role of empathy – or 'sympathy' as he called it – and altruism in human affairs: 'Sympathy . . . cannot, in any sense, be regarded as a selfish principle.'[63] A few years earlier, in *A Treatise of Human Nature*, David Hume anticipated our shuttling between cognitive and emotional empathy when he wrote:

> When I see the effects in the voice and gesture of any person, my mind immediately passes from these effects to their causes, and forms such a lively idea of the passion, as is presently converted into the passion itself. In like manner, when I perceive the causes of any emotion, my mind is convey'd to the effects, and is actuated with a like emotion.[64]

And Jean-Jacques Rousseau, Smith's and Hume's French contemporary, brilliantly foretold our modern research into the human sense of fear when he observed that the sight of pain is more powerful than the sight of happiness: it's a prime source of connection to others.[65]

As well as those philosophers who celebrate fellow feeling, some have condemned it as weakness. Friedrich Nietzsche hated compassion, women and the public masses, whom he never stopped calling 'the bungled and botched'. Instead he loved the will to power, 'great men' and the exploitation of the many by the few. Towards the end of the Second World

War, when large parts of the world found themselves in the grip of a Nietzschean experiment, the humanist philosopher Bertrand Russell saw clearly what was lacking:

> Sympathy, in the sense of being made unhappy by the sufferings of others, is to some extent natural to human beings; young children are troubled when they hear other children crying . . . An ethic such as that of Christianity or Buddhism has its emotional basis in universal sympathy; Nietzsche's, in a complete absence of sympathy . . , I dislike Nietzsche because . . . the men whom he most admires are conquerors, whose glory is cleverness in causing men to die. But I think the ultimate argument against his philosophy lies not in an appeal to facts, but in an appeal to the emotions. Nietzsche despises universal love; I feel it the motive power to all that I desire as regards the world. His followers have had their innings, but we may hope that it is coming rapidly to an end.[66]

Artists have also investigated empathy, just as profoundly as the philosophers. The nineteenth-century novelist George Eliot thought deeply about what she called 'the sympathetic imagination':

> The greatest benefit we owe the artist, whether painter, poet or novelist, is the extension of our sympathies . . . Art is the nearest thing to life; it is a mode of amplifying experience and extending our contact with our fellow-men beyond the bounds of our personal lot.[67]

And in a letter Eliot wrote of her own ambition as a novelist:

> the only effect I ardently long to produce by my own writings is that those who read them should be better able to imagine and to feel the pains and joys of those who differ from themselves in everything but the broad fact of being struggling, erring, human creatures.[68]

———————— • • • ————————

George Eliot, Neuroscientist?

If we look in what is arguably Eliot's greatest work, *Middlemarch*, we find a masterpiece brimming with carefully defined and explored representations of emotional states. She intuitively anticipated the discoveries of the twentieth and twenty-first centuries, about how the empathy instinct works:

Theory of Mind
'"What's the matter? You are distressed. Tell me pray." Rosamond had never been spoken to in such tones before. I am not sure that she knew what the words were: but she looked at Lydgate and the tears fell over her cheeks . . . This was a strange way of arriving at an understanding, but it was a short way.'[69]

Perspective-taking
'[Dorothea] constantly considered Sir James Chettam from Celia's point of view, inwardly debating whether it would be good for Celia to accept him.'[70]

Failure of perspective-taking

'[Mr Casaubon's] experience was of that pitiable kind which shrinks from pity, and fears most of all that it should be known: it was that proud narrow sensitiveness which has not mass enough to spare for transformation into sympathy, and quivers thread-like in small currents of self-preoccupation . . .'[71]

The potential for burn-out

'That element of tragedy which lies in the very fact of frequency, has not yet wrought itself into the coarse emotion of mankind; and perhaps our frames could hardly bear much of it. If we had a keen vision and feeling of all ordinary human life, it would be like hearing the grass grow and the squirrel's heart beat, and we should die of that roar which lies on the other side of silence. As it is, the quickest of us walk about well wadded with stupidity.'[72]

— • • • —

So writers and philosophers, from the Enlightenment to the twentieth century, wanted to define what makes us tick and why our societies function. They got very close to the truth. In Chapter 8 we'll see how arts and culture, with the telling and receiving of human stories, continue to promote and refine our empathy instinct. But now let's turn to the nurture and the nature of empathy. An American psychologist can help us introduce the next chapter. Dacher Keltner was intrigued by Darwin's belief that benevolence and compassion are an evolved part of human beings. Keltner conducted an experiment to see if compassion could be communicated non-verbally, demonstrating whether we're programmed for positive as well as negative behaviour. Strangers were asked to communicate emotions – love, gratitude, compassion – just via touch. They were screened off from each other but could reach through a hole to touch. More often than not those on the receiving end correctly identified the emotion being tangibly expressed: 'compassion is deeply rooted in our brains, our bodies, and in the most basic ways we communicate. What's more, a sense of compassion fosters compassionate behaviour and helps shape the lessons we teach our children.'[73]

3

THE NATURE AND NURTURE OF EMPATHY

In 2006 a neuroscientist was scrutinising brain scans of Alzheimer sufferers. As a control James Fallon had included a scan of his own, healthy brain. He got a surprise: 'I had the brain imaging pattern . . . of a full-blown psychopath.'[1] Since he was then working on the rather different subject of dementia, he didn't stop to think about it. Until 2011, by which time he had moved on to a study of serial killers. Unsurprisingly, several of them demonstrated lower than normal levels of activity in the frontal lobe of the brain, which is crucial for empathy and self-control. Fallon wanted to compare these results with a more normal cohort of people and so he used scans he'd taken of his family members. Of all the scans he was looking at – brothers, aunts *and* the convicted murderers in his study – his own stood out as the classic psychopath. This time he investigated further by testing his DNA. He found he had several high-risk alleles (gene variants which can be passed down from parents to children) for aggression and low empathy. So then Fallon began tracing his antecedents. And when he shook his family tree, no fewer than seven murder suspects fell out. Including Lizzie Borden who, in 1892, was tried for the axe murder of both her father and stepmother in Massachusetts. Not only did she later become the subject of a ballet, Lizzie was also celebrated in contemporary doggerel:

> *Lizzie Borden took an axe*
> *And gave her mother forty whacks.*
> *When she saw what she had done,*
> *She gave her father forty-one.*[2]

Lizzie was acquitted; but it's thought she might not have been in the modern era of forensics.

NATURE VERSUS NURTURE IS YESTERDAY'S DEBATE

James Fallon pondered why he hadn't gone into the family business, instead becoming a respected professor. If psychopathy was in his nature how had his nurture prevented a criminal career? In 2013 he went on to publish a book, *The Psychopath Inside: A Neuroscientist's Personal Journey into the Dark Side of the Brain*. He recalls teachers telling him there was something evil about him and how the police always seemed to let him go when he got into scrapes as a teenager because he impressed them by showing no fear. He concludes that he's a 'pro-social' psychopath with what psychologists call 'aggressive narcissism' and 'fearless dominance'. This is often displayed by natural leaders such as Kennedy, Roosevelt,

Clinton and, we might guess, Blair. But his most important insight is that it was the love and positive influence of his mother when he was young which saved him from a family tradition: 'That is why I tell my 97-year-old mother that the book I wrote about a young boy who could have turned out to be quite a danger to society . . . is not about me, it is about her.'[3]

James Fallon's story is the perfect illustration of a truism which it took us the best part of 2,000 years fully to acknowledge: that we are all the product of *both* our nature and our nurture, and the interplay between the two is critical. This has profound lessons for us about how we can engender empathetic citizens from positive parenting.

If you want, you can blame Adam in the Garden of Eden for the fatalistic idea of original sin. St Augustine certainly did, arguing that the sin we inherit from Adam makes us a *massa damnata* (a mass of perdition, a condemned crowd).[4] Augustine was arguing against others who said that humanity might have had some potential for good without the intervention of God and Christ. That view wouldn't have sold many Bibles. And centuries later the Protestant movement pushed Augustine's idea just as hard, with a particular emphasis on sex. Martin Luther assured us that 'men are full of evil lust and inclinations', while John Calvin described our natural state as one of 'total depravity'.[5] In the Enlightenment, philosophers rebelled against this fire and brimstone, asserting the primacy of nurture. John Locke argued that a child was 'only as white Paper, or Wax, to be moulded and fashioned as one pleases'.[6] And Rousseau said that children who make mistakes do so because they are 'innately innocent', only becoming corrupted through experience of the world.[7] Today we have an increasingly sophisticated view as we knit our knowledge of gene inheritance in with our understanding of how we develop as infants and toddlers. Matt Ridley wrote the best case for this symbiotic philosophy in his 2003 book *Nature via Nurture*:

> Genes are designed to take their cues from nurture . . . your genes are not puppet masters pulling the strings of your behaviour but are puppets at the mercy of your behaviours . . . [Genes] may direct the construction of the body and brain in the womb, but then set about dismantling and rebuilding what they have made almost at once – in response to experience. They are both the cause and the consequence of our actions.[8]

You may have noticed that we're prone to excess: in religion, astrology, philosophy and child-rearing. We seize on theologies and theories as we desperately seek comforting certainty and simplistic panaceas. When arguing for us to give due credence to our increasing knowledge of genes and inherited brain functions, Simon Baron-Cohen warns against the particularly strong, late twentieth-century swing away from nature to nurture: 'both biology and environment are important. Indeed, the idea that empathy is wholly environmental is a far more extreme and radical position to adopt.'[9]

And Steven Pinker takes a more mordant view: 'the Nurture Assumption developed a stranglehold on professional opinion, and mothers have been advised to turn themselves into round-the-clock parenting machines, charged with stimulating, socialising, and developing the characters of the little blank slates in their care'.[10]

The nature-versus-nurture battleground has often been one of tracing intelligence and educational achievement among twins – identical twins separated at birth and as between identical and non-identical twins. The most recent studies all have their battery of statistics pointing to the common-sense conclusion that who your parents are and how you're brought up are both important. An ambitious team of scientists led by Danielle Posthuma in Amsterdam analysed 2,748 twins studies covering millions of individuals. In 2015 she concluded that inheritance and upbringing had equal importance.[11] Other academics dispute this 50/50 outcome (such disputes are meat and drink to this breed), but no one rejects the idea that both are involved.

Graham Music is a child psychotherapist working at the Tavistock Clinic in London. He's taken an interest in attention deficit disorder (ADHD) in children. This is seen as a major problem in some schools, and the prescription of calming drugs such as Ritalin has become widespread in the US. Many of us would suspect that such phenomena are down to neglectful or inconsistent parenting. Up to a point. In Music's book *Nurturing Natures*, he talks about a gene whose form makes it more or less likely a child will suffer from ADHD. It's called DRD4 and neuroscientists have discovered that a long version of it can lead to a child compulsively seeking novelty and finding it difficult to concentrate. This version of the gene is more common in peoples which have a history of major migration and it's speculated that such an instinct would be useful in exploring the opportunities of a new territory. But perhaps Music's most interesting observation is that children with the long form of DRD4 may never exhibit the symptoms of ADHD if brought up in a loving family.[12] When it comes to nature and nurture, one's driven to say, 'It's both, stupid.'

So, before we explore the latest thinking on parenting and how we can nurture our children in their early years, we need to understand what we inherit and are born with: 'the fault . . . is not in our stars, but in ourselves . . .'.[13]

NATURE STUDIES

Until they died recently we owned two Border Terriers. They shared many characteristics, including enjoying a bit of mayhem. (Borders have been described as quick to learn and slow to obey.) But they were also different in material ways. We didn't know much about Daisy's antecedents except that she came from a long line of highly domesticated show dogs. She hated water. Gypsy, who arrived as a puppy two years later than Daisy, by contrast, loved swimming. We knew more about her background because we met her mother at the Somerset farm where Gypsy had been born. We were told the parents had lived a happy life hunting around the farm and diving into the pond to harass the ducks. I remember that Gypsy was kept with her siblings in the farmhouse kitchen and not allowed into the lounge. But there in the lounge I saw Gypsy's mother adopt a very distinctive piece of behaviour: jumping on to her owner's lap and resting her head precisely between the knees. Gypsy would never have seen this, but throughout her life she had a need to do exactly this, not sitting sideways or in reverse, but in exactly the same way. Daisy hated sitting on anyone's lap. I often reflected how we inherit more than our physical characteristics from our parents and grandparents.

We now know that a tendency towards anti-social behaviour or an instinct for empathy can also be inherited – a frequently quoted twins study was carried out between 1979 and 1999 by Thomas Bouchard at the University of Minnesota. He tracked sixty pairs of identical twins who had been separated in infancy and reared apart. Of course everyone loves the personal stories of apparently extraordinary similarities – in this instance, of Oskar and Jack. Born into a Jewish family, they were then adopted. Oskar was brought up a Catholic in Nazi Germany and joined the Hitler Youth. Jack grew up in a Jewish family in Trinidad. When united as adults they were not only similar in gait and speech. Both were wearing navy-blue shirts, both liked dipping hot buttered toast in coffee, both flushed the toilet before as well as after use and both had a taste for spicy food. Anecdotally they were unsurprisingly like two peas in a pod and we may love dwelling on these quirks. Twins are much more rarely separated at birth these days but the turmoil of the 1930s, as well as the adoption policies of the day, meant that Bouchard found a goodly number of such twins in the older generation. One of the things all these twins were assessed for was aggressive tendencies – by their own estimation, by that of their peers and via the monitoring of any criminal records. Bouchard's conclusion was that more than a third of the differences between the twins, in terms of aggressive behaviour, could be accounted for by the make-up of their genes. Steven Pinker points out that a 1994 study of children adopted (and thus not brought up by their own family) suggested that more than half of aggressive behaviour is down to our inheritance. Similar results emerge from tracking and analysing the differences between identical and non-identical twins.

A pair of American behavioural geneticists later conducted a survey of a hundred studies which looked at inherited aggression. Soo Hyun Rhee and Irwin Waldman then singled out a smaller number which specifically analysed overtly hostile behaviour, such as fighting, bullying and cruelty to animals, rather than more generally anti-social traits. They added in other twin and adoption studies focusing on criminal behaviour too. They concluded that a little less than half of aggression and rather more than half of criminality can be attributed to our genetic inheritance. Pinker concludes: 'The exact numbers should not be taken too seriously, but the fact they are all substantially above zero should be. Behavioral genetics confirms that aggressive tendencies can be inherited . . .'[14]

* * *

The 'Warrior Gene'

Serotonin is a well-known neurotransmitter, one of several 'chemical messengers' in our brains. If we have too little of it we get depressed. The right amount puts us in a good humour and too much makes us aggressive. We have a gene called MAOA (monoamine oxidise-A) which breaks down serotonin, ensuring that not too much of it builds up. Members of the historically warlike Maori people more commonly have a version of the gene which is less effective at breaking down serotonin. This version is called MAOA-low. And the press have dubbed it the 'Warrior Gene'.

In extremely rare cases the MAOA gene experiences a mutation known as Brunner Syndrome, after the geneticist who studied a troublesome Dutch family in the early 1990s. He investigated five men in the family who did not have a functioning MAOA gene and had been found guilty of exhibitionism, attempted rape and arson. One tried to run over his superior at work, another forced his sister to strip at knifepoint. This behaviour was found to be intergenerational, as the defective gene was passed down in the family. In other studies, mice which had their MAOA gene deleted became much more aggressive. And carriers of MAOA-low have been shown to have underdeveloped amygdalae and anterior cingulates – both important components of the empathy circuit in the brain.

The behavioural psychiatrist Avshalom Caspi has also studied children who have been abused. He found that those with MAOA-low were quite likely to display anti-social behaviour later on while those with the more prevalent MAOA-high were much less likely to, despite their terrible experiences.

Underlining just how important nature and nurture are, and how sophisticated the interaction is between the two, a study as far back as 1955 indicated that adopted children whose adoptive and natural parents both had criminal records were 40 per cent likely to go on to offend. This fell to just 12 per cent if it was only the biological parents who were convicted criminals – in other words, if they were brought up in a better home.

The MAOA gene is still the subject of much research and debate, reminding us how novel but promising the field is.[15]

———————————— • • • ————————————

In Cambridge, Simon Baron-Cohen is discovering more about the elements of the empathy instinct which are inherited, or not inherited, all the time. He's investigated people he describes as having 'Borderline Personality Disorder' or Type B. He quotes the title of a book on the subject, *I Hate You, Don't Leave Me*, as summing up their condition perfectly. Type Bs swing rapidly from craving comfort and love from others to lashing out in what they see as self-protection. They might make up 30 per cent of those committing suicide and as many as half of drug abusers. His research suggests that the condition is 70 per cent hereditable and 30 per cent a result of abuse and neglect in childhood.[16]

Baron-Cohen has so far isolated four genes associated with empathy, including GABRB3 which regulates an important neurotransmitter in the brain. Certain sequence variations in this gene have been shown to play a key role in causing Asperger's Syndrome.[17] But his team have now shown that other variations in the same gene affect the emotional intelligence of us all.[18] Another revealing project is Baron-Cohen's identification of 500 women who had the amniocentesis test in pregnancy (the extraction of amniotic fluid from the womb to test for abnormalities in unborn babies). This meant that there were samples kept which could also be analysed for testosterone produced in the womb. Following up on these 500 children as they've grown, Baron-Cohen has demonstrated that the less testosterone there was during pregnancy, the higher their empathy level is (as measured by his own Empathy Quotient test).[19] Another revelation from this study is that the babies who'd experienced lower levels of testosterone in the womb offer more eye contact with their mothers at twelve months and have superior language skills at twenty-four months (testosterone of course is seen as an especially male hormone which makes men bolder and more risk-taking).[20]

So our emotional intelligence can be influenced by purely inherited genes and also by our experience in the womb. As we've learnt, our behaviour is influenced by thousands of genes, many of whose effects have not yet been identified. We also generate around sixty mutations in our genome with each generation. As Pinker puts it: 'We are all mutants, so our genes may have an even bigger role in shaping us and our children than we thought: not just the ones we inherited from our ancestors but the ones we mangled ourselves.'[21]

- - - • • • - - -

Moral Babies

Babies apparently have an inherent sense of fairness, of right and wrong. Paul Bloom, a psychologist at the Yale Infant Cognition Center, conducted an experiment with one-year-olds. He performed a sort of Punch-and-Judy show for them. One puppet rolls a ball to another 'nice' puppet who returns it. The puppet with the ball then rolls it to a third character. This 'nasty' puppet runs off with it. Afterwards the kids were shown the nice and nasty puppets each with a treat in front. They were invited to remove one treat and a majority of them punished the nasty puppet by removing its treat. In fact, one toddler, with a particularly keen sense of justice, leant over and smacked the nasty puppet on the head.

What's so fascinating about this study is that the babies were not having something they wanted taken away from them personally. That would predictably cue distress or outrage. They were watching it happen to someone else and having to project their thinking onto that third-party situation. On top of that, it was a dramatic representation of reality that they had to understand. Their sense that reciprocity is fair, even moral, is surely based on identifying with the plight of the generous puppet who offers the ball in play and is rejected, even cheated. The empathy instinct starts early. Bloom wrote the experiment up in a 2013 book, *Just Babies: The Origins of Good and Evil*.

⸺ • • • ⸺

It's now indisputable that along with our height, the colour of our eyes and our intelligence, we also inherit emotional and social traits. There's so much more to discover about this, as genetics and neuroscience develop. But this makes our nurture even more critical. Precisely because we are born with differing levels of the empathy instinct, we need to work harder and more shrewdly on how every child is brought up. In this way we can produce not just individuals who can function in society, but people who are happy, fulfilled, both loved and loving. So let's turn to nurture.

NURTURE – THE OTHER PART OF THE EQUATION

Konrad Lorenz won the Nobel Prize for Physiology in 1973. His pioneering work with geese was about 'imprinting', the way that very early experiences shape us dramatically. At the age of six, Lorenz and a friend were given two newly hatched ducklings. From that moment on the chicks followed the pair around as though they were their parents. As an adult Lorenz studied goslings and discovered that for this adoption to take place the encounter between fowl and human had to take place between fifteen hours and thirty-six hours after hatching. He'd identified the means by which chicks become attached to their parents. What we now know is that this relates to a part of the brain called the IMHV (*intermediate and medial hyperstriatum ventrale*). In the first few hours after birth, the brain is in ferment and completely susceptible to early experiences. A neurotransmitter, GABA, is released and then switched off again – hence the precise window for hatchlings to bond. It's been shown that, if the IMHV malfunctions, no imprinting will occur. Just as you can't leave the nurture out of nature, neither can you leave the nature out of nurture. Think about how many physical and emotional experiences we go through in the first years of our life. An example is the way accents in speech are imprinted on us by those around us. It's been shown that some time between the ages of fifteen and twenty-five we adapt rapidly to the argot of our environment. But thereafter this malleability fades and we're stuck with our basic vowels for life.[22]

At about the time Lorenz was receiving his Nobel Prize

two researchers at the Californian Institute of Technology were doing some equally significant experiments, not on fowl but on fruit flies. Chip Quinn and Seymour Berger conditioned the flies by pumping a smelly chemical into their container, followed by an electric shock. They showed how the flies learnt the import of the smell and the moment they detected it they would take wing to avoid the shock. Later studies showed that flies without the genes for laying down a memory were unable to behave in this way.[23] Again we can say: it's both, stupid.

The twentieth century, the era of Freud, Jung and Spock, abounded with theories of child psychology. None was so deluded as as that of the behaviourists, a school of thought founded by the American John Watson in the 1920s. He didn't approve of maternal love and he believed fussing mothers instilled weakness in an infant. He railed against the 'over-kissed child'. His classic experiment was with 'little Albert', a hapless boy selected by Watson to display the genius of Watson. The twenty-month-old was given a white rat to play with. Albert became very attached to the rat. But then Watson and his assistants started banging a steel bar with a hammer every time he reached out for the rodent. Albert cried. Then they made the noise every time the rat appeared. Albert cried again. Finally, Albert was conditioned to cry whenever the white rat appeared, without the noise. He also developed a phobia for anything white and fluffy, including a pet rabbit and even a white coat.[24] Watson argued, much as John Locke had with his 'white Paper, or Wax', that children were merely a product of their environment:

Give me a dozen healthy infants, well-formed, and my own special world to bring them up in and I'll guarantee to take any one at random and train him to become any type of specialist I might select – doctor, lawyer, artist, merchant-chief and, yes, even beggar and thief, regardless of his talents, penchants, tendencies, abilities, vocations, and race of his ancestors.[25]

Watson advocated the setting up of baby farms, the better to nurture his model army of perfect children. As it happens, the Communist dictator of Romania did just that forty years later.

———————————— ● ● ● ————————————

The Romanian Orphans

In 1989 Nicolae Ceaușescu's dictatorship crumbled and he was shot by firing squad. Among the terrible legacies he left behind were 170,000 disowned children in soulless state orphanages. Ceaușescu had been determined to boost the birth rate of Romanian families, so he despatched a team of state gynaecologists, known as 'the menstrual police', to visit homes to encourage bigger families and discourage contraception.

When these additional children were born to poor families they were rejected, and so state orphanages were set up to house them. These were underfunded and understaffed. So the children were kept in cribs and never picked up or shown affection, in case they might demand more. They were dressed alike, fed alike, had the same haircuts regardless of gender and were marshalled on to potties every few hours. Distressing news footage, from when these asylums were opened up to public scrutiny, shows ranks of moaning, inarticulate children with pitiful, zombie-like demeanours.

An American child psychologist, Charles Nelson, assessed 136 of these unfortunate kids, aged between six months and three years. He found that their IQs were way below par for their age, that they had few language skills and dramatically reduced neural activity. An American couple, Carol and Bill Jensen, adopted three of the four-year-olds. In the car, after they had been picked up for the first time, the children made strange noises. Carol asked the driver what language it was, but was told their gibberings were not Romanian nor apparently any known language.

What Charles Nelson and the Jensens showed over time was that these children were young enough to recover and lead normal lives – once, that is, they were nurtured humanely. Empathy 1, Behaviourism 0.[26]

• • •

John Watson himself, it is said, had a violent adolescence, was a faithless husband and a domineering father.[27] Had we had the benefit of fMRI scanners in the 1920s my bet is that we'd have seen a woefully underperforming empathy circuit in the great man's brain. He was followed by B. F. Skinner who, more alarmingly, was called a 'radical behaviourist'. Skinner also argued that babies simply receive information from their environment, adding nothing from any innate knowledge or instinct. He believed that the sole reason an infant loves its mother is the nutrition in her breast, and he experimented by confining his own daughter, Debby, in a dark box.[28] Yes, you can shudder at this point. If we think of Watson and Skinner as the arch-nurturists, we can thank two primatologists for reasserting the empathy instinct. The first is Harry Harlow, who kept monkeys at the University of Wisconsin.

Harlow found that baby monkeys taken from their mothers and reared in isolation soon became mentally disturbed and socially handicapped. In further experiments with eight babies, he demonstrated that they preferred to hang on to more sympathetic, realistic cloth models of a mother even when there was an adjacent wire model which dispensed milk for them. When he revealed his findings in 1958, he provocatively entitled the lecture 'The Nature of Love'. Then in 1980, also at Wisconsin, Susan Mineka investigated how it is that monkeys reared in the wild fear snakes and ones brought up in the lab don't. She found that the domesticated baby monkeys would also be frightened by snakes if they saw alarm in an adult. This is known as 'parallel learning'. But in further, ingenious experiments she proved that you could not make such monkeys fear flowers, even when they were shown adults apparently traumatised by them. Matt Ridley calls this one of the great experimental moments in psychology: 'It shows that there is a degree of instinct in learning, just as imprinting shows that there is a degree of learning in instinct.'[29]

The neuroscientist David Eagleman contrasts the relatively 'finished' brains of newborn giraffes and zebras, which have to be able to keep up with the herd right away, with the unfinished brains of human babies. We're hardwired for basics like breathing, crying, hearing and reacting to faces, but remain helpless as our brains go through the process of being moulded by our environment. Adults and babies have the same number of brain cells, but they're connected differently. Eagleman says that as many as two million new connections, or synapses, are made every second in an infant brain. By the age of two a child has 100 trillion of these synapses. These are then pruned back until maturity, at which time the brain has half as many.[30] And the psychiatrist Iain McGilchrist suggests that the right frontal lobe, the part most associated with social understanding and empathy, expands rapidly in the second six months of life when the baby experiences an intense relationship with its mother.[31] This is how a toddler, by the age of two, will have instilled the sense of self we looked at in Chapter 2, necessary to recognise other people as separate, with their own individual needs. In other words, the development of theory of mind.

There are two very instructive studies, both carried out in London, about how damaging early deprivation during this period is. Just after the Second World War a child psychologist at the Tavistock Clinic researched a group of young offenders, many from broken or troubled homes. John Bowlby entitled his report *Forty-Four Juvenile Thieves, Their Characters and Home Lives*. He demonstrated how early attachment between infants and caregivers, or lack of it, is a predictor of future moral development.[32] The malign consequences of parental rejection and the benign results of parental affection were further underlined in 2011 when Eamon McCrory scanned the brains of forty-three children at University College London. Twenty had been exposed to family violence and twenty-three had not. Those who had been maltreated showed the same pattern of brain activity as soldiers returning from combat. In essence, post-traumatic stress disorder.[33] They were subject to the same anxiety and depression. When Simon Baron-Cohen reflects on the work of Bowlby and others he points out how loving parents, usually mothers, give their children a lifelong 'internal pot of gold' to sustain them.[34] Who does that remind us of? James Fallon, at the beginning of this chapter, thanking his mother for saving him from the family genes.

A perfect conclusion to our look at how nature and nurture interlock is the work of an American child development expert, Gene H. Brody, which I first came across in Siddhartha Mukherjee's fascinating book *The Gene: An Intimate History*. At the University of Georgia, Brody has been studying intervention programmes for problem families. His work draws on the revelations we're now getting from genetics. Serotonin is the neurotransmitter associated with happiness and well-being. Because it helps maintain our mood balance, a deficit can lead to depression. There's a 'transporter' gene that's been identified, 5HTTLPR, which assists the distribution of serotonin across our brain neurons. But there are two versions ('alleles') of 5HTTLPR: 40 per cent of us have the short allele, and 60 per cent the long. The short one is not as efficient in helping the transportation of serotonin and people with it suffer more often from depression, alcoholism and other problems.

In 2010 Brody recruited 600 African-American families from a very poor, rural area in Georgia. Their locality was described as 'overrun by delinquency, alcoholism, violence, mental illness and drug use'.[35] Divided into two groups, the first had regular counselling, emotional support and extra education. The second, control group was left alone. But all of them had had their 5HTTLPR gene sequenced in advance. Unsurprisingly, those with the short version in both groups were twice as likely to binge on drink and drugs, be sexually promiscuous and display other destructive habits. What was much more revealing was that those in the intervention group with the short allele were also the most likely to respond and benefit from the intervention.[36] This finding was confirmed by a similar study of children emerging from Romanian orphanages into foster care. Those with the short version of 5HTTLPR prospered, becoming more obedient and less aggressive by the age of four and a half than children with the long version. The latter improved too when in a family, but never as dramatically as those with the short allele.

These studies raise all sorts of ethical questions which are being hotly debated. What is normal? Should all, or even any, children be tested in this way? Would gene profiling condemn some children to lifelong discrimination? All important questions, but for our purposes we have a clear demonstration that both what we inherit *and* how we're treated have a critical influence on our prospects. Marinus van IJzendoorn of Leiden University in the Netherlands was one of the first scientists to do genetic research on how children's susceptibility to their environment differs between individuals. Despite his breakthroughs in the lab he also said, 'Neglect of the environment is a big misunderstanding and, in the end, children suffer . . .'[37]

BRINGING UP BABY

The empathy instinct is an essential life skill. We've learnt that we are born with it, to a varying degree, and that the early years of our life can make it flower or wither, sometimes severely. As two American psychologists put it:

> Deeply rooted instincts for empathy become increasingly refined and regulated as attachment and bonding with the caregiver prepare the child for later empathic connections outside the family setting.[38]

So what are the critical stages for nurturing infants and how can we, as a society, ensure they're more widely understood and cultivated? An authoritative analysis of our early development was published in 2000 by Martin Hoffman, a clinical psychologist at New York University. In *Empathy and Moral Development* he identifies five key stages which echo the key elements of empathy we looked at in Chapter 2:

1. *Newborn reactive crying*: From one day old, a baby will cry at the sound of another baby wailing. This emotional contagion works when tested with recordings as well, but less so if the audio is of the baby's own crying.

2. *Egocentric empathic distress*: From ten months old, and sometimes slightly earlier, the infant will respond to another's emotions as though they are their own. For instance, if they see someone obviously in physical pain they'll pout, start crying and possibly seek solace from their mother.

3. *First sense of feeling not their own*: From around thirteen months we understand someone else is distressed but still react as though it's our own upset. An example would be taking another crying toddler by the hand and leading them to our mother, where *we'd* expect comfort, even though the other toddler's mother is in the room.

4. *Theory of mind*: From eighteen months to two years, toddlers can identify others' feelings as separate from their own. It's closely linked to the ability to recognise yourself in the mirror. This sense of self assists us to define others as discrete. It's a skill which then remains with us all our lives, whereas the first three phenomena are merely necessary steps towards this point.

5. *Mentalisation*: From five years old a child will understand that other people have a life beyond the immediate situation. Mature empathy involves a sense of self, a sense of others and an understanding of the relationship between the two.[39]

I'm looking in the indexes of the baby-care manuals we used when our children were small, in the mid-1980s. In one I can see Eczema, Emergencies and even Enemas, but I can't see Empathy. In another there's a section on 'anti-social babies' which contains the advice that maternal attention can overcome such traits, but it shows no understanding of autistic inclinations. The books were fine for their time, both helpful and solicitous, but they are based on the science of three decades ago. They look rather limited today. What about the current leading manuals? Looking at fifteen publications in

Waterstones bookshop reveals that eight actually reference empathy by name and the others have good, sound advice on emotional and social development.[40] So we're making progress and learning from all the recent research on empathy. And we know from the work of Bowlby and McCrory what happens if parents neglect or abuse babies in these crucial years. What are some of the critical elements of good parenting? How can we help develop the internal pot of gold which engenders resilient, empathetic individuals?

Jack Shonkoff set up the National Scientific Council on the Developing Child in the US. He says that cognitive, emotional and social capabilities are highly intertwined with general physical and mental health. Drawing on the mountain of early-years research available, he says there are three essential foundations:

First, a stable and responsive environment of relationships providing nurture, consistency and enriching interactions with adults.

Second, safe and supportive space allowing secure exploration and the development of social connections in and around the family.

Third, good nutrition for the mother before conception, through pregnancy and on for the baby through the early years.[41]

If we can detect more than a whiff of motherhood and apple pie in this list, then we should stop to think how many babies in the world lack one, two or even all three of these advantages. And then pause to consider what effect it has on them and their behaviour as adults. Martin Hoffman argues that when we give young children affection it doesn't only make them feel secure and good about themselves, it makes them more open to the needs of others. The emotionally deprived child is more likely to be self-absorbed and needy. Shonkoff talks about 'serve and return' – when an adult responds to babbling, laughter or gestures with eye contact, words, hugs or their own seemingly inane baby noises. Via these apparently inconsequential exchanges, neural connections are built and strengthened in the child's brain. The absence of such dialogue not only impedes development, it can also lead to harmful stress.[42]

A popular self-help book, written in 2012 by Noël Janis-Norton, offers a useful focus here with what she calls 'reflective listening'. It came out of her realisation that many interchanges in the family are driven by the child's right brain and the parent's left – an emotional impulse met with an ultra-logical response. Janis-Norton's four steps of reflective listening promote a more sympathetic response from parents or carers. The first is to put your own wishes and emotions to one side, the second requires stopping what you're doing to look at the child, the third is to get your theory of mind into gear and imagine what your child is feeling by saying something which reflects this, and the last builds on this to support your child's wishes, with imagination or even fantasy ('Wouldn't you like a magic wand?').[43] The truth is we're often too busy to focus in this way. I'll make a confession: I could have done with reading this before we had our first child, and it took me some time to jolt myself out of my previously childless, self-gratifying regime. By the time the second came along I think I'd worked it out.

Hoffman also talks about the dangers of over-protection.

Allowing highly socialised children to experience a variety of emotions increases their ability to empathise. But only up to a point. Shonkoff agrees that being mildly stressed is a normal part of development. For a young child this might be a first day at nursery or getting an injection. It quite naturally provokes increased heart rates and heightened hormone levels. Even the stress which results from some sort of injury, death or other disaster can be coped with if it's limited in duration and buffered by strong, reassuring adult relationships. But he defines 'toxic stress' as exposure to prolonged adversity such as physical and emotional abuse or chronic neglect. This extended activation of the body's stress-response systems can disrupt the development of brain architecture and result in cognitive impairment. Such an emotional deficit has now been shown to make a range of adult afflictions more likely: heart disease and diabetes as well as drug addiction and depression.[44]

All the research points to a crucial common factor in resilient children: at least one stable and committed relationship with a supportive parent, caregiver or other adult. As I write these words I'm thinking of my father, born in 1920, and his younger brother, born in 1923. The years just after the First World War were turbulent. A whole generation of men returned from the conflict with what today we'd recognise as post-traumatic stress syndrome. My paternal grandfather came back from the Western Front and married in 1919, aged just twenty-three. When his wife sued for divorce, less than four years later, the petition described his heavy drinking and violent behaviour towards her. After the divorce had been granted, my father never saw him again.

And he hardly saw his mother either. She had a liking for gin, sex and the cash required to obtain them. She took up with a man who'd fiddled the foreign exchange markets to pocket a cash fortune (and then they fled to the south of France). The two young boys were effectively orphaned. But their maternal grandfather took them in. He was by now married to his second wife, someone who had no blood relationship to the brothers. 'Aunt Peggy', as she was known, became their mother and brought them up. She gave them their internal pot of gold. In the fashion of the day, she was pretty strict. But we know that healthy emotional development is not merely a question of indulgence.

In fact, making clear to young children the consequences of their more anti-social behaviour, sometimes rather sharply, is a very important part of cultivating the empathy instinct. Hoffman's advice is to make children adopt the perspective of a harmed child, so they realise the distress their behaviour has caused. This promotes empathy-based guilt – a feeling of intense disesteem for having harmed another. As the child grows up, the frequency of discipline decreases as the child increasingly internalises a sophisticated calculation: the satisfaction they'd gain from an anti-social action compared to what they'd lose or suffer by way of guilt. Building this kind of cost-benefit analysis into a child's thinking is a question of patient explanation, not summary punishment. This is how Simon Baron-Cohen puts it:

Parents who discipline their child by discussing the consequences of their actions produce children who have better
moral development, compared to children whose parents use

authoritarian methods and punishment. And parents who use empathy to socialise their children also produce children who are less likely to commit offences, compared to the children of parents likely to use physical punishment.[45]

EMPATHETIC CITIZENS

It's indisputable that what happens to us between birth and the age of three has a massive effect on the course of our lives. And although we can learn to read and write at five, seven or even nine, if our emotional life goes wrong as the brain develops in the early years, then it dramatically narrows our life chances. Up to the 1990s we virtually ignored the pre-school years in educational policy, preferring to believe that it was just down to families. But some families need help, and coming into contact with the state, via education or social services, can provide that. The Americans woke up to this long before us. It was in 1965 that the US President Lyndon Johnson funded the Head Start programme, aimed at pre-school children from deprived backgrounds. Johnson was as liberal as he was foul-mouthed, a hawk in foreign policy but a dove at home. Head Start spawned many similar programmes, where expert mentors could help with the nurturing of young kids and their families. One in Ohio embarked on an intriguing long-term study which caught the eye of social reformers in Europe in the 1990s. The HighScope Perry Preschool Study followed thousands of children who'd been the subject of intervention, comparing them to a similar cohort who'd not been put into such a programme. When they reached the age of forty, well into adulthood, the results were stark. The HighScope children were more likely to hold down a job, committed fewer crimes and were more likely to have graduated from high school.[46] There's conflicting evidence on the value of pre-school nurseries. But a 2016 study conducted in Bologna suggests that while they're beneficial for children from disadvantaged backgrounds, they actively hold back children from high-functioning families. The reason is that early nurseries reduce valuable contact with engaged parents.[47]

When the Labour government came to power in the UK in 1997 it instituted Sure Start, in which 3,500 pre-school nurseries were to be set up by local authorities in areas of need. At their best they supported families as well as socialising young children. As local authorities have come under sustained funding pressure since the credit crunch, perhaps a quarter of these have now closed. The coalition government of 2010 took a different approach.[48] Indeed, I remember being in 10 Downing Street in late 2011 (in my case, for a low-level meeting about promoting the creative industries) when some very senior civil servants burst into the room. 'Is this Troubled Families?' they asked. It turned out that the Troubled Families programme was being discussed in the much bigger room downstairs. They were embarking on a very ambitious scheme to try to tackle the most dysfunctional families in the country, given a sense of urgency after Britain's widespread civil riots in 2011.

The idea was that 120,000 very challenged families cost the state £9 billion a year in terms of their intensive need for welfare payments, for addiction and child poverty services and for educational interventions, as well as because of their disproportionally high contribution to crime. The public finances may be very important, but we might add, or indeed say first, that the sheer misery of children caught in this trap is something we should all want to alleviate. Local authorities were funded to the tune of £450 million to recruit 'family coaches' to try to turn around individual families. In some cases they have apparently been successful. The *Guardian* reported one case study in Brighton.

Sylvia Newton was pregnant with her fourth child and, in her own estimation, was depressed and not coping. Her existing children were well known to the police for their anti-social behaviour and truancy. Becky Williams became their family coach. She sorted out their benefits so they were better supported, got repairs completed to their council house and, crucially, connected Sylvia and her husband to agencies that could help them with better parenting. There's no question the process helped the Newtons turn their lives around, and they point to nine police call-outs in a six-month period leading up to the intervention, and none afterwards.[49] There have been heated debates about how effective the whole Troubled Families programme has been.[50] But in 2016 the Prime Minister, David Cameron, announced its extension to another 400,000 families. In a remarkable speech – remarkable, that is, for a politician and a Prime Minister – he said:

First, when neuroscience shows us the pivotal importance of the first few years of life in determining the adults we become, we must think much more radically about improving family life and early years. Second, when we know the importance of not just acquiring knowledge, but also developing character and resilience there can be no let-up in our mission to create an education system that is genuinely fit for the 21st century. Third, it's now so clear that social connections and experiences are vitally important in helping people get on. So when we know about the power of the informal mentors, the mixing of communities, the broadened horizons, the art and culture that adolescents are exposed to, it's time to build a more level playing field with opportunity for everyone, regardless of their background.[51]

How Finland Does It

There's a toy-shop chain in the UK shrewdly named the Early Learning Centre. It plays on parents' neuroses about their little ones' intellectual development. They think it's never too early to nurture the next generation of Einsteins and Hawkings. But in Finland they've understood that positive emotional development is not only more important to begin with, but also a great influencer of happy, fulfilled and achieving children. Their early-years educational goals are defined as 'promotion of personal well-being, reinforcement of considerate behaviour and action towards others and gradual build-up of autonomy'.

Traditionally Finnish children don't go to formal elementary school until they're seven, a couple of years later than the US and UK. But before that they have a legal right to day-care for babies and toddlers and then a year of pre-school kindergartens for six-year-olds. Five- and six-year-olds are not routinely tested. In their early years they get to play a lot as well as being started on literacy and numeracy. The accent is on learning how to learn and caring for others. Their activities are based around exploration and self-expression.[52]

Educationists are a bit fed up with hearing how well Finnish children perform in international league tables, and the results certainly fluctuate from year to year. But a country which used to have low educational attainment now rates quite highly. A system which is specifically designed around empathy and the production of good citizens deserves serious study. All the world's research now points to the importance of developing social skills first. Harvard's Center for the Developing Child promotes 'laughter, hiding games, imaginary play and story-telling'. In the UK there's even a Baby Laughter Project, singling out this most joyous, most intense of emotional exchanges.[53]

— • • • —

There will always be plenty of debate as to whether a government has the policies to live up to its rhetoric. But it's certainly a start to put neuroscience, and by implication the empathy instinct, at the heart of political thinking. One of the architects of the original Troubled Families programme was Steve Hilton, no longer in Downing Street but now the author of a book, *More Human: Designing a World Where People Come First*. In it he considers the plight of people forced to rely on welfare, of addicts and of convicted criminals: 'One thing we can now say with confidence is that for a vast majority of them, adverse childhood experiences – and the toxic stress that goes with them – are part of their story; part of their circumstances . . .'.[54]

It's one thing to direct society's efforts to a small number of extreme cases. It's quite another to try to ensure that everyone benefits from the new understandings of this century. Finland is a case in point. In Britain the most recent definition of what good education is before the age of five was published in 2014. The Department for Education's *Statutory Framework for the Early Years Foundation Stage* attempts to set down standards for 'learning, development and care for children from birth to five'. Under the heading 'Personal, social and emotional development' it outlines how they should have developed in three areas: self-confidence and self-awareness, managing feelings and behaviour and, lastly, making relationships. Then there's something called the Early Years Foundation Stage Profile which, when translated, is a mandatory assessment of each child in the year they become five.

These standards are well thought through, but they certainly lag behind the new thinking expressed by David Cameron. The appearance of the word *empathy* would be a start. In the future we'll have to be much more exacting and precise about assessing the emotional intelligence of young children and deciding on the best way to help those in difficulty. And we've yet to find a way through a number of dilemmas. For instance, much of welfare policy is now based around the idea that you can tackle poverty if you increase childcare provision and get mothers back to work. But this means, of course, less critical contact between parents and children. Hilary Cremin is a former primary school teacher and now a researcher at Cambridge University. She's certain that the thinking which should inform future policy must put the child and parental relationship before anything else. Cremin would like to see longer paternity and maternity leave, fathers made more accountable for their offspring, and grandparents being given a more central role, filling in the gaps. These are big propositions and would face both opposition and difficulty in execution. But, as we've learnt, is anything more important than the nurturing of fulfilled children who'll go on to become empathetic citizens? Here's David Cameron again, in his 2016 speech:

Thanks to the advent of functional MRI scanners, neuroscientists and biologists say they've learnt more about how the human brain works in the last ten years than in the rest of human history put together. And one critical finding is that the vast majority of the synapses, the billions of connections that carry information through our brains, develop in the first two years. Destinies can be altered for good or ill in this window of opportunity.[55]

4

THE DIGITAL DYSTOPIA

In 2016 Facebook added six new emojis to their platform. Previously you could only 'like' with their thumbs-up sign. Now you could also 'love', 'laugh', 'go yay', 'wow', 'cry' and 'be angry'. The founder of Facebook, Mark Zuckerberg, said:

> What [people] really want is to be able to express empathy. Not every moment is good, right? And if you are sharing something that is sad . . . then it might not feel comfortable to 'Like' that post.[1]

At about the same time Facebook released the results of an analysis they'd carried out of thirty million status updates on the service and other users' reactions to them. More than a third of the updates expressed a negative emotion and, in those cases, the vast majority of responses from friends contained supportive words, such as 'bless', 'luck', 'strength' and 'sympathy'. Facebook said that these posts contained two and a half times as many supportive words as reactions to other posts. They regarded this as evidence of empathy between users, particularly in circles of 'friends'.[2]

This sounds very positive, doesn't it? If we think about all the benefits of the world wide web – infinite search and learning, whole new sectors of industry, instant communications, dating and social media, online shopping, price comparison, online travel booking – we might count ourselves fortunate to live in the twenty-first century. However, here's another statistic: it's estimated that one in five children in Britain under the age of eleven has a Facebook account.[3] Facebook's own terms of service may require registered users to be over thirteen, but there's no way of enforcing this at the moment. Who are these children in contact with? Are they emotionally prepared for the potential aggression and hostility? What else are they accessing on the web? With all the positive aspects of the digital age come cyber-bullying, hard-core porn, radicalisation and other forms of extremism. The web services we all access – email, text messages, Facebook, LinkedIn, Snapchat, Instagram, WhatsApp, Twitter – are significantly different from a telephone or a face-to-face encounter. With the latter we deploy our empathy instinct to pick up on and respond to a thousand clues and nuances in the facial expressions and tone of voice of our interlocutor. Text-based communication is stripped of that vital information and a choice of six emojis doesn't come anywhere near the infinite nuances of speech and visage. It's easy to attack or offend in a textual interchange because you can't see the real effect your words have had. I noticed how the culture of Arts Council England changed in 2014 when we moved from an old-fashioned 'cubby-hole' set of offices to an open-plan building. Staff were able to talk face to face much more, rather than emailing colleagues who'd sat on different floors, behind partitions and out of sight. A short conversation can save a lengthy exchange of emails and, more crucially, is a much more effective and human interchange.

We can connect with more people more quickly than has ever been possible in the history of mankind. But we're in danger of entering a new world of text and social media where empathy becomes a forgotten quality. Digital narcissism is all about me and what I'm experiencing, regardless of you and how I affect your feelings. How can we prevent this anti-society dominating our lives?

THE DOWNSIDE TO THE DIGITAL ERA

Why would Steve Jobs, the man who led Apple and revolutionised our use of technology in the early years of this century, not give an iPad to his children when they were first issued? 'We limit how much technology our kids use at home', he said. He preferred to make sure his brood ate together around a big family table every evening. Why would Chris Anderson, former editor of *Wired* and now chief executive of a robotics company, place time limits and parental controls on all his children's devices? 'We have seen the dangers of technology first hand. I've seen it in myself, I don't want to see that happen to my kids.'[4] Dimitri Christakis analyses children's use of media and points out that in 1970 the average age for children to begin watching television was four years old. Now it's four months.[5] We saw in the previous chapter how critical the first two years of life are for brain formation and establishing positive emotional pathways. This only happens as a result of warm, intense, personal relationships between parent and child.

In 2016 Michele Borba published *UnSelfie: Why Empathetic Kids Succeed in Our All-About-Me World*. She says that, on average, eight- to eighteen-year-olds are plugged into digital media devices for more than seven and a half hours a day. She estimates that three-quarters of all children of eight and younger in the US have access to a smart mobile device in the home:[6]

> The single best predictor of healthy emotional interactions is a lot of face-to-face communication; it's also the best way to learn emotions and develop human-contact skills. Staring at computer screens, texting, tweeting and messaging do *not* teach kids their Emotion ABCs.[7]

Borba quotes a survey which shows the time spent socialising as a family is rapidly diminishing and another, shockingly but unsurprisingly, which found that 62 per cent of school-age children said their parents are too distracted when they talk to them. The top distraction? Mobile phones.[8] A study in the journal *Pediatrics* scrutinised families in fast-food restaurants. When parents' mobiles were out in their hand (which was much of the time) their engagement was with the device and not the children.[9] Perhaps the only way the children can get their parents' attention in this digital dystopia is to contact them via their own smart devices, even though they're sitting opposite each other!

The most digitally connected nation on earth is thought to be South Korea, where 64 per cent of all teenagers have a smartphone. One in five of them now uses their device for more than seven hours each day. Something really sinister appears to be happening there. They've come up with a chilling name for a new affliction: digital dementia. It refers to a deterioration of cognitive abilities akin to having suffered a head injury or psychiatric illness, as Byun Gi-won, a doctor at the Balance Brain Centre in Seoul explains: 'Over-use of smartphones and game devices hampers the balanced development of the brain . . . heavy users are likely to develop the left side of their brains, leaving the right side untapped or underdeveloped.'[10]

As we saw in Chapter 2, the right side of the brain is central to processing emotions and others' pain, to implicit meaning and humour, to appreciation of music and to self-awareness. Its failure to develop can also diminish attention and memory span. A German neuroscientist is equally worried about the situation in Europe and actually wrote a book with the title *Digital Dementia*. Dr Manfred Spitzer warned parents and teachers about allowing children to spend too long on laptops and mobile phones. He argues that resultant deficits in brain development can become irreversible and lead to a state of addiction.[11]

A 'mobile' generation is now growing up for whom online communication is simply the norm. This allows children and teenagers to contact practically anyone anywhere in the world. It's rapid and, once committed as text, image or video, the content is virtually indelible. Just think about how different and how overwhelming this is compared to all previous generations in humanity's history. If you've ever tweeted you'll know how frequently you experience aggression and hostility from people you've never met. It's almost as though every passing thought, every fleeting impression which might be uncharitable but soon forgotten, is now spewed out for all to see. Seventy-three per cent of Americans now say they've witnessed online abuse and 40 per cent have actively complained about it, according to a 2014 survey. Two-thirds of the incidents occurred on social networking sites. Young adults were the most likely to be affected, with young women coming in for the most unpleasant treatment: among complainants in this category 26 per cent had been stalked online and 25 per cent were the target of sexual harassment. Half of all those who'd been subjected to cyber-bullying did not know the person getting at them.[12]

The *Guardian* is one of the most visited news websites in the world. For ten years its readers have been able to leave comments at the bottom of articles. I have written a number of 'op-ed' pieces for its Comment section over the years but I never read the reactions from its gentle readers, which are sometimes too brutal to cope with. When others say to me, 'That was a bit harsh in response to your piece . . .', I can always respond, 'I wouldn't know, I haven't read it.' I'm hardly a blushing media debutant. I started working in BBC News forty years ago and have been roundly abused by the *Daily Mail* and others for my efforts at television production on many occasions. But the sheer negativity and low emotional intelligence of some reader reactions is better avoided, even by the most hardened hack. In April 2016 the *Guardian* did an analysis of seventy million comments posted over a decade.

Almost one and a half million had been blocked by moderators for violating the publication's community standards. Some had contained threats to rape, maim or kill. Some were judged 'crude, bigoted or just vile . . . too often things are said to journalists and other readers that would be unimaginable face to face'. The *Guardian* also reported that, although the majority of its opinion writers have been white males, those who received the highest levels of trolling and abuse were eight women and two black men. Two of these women and one man were gay and, of the women, one was Muslim and another Jewish. The tribal behaviour we looked at in Chapter 2, with all its unbridled prejudices, is given free rein in this empathy-free, digital dystopia.[13]

The referendum campaign in the summer of 2016 brought home to many people how online communications had coarsened and, in some cases, poisoned political discourse. Much of the debate was threatening and *ad hominem*. This was little surprise to some female MPs who had been suffering abuse for years. Jess Phillips, the MP for Birmingham Yardley, once had 600 threats of rape on Twitter in one evening. The MP for Walthamstow, Stella Creasy, suffered similarly, and one of her abusers was eventually prosecuted. As was the man who sent a Facebook message to the Dewsbury MP, Paula Sherriff: 'Dead girl walking. Hope you get raped. We got your phone number and details.'[14]

Facebook and Twitter work quite hard to deal with complaints, take down offensive posts and ban some frequent offenders. But this cannot prevent abuse. When Nicola Brookes commented on an *X Factor* contestant on Facebook, a fake profile of her was created saying she was a prostitute, a drug dealer and a paedophile. With the support of her friends she managed to cope with it, but then she is an adult.[15] In the US Hope Witsell, aged thirteen, sent a topless image of herself to her boyfriend. This was intercepted by someone else using his phone and circulated. She was bullied at school as a 'whore' and committed suicide.[16] Tyler Clementi, an eighteen-year-old music student in New York, was videoed by a room mate conducting a gay liaison. When the video was sent around online he threw himself off the George Washington Bridge.[17] There is a long list, now, of young people who have been persecuted in a way that would not have been possible until this century. And to a lesser or greater extent millions are affected. It represents a failure of empathy, an inability to put yourself in someone else's shoes to imagine how they feel, compounded by the impersonality of digital communications. Between 16 and 30 June 2016, before and after the UK's European Union referendum, the police reported a 40 per cent increase in hate crimes compared to the same two weeks in 2015.[18] Not long before that the Chief Constable of Essex, Stephen Kavanagh, talked about an explosion of online crimes – trolling, racial and homophobic abuse, underage sexting – which were not even imaginable when he started as a policeman in 1985.[19] He also mentioned what has become known as 'revenge porn'.

'Could you help? I'm in trouble.' The person calling the Revenge Porn Helpline is a woman in her forties. A man she's had an affair with has posted compromising pictures of her online and shared them via social media with her children, husband and wider family. She's sitting in bed with a bottle of vodka, contemplating suicide. The helpline was set up by Laura Higgins in 2015 and has thousands of calls a year. There are twelve sites she knows of which encourage men to post images of former wives and girlfriends. One advertised itself as a forum for pictures of 'cheating slut wives'. Higgins says that this is a worldwide phenomenon, and increasingly local fora are being set up for explicit images to be posted and shared.[20] There are now laws specifically prohibiting revenge porn in both the US and the UK. In 2015 Kevin Bollaert became the first man to be prosecuted for setting up a site which not only hosted the pictures but explicitly linked them to the victim's social media profile and residential address. He even tried to extort money from victims to take the images down.[21] But despite the efforts of the law, it remains several steps behind the rapid growth of these painful outrages. Figures released in April 2016 showed that only about 10 per cent of cases reported to the police led to a charge (three of the alleged victims were as young as eleven).[22] Revenge porn is especially shocking and profoundly hurtful because, unlike other online abuse, it represents the betrayal of confidences and a gross breach of trust.

• • •

Radicalisation

In the summer of 2016 a series of attacks on civilians took place across mainland Europe. They appeared to have two common factors: that the perpetrators had been radicalised online and that the extremists doing it were preying on unstable individuals with mental-health problems.

Since the advent of the rogue state Isis, we've become all too familiar with extreme online propaganda. The Quilliam Foundation describes itself as 'the world's first counter-extremism think tank set up to address the unique challenges of citizenship, identity and belonging in a globalised world'. A paper from Quilliam in December 2015 (*Youth Led Pathways from Extremism*) said this:

> extremist groups have a well-defined business model, in which digital platforms guide their strategies: they know their audience and have a clear, strong message backed by a 'sophisticated and global' marketing scheme. This allows them successfully to target vulnerable groups, particularly youth, who are in transition and searching for meaning or purpose . . . Their message attracts members, who are able to 'like' 'friend' 'share' 'follow' or 'link' with the ideologies and hope purported by online recruiters . . .[23]

American communications experts point to how Isis videos use empathy, for example by showing a handsome soldier visiting injured people in hospital. Quilliam says that negative measures to try to prevent this indoctrination – deleting, blocking, filtering, taking down content – are ineffective. The material reappears just as quickly elsewhere. More encouraging has been the 'counter-speech' movement. Bloggers, comedians and other digital media stars are exposing the waves of extremist propaganda, often with the potent weapon of ridicule. Take a look, for instance, at the work of Humza Arshad on YouTube.

A controversial UK government scheme called Prevent now

places a duty on schools to identify children who are vulnerable to radicalisation. Attempting a slightly more positive approach, the then Education Secretary, Nicky Morgan, also launched a new site in early 2016. EducateAgainstHate, she said, would counter extremists' 'sophisticated social media strategies [allowing] them to spread their lies and propaganda on an unprecedented scale'.[24] It's a start, but Quilliam points to a broader strategy of empathy education that's also needed:

> A vital component to countering abusive, violent and anti-social behaviours is the presence, activation and application of empathy. In the setting of extremism recruitment, this essential human attribute may very well be the key to thwarting radicalisation and extremist behaviours. Despite this critical importance, few if any, programs exist with the sole purpose of building empathy among children and youth. It is therefore essential that programs and content be incorporated into government, NGO and other efforts designed to thwart extremism recruitment and youth radicalisation.

— • • • —

More broadly, pornography is ubiquitous on the world wide web. There's particular concern as to what effect this has on children and young people, since the images are just a tap away on a smartphone. In the Queen's speech of May 2016, setting out the UK government's latest legislative programme, a law was promised forcing porn sites to get all users to verify that they are over eighteen. The speech revealed that one in five children, aged eleven to seventeen, had seen pornographic images which upset them.[25] The NSPCC released two reports in 2016 with equally worrying findings. Twelve per cent of children surveyed had made videos, for sharing, of their own bodies or sexual activity and 9 per cent regarded themselves as being addicted to pornography. Slightly more than half of all children surveyed had seen pornographic images and, of them, nearly all had started doing so before the age of fourteen. Peter Wanless, the NSPCC's Chief Executive, issued a warning: 'Exposing children to porn at a young age before they are equipped to cope with it can be extremely damaging. Industry and government need to take more responsibility to ensure that young people are protected.'[26]

In the summer of 2016 the Chief Executive of the children's charity Barnardo's, in a report called *Now I Know It Was Wrong*, warned that around a third of sexual abuse now experienced by children is perpetrated by those who are themselves under the age of eighteen.[27] Javed Khan said: 'We have left children to navigate their way through online pornography and decide what is right and what is wrong . . . Even parents who provide loving homes don't necessarily know how to keep their children safe online.'[28]

Porn may be particularly disturbing for young children going through puberty. But its sheer ubiquity means it connects with people of all ages. Some researchers in Amsterdam showed a good deal of fortitude, in 2013, by analysing the 400 most watched internet porn videos at that time (it was 108 hours of material). Most featured sex between a man and a woman, 17 per cent showed group sex, spanking appeared in more than a quarter of the footage and gagging in a fifth. Other sorts of violence were rare. However, around one in twenty did show non-consensual sex. Women were often depicted as merely instruments of male pleasure, but men were also frequently dehumanised because their faces were rarely shown.[29] Fortunately, most people do not find their way to the more appalling examples of pornography, often on the dark web. Graham Coutts strangled Jane Longhurst in Brighton in 2003 and was found to have previously collected 800 images of strangled, suffocated or hanged women. In 2013 Jamie Reynolds hanged seventeen-year-old Georgia Williams at his Shropshire home and, when apprehended, was found to have assembled seventy-two violent videos and 17,000 still images. It is thought that there are around 100,000 'snuff' sites online containing stills and videos of killings, cannibalism, necrophilia and rape.[30] But it's one thing to be repelled by these profoundly disturbing libraries, quite another to prove they cause violent behaviour, rather than merely satisfy existing perversions.

Gail Dines is a leading campaigner against pornography. She's clear about the significance of this new phenomenon: 'We are now bringing up a generation of boys on cruel, violent porn and, given what we know about how images affect people, this is going to have a profound influence on their sexuality, behaviour and attitudes towards women.'[31]

But in an article in *Psychology Today* in 2014 Dr David Ley quoted Dutch research which suggests that aberrant sexual behaviour among teenagers is nearly all caused by factors other than the consumption of pornography. He agrees that common sense dictates we don't want children to watch pornography intended for adults, not least because it might confuse them or warp their ideas. But he argues there's as yet no evidence of a direct effect.[32] Nevertheless, the Max Planck Institute in Berlin has shown that the brain can change as a result of such consumption. The more a group of healthy men watched porn the lower the activity in their brains' reward centres was. The brain needed more dopamine each time to feel the same effect, which could mean we seek out more intense porn to get the same high.[33] Two other studies, one in Cambridge and the other in Germany, have investigated the effect of porn on the brain in more detail and have confirmed it to be very similar to the way in which drug addicts need more to create the same effect, and also to the way in which their striatum (a crucial part of the reward system) shrinks over time.[34]

It is a 2013 study from the Children's Commissioner for England which has probably set out the most rational conclusions based on what we know up to this point. It was entitled *Basically . . . porn is everywhere* and concluded:

Exposure to pornography affects children and young people's sexual beliefs . . . [it] has been linked to unrealistic attitudes about sex; maladaptive attitudes about relationships; more sexually permissive attitudes; greater acceptance of casual sex; beliefs that women are sex objects; sexual uncertainty; and less progressive gender role attitudes . . . we can conclude that exposure to sexualised and violent imagery affects children and young people; however, the ways in which they may be affected and how long-lasting the effects may be are debatable.[35]

The maladaptive relationships the Commissioner talks about show that the most important issue of pornography is not criminal behaviour, but one of empathy and fulfilling relationships.

Another affliction challenging our digitally challenged adolescents is the growing prevalence of eating disorders. It's thought that as many as 725,000 Britons may suffer from an eating disorder, and hospital admissions in the past decade have grown by a third.[36] The Chair of the Nutrition Committee at the Royal College of Paediatrics and Child Health, Dr Colin Michie, thinks a reason for the growing problem is children's increasing use of mobile phones and the baleful influence of 'perfect' celebrity bodies constantly paraded.[37] While there are some excellent websites that attempt to help sufferers recover a more normal attitude to diet and body shape, there are also a greater number of pernicious 'slimming' sites which peddle every conceivable myth about what is healthy, and several inconceivable ones. Even more sinister are the 'pro-ana' and 'pro-mia' sites which positively advocate eating disorders as a legitimate lifestyle choice. Many of these sites and the blogs on them are created by young women – an EU study in 2011 suggested that more than 10 per cent of eleven- to sixteen-year-olds had seen a pro-ana site.[38] Emma Bond wrote a report on them (*Virtually Anorexic – Where's the Harm?*):

> Online anonymous environments allow people to express views about their disorder that would be judged negatively in other surroundings. 'Pro-sites' for those with positive beliefs about stigmatised behaviour exist for other behaviours also

such as drug use, self-harm and suicide. Thus cyberspace has emerged as a critical context for the construction of alternative identities and narratives relating to eating disorders.[39]

The latest thinking on anorexia looks beneath the severe weight loss and restricted food intake to ask whether the condition itself may be a form of autism. As Professor Baron-Cohen points out: 'A characteristic of anorexia that many clinicians and parents instantly recognise is the self-centred lack of empathy, even though this is not one of the diagnostic criteria.'[40]

I should repeat that the internet era has brought us many extraordinary benefits. But it is a medium like no other that mankind has ever dealt with. You know that person you see drinking alone at one end of the bar, whom you instinctively avoid? He thinks Elvis is still alive, or that Paul McCartney is dead or that, in the words of Donald Trump, 'There's something going on.'[41] The extraordinary thing about the world wide web is that all those solitary drinkers and fellow paranoid delusionists can for the first time find one another. They can reinforce one another's wilder fantasies. And to add fuel to the online fire, there's something about the medium that is fundamentally unempathetic, divorced as it is from genuine human interaction. Hence the prevalence of cyber-bullying and soulless porn. This is the Tower of Babel that the mobile phone is giving our children unfettered access to. We can't disinvent it, but what can we do to protect them?

Virtual Reality

We should not let the challenges of technology blind us to its many benefits. Virtual reality (VR), still in its infancy, enables us to don a headset and see video of a 360-degree environment. You can turn left, right or look behind you. Chris Milk has given a TED Talk about VR which you can view online. He describes how he collaborated with a United Nations agency to make a film about a twelve-year-old Syrian girl called Sidra living in a refugee camp just over the border in Jordan. *Clouds Over Sidra* explores her hopes and fears in a compelling way. This is how Milk articulates it:

> You're looking around through this world . . . And when you're sitting there in her room, watching her, you're not watching it through a television screen, you're not watching it through a window, you're sitting there with her. When you look down, you're sitting on the same ground that she's sitting on. And because of that, you feel her humanity in a deeper way. You empathise with her in a deeper way.[42]

Milk took *Clouds Over Sidra* to Davos to show to the influential decision-makers at the World Economic Forum. Now he's shooting further pieces in Liberia and India:

> It connects humans to other humans in a profound way that I've never seen before in any other form of media. And it can change people's perception of each other . . .

It's a machine, but through this machine we become more
compassionate, we become more empathetic, and we
become more connected. And ultimately, we become more
human.[43]

There's now a creative agency in New York, set up in 2015,
called empatheticmedia.com. They use VR to make immersive
reports for clients such as the *Washington Post* and Associated
Press. They believe it's a new sort of journalism which 'fosters
empathy between storytellers and their subjects'.

VR even has the potential to make us more sympathetic to
nature. Some American universities have been busy inserting
people into otherwise inaccessible natural environments.
Researchers at Stanford have made a thirteen-minute video of
an ocean in which the viewer is turned into a pink coral (really).
As the video progresses, a century of acidification causes the
organisms surrounding the reef (snails, urchins, bream) to interact
less and less with 'you', the coral, and eventually die out. Early
results from studies on these encounters show that giving people
such a visceral experience of what humans are doing to their
planet has a significant effect on their attitudes.[44]

• • •

REGULATION AND SELF-REGULATION

At the dawn of the internet age, during the dotcom boom,
we were told by starry-eyed digital soothsayers that we were
entering a brave new world that was free, unmediated and
could not be regulated. This was never true – in the end we
move to govern all areas of human concourse in the interests

of society. Now, in matters of copyright and piracy, privacy and data protection, theft and fraud, libel, harm and offence, the law intervenes in the internet. But it's neither easy nor simple.

There's a debate about whether we have the laws we need but apply them poorly, or whether we need an overhaul of the statutes themselves. techUK, which represents 900 British technology companies, argues that existing legislation is 'fit for purpose' but that police and prosecutors need better knowledge and skills to apply it. There is some evidence for this. In the first six months after the new law prohibiting revenge porn was enacted, 1,160 cases were reported in England and Wales, but there were only eighty-two prosecutions and seventy-four cautions. As we've seen, three of the alleged victims were just eleven years old, which makes us wonder how widespread the problem is and whether the law alone can tackle it. Indeed, a learned discussion around whether the revenge-porn definition should be expanded from 'exposed genitals' to include 'breast and buttocks' reminds us how difficult it is to define human behaviour in legislation.[45]

Chief Constable Stephen Kavanagh, who leads for the police on cyber-crime, agrees that the police need to become much better at applying the law. But he also says that they are struggling with thirty relevant pieces of legislation, from the new revenge-porn offence to the 1990 Computer Misuse Act to Victorian decrees as far back as 1861.[46] Kavanagh says that only 7,500 police officers out of 100,000 nationally are properly trained to deal with cyber-crime while an 'unimagined scale of online abuse' threatens to overwhelm them. For him the answer is better training but also rationalised legislation:

Often victims don't know how to articulate what happened to them, they aren't clear what the offence is, if there is one. When they get an ambiguous response from the police, it undermines their confidence about what has happened . . . so the law needs to be pulled together and the powers consolidated into a single place.[47]

In October 2016 the Crown Prosecution Service issued new social media guidelines, in order to consult on how the law should tackle hate crimes. They also suggested care in not criminalising under-eighteens wherever possible. Meanwhile the EU has enacted some sweeping data-protection legislation, due to take effect in 2018, obliging social networks to get parental consent for all users under the age of sixteen. The networks face fines of up to 4 per cent of their global turnover if they fail to do so.[48] It remains to be seen how enforceable this is and, following the UK's decision to leave the EU, it may never apply in Britain anyway. Voluntary actions by Twitter and Facebook – responding to complaints, taking offensive material down and banning frequent offenders – are also very important. But since cyber-criminals are persistent and canny they soon reappear under another moniker. So prevention is going to be more valuable than cure and much of it will depend on smart, well-designed technology.

Apple's iPhones have taken the lead over Android devices in offering parental controls which can filter the online traffic of children. Apple have an 'Ask to Buy' feature. When this is enabled, any child downloading an app or making a purchase within an app will trigger a notification to the parent's phone. They can then allow or deny the transaction. In the iPhone's

'Settings' there's also an option called 'Restrictions' allowing the enabling and disabling of various features. For instance, you can restrict the Safari browser from loading websites with adult content. The drawback of placing filters on devices is that parents need to be a bit tech savvy to do it.[49] The alternative is to place the filters on at the network level. After chivvying from David Cameron, Sky, Virgin Media and other broadband suppliers implemented an unavoidable choice for customers when turning on their connection for the first time. You have to opt in to watch pornography, if that's what you want. Later Sky went a step further and started blocking all adult websites for all subscribers who had not responded to the opt-in choice.[50]

The UK Council for Child Internet Safety (UKCCIS) is a group of more than 200 organisations drawn from government, industry, the legal profession, academia and the charity sector. It helped broker the new generation of broadband filters. In 2016 it also published a guide to help online services protect minors and a separate guide for parents:

A childhood with the internet is still a relatively new experience . . . The immediacy and reach of social media has opened up all kinds of positive opportunities for children as they grow, but also the possibility of considerable harm. Bullying, child sexual abuse, sexual grooming, trafficking and other illegalities can, and do, thrive if left unchecked.[51]

A Home Office report as far back as 2010 recommended more digital literacy lessons in schools, and learning to navigate social media is certainly becoming an essential life lesson.[52] There are also differing opinions about the age at which children should be given access to smartphones. Some as young as four and five have them. But a piece in the *Huffington Post* in 2015 suggested they should be banned for children under twelve.[53]

What happens in the home is even more important than in school. The UKCCIS has identified that parents need as much internet education as their children. And a website, parentzone.org.uk, has been set up to assist this. In her book Michele Borba reminds us constantly to check our digital habits and those of our family, to set 'unplugged' times and to eat together as a family. This is something the late Steve Jobs had worked out for himself when he thought about his own family, understanding the profound value of uninterrupted 'face-to-face' time. In this way we can educate our children in the perils as well as the benefits of the internet age. But if our education system truly embraces the empathy instinct, it will offer much more than prohibitions and preventions.

THE POWER OF EDUCATION

Two decades ago a Canadian teacher, Mary Gordon, became very interested in the emerging science of empathy. How could it be harnessed in mainstream education? She persuaded a local school to allow a mother to bring her young baby into class every three weeks throughout the school year. A trained instructor coached the pupils to observe the baby's development and label its feelings. The children were, in the process, able to identify and reflect on their own feelings and the feelings of others. The idea spread and became known as Roots of Empathy in all the schools which introduced it, for four-year-olds up to thirteen-year-olds. From Canada it has now spread to the US, the UK, Germany, Switzerland and New Zealand. More than 800,000 children have benefited from it. A large study in its country of origin, carried out by the University of British Columbia, found that children who had taken the course exhibited less 'proactive aggression' – that is, the selfish use of aggression to get what you want.[54] Other evaluations have also revealed increases in social and emotional knowledge, increases in pro-social behaviour and lasting results. This is how the Roots of Empathy programme now defines its mission:

> to build caring, peaceful and civil societies through the development of empathy in children and adults . . . part of our success is the universal nature of the program; all students are positively engaged instead of targeting just bullies or aggressive children.[55]

• • •

Chess

We might regard the game of chess as the ultimate triumph of the systematising types, brilliant at maths and logic but a bit slow on the emotional uptake. Michele Borba visited a school in Yerevan in Armenia and came to a different conclusion. This is the first country in the world to make chess compulsory for every child from the age of six. Borba watched as the young pupils sat face to face in their weekly class. She reminds us in her book that playing chess has always been credited with increasing concentration, memory and reading and maths scores. But now there are studies which show that chess is associated with socio-affective development as well:

> As I watched two first graders named Narek and Arman, I recognised that chess is also a powerful way to cultivate empathy's cognitive side. They played face-to-face, imagined their opponent's next plays, tuned in to emotional cues ('Does he look confident, hesitant, or anxious about that move?'), and predicted 'if-then' scenarios ('If he moves that piece, then . . .'). Narek and Arman were learning essential perspective-taking skills, but also having fun and building relationships.[56]

These benefits seem to have been tacitly acknowledged by the news that the artificial intelligence industry, rapidly developing their chess-playing robots, are now trying to programme empathy and emotional expression into them.[57]

Borba encourages all parents to seek out any board or card games that help their children step into another's shoes.

———————————————— • • • ————————————————

We learnt in Chapters 2 and 3 how children who have been abused in some way, or who are on the autistic spectrum, find it difficult to learn at school. Worse, they can disrupt others' learning too. In 2012 two academics systematically reviewed more than fifty studies of parental maltreatment of children and the resultant difficulty their offspring had in recognising and understanding emotions. By the time they're in primary school, up to the age of eleven, the evidence was clear: such children are seen as disruptive by classmates, causing more fights; they have a poorer social understanding of feelings, desires and cooperative behaviour; and they are generally less likely to help others.[58] If deployed, the empathy instinct can tackle this very important problem.

A year later, in 2013, Louise Bombèr and Daniel Hughes wrote an influential book about this, *Settling Troubled Pupils to Learn: Why Relationships Matter in School.* They say that we're often shocked by the behaviour of disruptive pupils and particularly their lack of remorse at the problems they engender. But we should remember that they need their own opportunity to have someone (in this case, the teacher) demonstrate empathy for them before they can do so for themselves and others. The danger for hard-pressed teachers is that they withdraw emotionally and resort to simply 'doing their jobs'. Bombèr and Hughes say that giving teaching staff time to reflect on their practice (much as happens with the Schwartz Rounds for doctors that we'll look at in Chapter 6), can allow them to think through responses to challenging behaviour from children who are stressed or traumatised. The authors offer the following four precepts:

1. Co-regulation leads to self-regulation: empathy can greatly assist a pupil in moderating his strong emotions.

2. Trust: empathy assists a pupil to trust our intentions.

3. Making sense of what's happening: empathy helps a pupil to make sense of his behaviour and ours.

4. Facilitating communication: empathy increases a pupil's readiness to communicate his inner life to us.[59]

Bombèr and Hughes conclude by asking whether it isn't time for empathy to be clearly written into our behaviour policy for all schools. They are not the first to focus on how a teacher's understanding of the empathy instinct could pay dividends. In fact, it forms the basis, whether explicitly or implicitly, of much of the practice of educational psychologists dealing with problem children.[60] But it is probably less understood by teachers themselves. This is why there are those, in both the US and the UK, now establishing programmes that bake empathy into the life and philosophy of a school. We'll look at the American Ashoka project in Chapter 8. Here in Britain, Miranda McKearney has founded the embryonic EmpathyLab. She used to run a literacy charity and sees phenomena such as cyber-bullying as evidence that a serious empathy deficit may be developing in young people. McKearney defines key empathy skills as emotion recognition, deep listening and conversation, valuing others' perspectives and feelings and, finally, pro-social attitudes and behaviours. There are a small number of primary school head teachers who already subscribe to an overt application of the empathy instinct. One who runs a school of 750 in Sheffield told me that 60 per cent of her charges are on pupil premium, which is additional funding to raise the attainment of children from disadvantaged backgrounds.

She said that by definition they are deprived and so she needs to deploy the disciplines of empathy with them before she can begin to tackle their numeracy and literacy. Some of them are not able to socialise properly, not able to concentrate and thus not able to learn.

McKearney believes that literature and the telling of stories can promote this essential empathy and she has persuaded ten schools to pilot a range of activities. We visited two of them:

Netley Marsh is a small primary school for four- to seven-year-olds in the New Forest in Hampshire. The school has six core values, one of which is Openness ('I open my heart and mind to people and ideas that are different'), so the staff are already very interested in the empathy instinct. Matt Perrett, Head of Learning, teaches a class about 'point of view'. The children stand in a circle around a giant die. Michelle can see the number 5 from her angle. Jim can see number 2 and Hannah the number 6. Yet, of course, they are all looking at the same die. Recognition of the concept of different perspectives dawns on their faces.

In another class they're having an actual 'empathy lesson'. Four children are asked to imagine they're about to watch a film at home. But there's a sofa with only three places and only three bags of popcorn. One by one they're asked to imagine and articulate what it means to be the one left out. They do this by formally standing on different cardboard shoes in turn, each having a go at standing in the pair which represents the person excluded. There are also empathy cards given out for children who have displayed the instinct and a board inside the entrance with important empathy quotes.

In Britain's culture, emotion is often understated and so it's intriguing to hear Matt Perrett talk about how the children are responding:

> The kids really seem to love learning about empathy. When we asked them to put on an empathy show the other day, they made us a song and wouldn't let us leave at the end of the day until they'd sung it to us a few times: 'Empathy is good. Empathy is great. We love empathy. You should too.'[61]

Beck Primary School, for five- to eleven-year-olds, is situated on the outskirts of Sheffield. They've gathered thirty-six seven- and eight-year-olds in their school gym-cum-hall. Amy Willoughby, one of the teachers, has selected them carefully, with half of them being particularly empathetic and the other half being rather less so. Her idea is that one group might help the other. Their special guest this morning is the children's author Alan MacDonald. They're taken through a number of exercises the purpose of which is to help them identify emotions – how you would react to someone whose cat had just died; matching facial expressions to particular emotions; acting out particular emotions in a role-play. But the centrepiece of the session is MacDonald reading from his book *Trolls Go Home*. Derived from the *Billy Goats Gruff* classic, it imagines the troll family leaving Norway in shame and settling in England, having a particularly hard time of it in the suburbs. Are trolls 'grotesque, petrifying, ugly, slug-breathed' or might there be other adjectives to describe them? Should they bite their new teacher and might anyone befriend them to explain why this is not such a good idea?

Then Amy introduces the concept of 'empathy leaders' – children who watch out for others in the playground who look lonely or unhappy in some way. She asked those who wished to volunteer 'for this special honour' during the following week to talk to her. The acting Head Teacher of Beck said this of the programme:

Before the EmpathyLab came along we already knew we needed to focus on social and emotional skills because a majority of our students are on pupil premium . . . Empathy training is about giving our children social experiences that they don't always get enough of at home.[62]

●●●

Volunteering

Anthony Bloomfield is sixteen and has been laying a new path in a community garden in Bristol. He's given three weeks of his time to the National Citizen Service, a government initiative which works with local charities to create volunteering opportunities for young people. 'This has changed my life for the better,' he's quoted as saying in an *Independent* piece about the project. There are now a range of such schemes offered by several groups – vinspired, the British Youth Council, the Prince's Trust, the WRVS – and they offer a number of benefits. There's the training, the benefits of being mentored, of establishing a wider network and an introduction to the disciplines of work. But the reporter from the *Independent* saw something else: 'At a time when bullies stalk teens on Facebook, there is a warmth that comes from these youngsters who are engaging with their peers face to face. It is striking to be among a group of young people who are not constantly looking at their phones. Social interaction takes the place of social media.'[63]

Young people who have volunteered through the National Citizen Service are then eligible to benefit from Head Start, rolled out in London, Birmingham and Manchester so far.[64] This offers workshops designed to boost employability and, crucially, hone interpersonal skills.

— — — — — — — — — • • • — — — — — — — —

As Miranda McKearney develops the EmpathyLab, she wants to offer more and more materials which will inspire activities in schools. One is the Empathy Oscars, where children nominate and vote for their favourite empathetic book characters. As she puts it, 'in the process of celebrating great acts of empathy in stories, children are encouraged to reflect on what empathy is, and how to put it into action'. It is based on the widely acknowledged idea that fiction – the telling of human stories – allows the reader to practise empathy and the theory of mind it requires. (We touched on this idea in 'George Eliot, Neuroscientist?' in Chapter 2, and we'll look at it in greater depth in Chapter 8.) McKearney's definition of the key elements of empathy is familiar to us: empathetic communication, the ability to value, feel, understand and respect other people's feelings, emotion recognition, strong imagination and the capacity for reflection. These are qualities which we explore throughout this book. And they are of interest to the thousands of neuroscientists, anthropologists and psychologists who are studying the empathy instinct around the world. But we are still, at the most, only halfway to understanding how the empathy instinct works. Equally, we're only beginning to get to grips with the new internet age and its effect on how we think and behave. If we can put the two bodies of knowledge together, as the pioneers quoted in this chapter are trying to do, then the benefits to our civil society will be immense.

ARTIFICIAL INTELLIGENCE

When the Mayor of Palo Alto in California, now home to Silicon Valley, writes to the President of the United States warning that technology is a 'Frankenstein monster' that threatens to 'devour our civilisation', we should sit up and listen. In fact, the technology he was referring to was industrial automation, and the President was Herbert Hoover, at the time of the Great Depression.[65] I doubt today's Mayor of Palo Alto would be caught expressing such sentiments, and yet current advances in artificial intelligence (AI) represent a far more profound challenge to humanity than any innovations in manufacturing seventy-five years ago. Then the fear was a loss of jobs in an already difficult time. Now, in the twenty-first century, AI similarly seeks to replace many tasks currently executed by people – advanced robots on production lines, drones in place of delivery drivers, driverless buses and trains, intelligent diagnosis and interventions in healthcare. But AI represents something far more profound. In the long term it could seek not just to replace humans, but also to replicate us – physically, intellectually, emotionally.

On the face of it, AI will be a great boon in the immediate future. The next stage of AI is 'machine learning' where computers understand us better and can anticipate as well as satisfy our needs. That sounds quite empathetic. But there is a further step, human-level machine intelligence (HLMI). A survey of the world's top AI researchers suggests that there's a 10 per cent chance it will have been achieved by 2030, a 50 per cent chance by 2050 and a 90 per cent chance by 2100 (babies born now will still be living and active then). Elon Musk, the electric-car billionaire, says AI is 'potentially more dangerous than nukes'. Stephen Hawking has said that 'the development of full artificial intelligence could spell the end of the human race'. Professor Nick Bostrom, author of *Superintelligence*, is both an evangelist for AI and a Cassandra:

> It's not just another cool gadget or another nifty little thing. It's the last invention humans will ever need to make . . . With the AI transition we will automate human thoughts, human brain power. It's hard to think of any area of human life that would not be impacted in some way.[66]

So Bostrom's warning is about computers acquiring a mind of their own and threatening human existence. But he reminds us that AI is a fact and his book is about working out how we control it before we unleash it further.

Can AI develop to such an extent that it's capable of performing all human jobs? A 2013 Oxford University study forecast that intelligent machines might be able to perform half of all US jobs in as little as twenty years. Its authors, though, cited psychologist as an occupation that was least likely to be replaced, owing to the human, empathetic qualities required.[67] It may be the ambition of AI developers to ape all human functions, but Dr Pamela Rutledge, Director of the Media Psychology Research Center in Santa Barbara, California, is sceptical thus far:

> Advances in AI and robotics allow people to cognitively offload repetitive tasks and invest their attention and energy in things where humans can make a difference. We already have cars that talk to us, a phone we can talk to, robots that lift the elderly out of bed, and apps that remind us to call Mom. An app can dial Mom's number and even send flowers, but an app can't do that most human of all things: emotionally connect with her.[68]

Jerry Kaplan, a Silicon Valley entrepreneur who also teaches a class in AI at Stanford University, believes similarly that work which involves meaningful personal interaction will not be affected. His example is that you don't want an undertaker robot to say, 'I'm sorry for your loss.'[69] Another Silicon Valley sage, Jamais Cascio, agrees:

> The kind of jobs that are the most difficult to replace with machines are the jobs that depend on empathy and human connection; things machines can't do reliably and effectively. So it will be much simpler to replace a university professor than it will be to replace a kindergarten teacher. It will be much easier to replace a surgeon than a nurse . . . the jobs that last are the ones driven by empathy and human contact.[70]

When the burden of systematising is removed from humans by intelligent machines, what do we have left? Already devices are having a telling effect. If you look at the percentage of US economic output that is represented by wages, it's at its lowest level since such measurements began in the 1950s. In 1964 a top technology stock was the telephone company AT&T. It employed thirteen times more people than Google does now, a company worth more today than AT&T ever was. Some believe that as technology develops it will invent new categories of job. But the evidence suggests that that won't be enough to enable mass employment.

Typically, employment has been seen as a measure of self-respect and societal esteem. When the steel industry collapsed in Youngstown, Ohio, in the 1970s there was a swift increase in spousal abuse, depression and suicides.[71] That was in a specific area and a particular industrial sector. AI represents a universal shift. The Astronomer Royal has written about whether we'll need 'massive redistribution of wealth so the benefits don't just go to the elite owners of robots'.[72] Some might argue that this process is under way when the internet economy is already dominated by a few enormous players. Nick Bostrom has asked how we'll be able to maintain the standards necessary for the welfare and stability a functioning society needs. A scientist at BBN Technologies has speculated that parts of the economy could be 're-humanised' as blue-collar and white-collar jobs are replaced by automated systems and that then there will be increasing demand for artisanal products – made by humans for humans:

In the long run this trend will actually push towards re-localisation and re-humanisation of the economy, with the 19th- and 20th-century economies of scale exploited where they make sense (cheap, identical, disposable goods) and human-oriented techniques (both older and newer) increasingly accounting for goods and services that are valuable, customised or long-lasting.[73]

Even if we sort out all those problems, can we handle much greater leisure? Only if we enhance the rewards of human relationships. Then we'd have the pleasure of living and loving, delights that empathy affords us. Unless by then we've allowed the digital age to expunge these most beautiful of sentiments. Bostrom posits that when computers can design computers, a sort of definition of AI, then the process of discovery might become rapidly accelerated. Such leaps as preventing ageing, which might have taken tens of thousands of years to achieve, could be realised in the immediate future, or so its evangelists speculate.[74] All the more reason to preserve our humanity – it might be good to live for ever, so long as it doesn't seem like it's for ever. The pleasure we take in each other may become even more precious than it is today. But only if we nurture the empathy instinct.

5

CRIME AND PUNISHMENT

In thirty years' time our judicial system will be unrecognisably different from that of today. Criminal courts will seek to connect with transgressors to change them, rather than punish them and send them on their way. Routine fMRI scans will identify psychopaths and others with an empathy deficit as people requiring special attention. There will be programmes to repair the parts of their brains which malfunction. 'Restorative justice', where victims and perpetrators come to terms, will be widely employed. And prisons will become places which reintegrate inmates into society, rather than isolate and alienate them. In health we can no longer afford the burgeoning demand for critical medicine, and a decisive shift is under way in favour of prevention rather than cure. So, with justice, we'll increasingly seek to prevent crime rather than punish it. This will mean putting much more effort into repairing broken families. Countless well-documented studies, particularly in the US, show how this early investment pays social dividends. As we saw in Chapter 3, training first-time mothers at risk in child-rearing and behaviour management (the empathy skills) showed that their offspring were less likely to get into trouble with the law as they grew up – as one report put it, thus helping to 'reduce the number of little trouble-makers and, in doing so, in the long term, the number of big trouble-makers'.[1] In his book about crime prevention Nick Ross points out that it costs twice as much to send teenagers to young-offender institutions as it does to send them to Eton. In America this equation is expressed as its costing far more to get sent to 'jail than Yale'.[2]

EMPATHY AND OFFENDING

Everyone agrees there's a link between a lack of empathy and breaking the law. But because neuroscience is still unlocking the functions and malfunctions of our brains, not everyone agrees how. It's not surprising: in all emerging areas of science there's always a welter of theories and counter-theories until the true picture eventually crystallises.

In 2003 Darrick Jolliffe wrote a Cambridge PhD thesis which scrutinised thirty-five studies on the subject. He could see that low empathy correlated with offending but concluded that both phenomena might be the result of other factors such as a disrupted family or poverty, or congenital charac-teristics such as low intelligence or impulsivity.[3] Jolliffe also thought that measurements of empathy varied a good deal. So he constructed his Basic Empathy Scale to try to regularise such studies. With its questions it tests for both low cognitive empathy ('It is hard for me to understand when my friends are sad') and for diminished affective empathy ('I usually feel calm when other people are scared'). Jolliffe's belief was that improving affective empathy – successfully experiencing someone else's emotions – is important in stopping a cycle of offending. This is certainly the case with psychopaths, but they comprise only one category of criminal. A Dutch study in 2014 argued that a deficit in cognitive empathy – understanding the emotions of others – is a greater influence.[4] And a large American research project probed the relationship between empathy and aggression, concluding that it's not clear cut at all. Its authors warned against too many therapies based simply on empathy while the data is still affected by measurement problems.[5] Work in progress.

Since completing his PhD, Jolliffe has explored a different characteristic that causes individuals to break the law: impulsivity. In his Basic Empathy Scale he has asked to what extent is a person daring by nature. Those who answer 'mostly' or 'always' have higher levels of offending. But, of these, some are higher in empathy and some lower. However, among people he's tested who are not very impulsive, there's a clear connection between empathy and crime: those with low empathy scores in this category are much more likely to be offenders. He summarises it as follows: 'Empathy and offending are related, but impulsivity overwhelms this.'[6] As we'll see, when individuals can understand the consequences of their impulsive behaviour this becomes an important deterrent. It helps prevent criminal behaviour. Most children learn this lesson at an early age and it means they can develop socially positive attitudes. It's why, as we saw in Chapter 3, an explanation is better than a smack.

So low levels of empathy can result in anti-social, criminal behaviour. But often one doesn't cause the other, rather they coexist: offending is sometimes caused by other factors which themselves can also give rise to defective emotional intelligence. More recently Jolliffe's work on how we can help people get out of a cycle of offending and reoffending has led to his comparing inmates of Wandsworth Prison with similar lawbreakers who were put on probation. Whatever caused them to offend in the first place he has a clear conclusion that, while prison may protect society from convicts in the short term, it does not rehabilitate them:

> If you fear for your safety, if you don't know when you can call home, if you're shut in a cell for up to twenty-three hours a day, you're not improving. You can't slam them up and hope they're going to change. People who've been to prison are more likely to reoffend than people who've been on probation, and more likely to reoffend more often.[7]

So how we treat people once they've offended is just as important an issue as why they offended in the first place.

ARE OUR PRISONS THE PROBLEM? CAN THEY BE THE SOLUTION?

Visitors to an art installation in a disused Victorian prison, in the autumn of 2016, saw at first hand the misguided origins of our modern penal system.[8] Reading Gaol was designed by George Gilbert Scott and opened in 1844. Single cells isolated prisoners for twenty-three hours a day, on the grounds that they might be a bad influence on each other. They didn't realise that this deprivation would be entirely counter-productive. Solitary confinement and lack of human contact are themselves very damaging. Reading's most famous prisoner Oscar Wilde later wrote, in *De Profundis*, of 'a thousand lifeless lives' and how it was 'always twilight in one's cell, as it is always midnight in one's heart'.

'Only one drug is so addictive, nine out of ten laboratory rats will use it. And use it. And use it. Until dead. It's called cocaine. And it can do the same thing to you.' This skilful piece of 1970s copywriting in the US created the voice-over for pictures of frenzied, narcotically poisoned rodents. It was part of a campaign meant to scare Americans off drugs, though the subsequent consumption of cocaine on that continent suggests it may not have worked. A Canadian psychologist at the Simon Fraser University in British Columbia had a completely different reaction when he saw it. Bruce Alexander wondered why the rats were all isolated in individual cages. Was this predicament, wholly unnatural for a social breed, in fact the cause of their galloping drug habit? So he conceived a study in which some rats were put in solitary confinement, as they had been in the television advertisement. Meanwhile a separate group were housed together in something he called 'Rat Park', a sort of idealised rodent resort with gourmet food, jolly wheels and lots of other rats to socialise and copulate with. In both environments were two bottles, one with water and the other containing a morphine solution. The results appeared to support Alexander's thesis.

Over a period of around sixty days the isolated rats drank nineteen times more of the morphine water than those in Rat Park. The latter much preferred plain tap water and didn't seem very interested in consuming the opiates, which tended to interfere with their exciting and fulfilling lifestyle. He also tried a number of other variations during the study. One involved some solitary rats to which he gave exclusively morphine water, for fifty-seven days. Then they were released into Rat Park with the same choice as before. They suffered withdrawal symptoms, of course, but most soon exercised a preference for plain water, allowing them to lead a normal life in the resort. Alexander concluded that addiction is probably caused by our reaction to oppressive circumstances, rather than being an inherent property of the drug itself. This was highly controversial and to begin with his findings were refused publication. Even when he eventually had the report accepted in 1981, it still caused a furore. Critics argued that the rats' behaviour could be down to genetic disposition as much as environment and alleged that Alexander's findings were difficult to replicate.[9] We needn't get bogged down in yet another nature-versus-nurture debate here, obsessing about the true causes of addiction. What is just as interesting is a simpler conclusion: rats shut up on their own, without normal social contact, were more likely to take drugs (it's an echo of Harry Harlow's unhappy monkeys, deprived of maternal contact). And what does that remind us of? Yes, our prison population, among whom drugs are rife. A recent report from the think tank the Centre for Social Justice (CSJ) said:

Prisons in England and Wales have a serious drug problem
. . . Drug-using prisoners are suffering from physical and
mental health conditions and their chances of rehabilitation
are slim . . . One of the chief purposes of prison is to reduce
crime. In this regard they are clearly failing.[10]

Although the incidence of traditional drugs such as cannabis
and heroin has fallen latterly, the use of legal highs has rock-
eted. These new psychoactive substances have had their
chemical structure altered to evade current drug laws. They
can therefore have unpredictable and life-threatening effects.
In May 2016, Britain's newly appointed Chief Inspector of
Prisons reported that synthetic cannabis is having a devas-
tating effect on prisons. Peter Clarke said prison staff had
told him this was wholly unlike anything they'd seen before:
'At the moment the situation appears to be getting worse not
better.'[11]

In April 2016 synthetic drugs were made illegal, but when
I was in contact with Clarke later that summer he said, 'In
the prisons I've been to in the past few weeks, they are still
readily available.'[12] The introduction of experimental Drug
Recovery Wings in some prisons has proved effective in
weaning inmates off drugs, particularly where all the staff are
trained in addiction therapies. A Department of Health evaluation observes that in these circumstances they trust the staff,
finding them to be 'approachable, empathetic and understanding'.[13] As we'll see, there may be strong arguments for
prisons, but they have to be run in a way which helps solve
crime, not fuel it.

Prison Works?

When he was Conservative Home Secretary Michael Howard made a speech in September 1993 which was met with roars of approval at the party's annual conference. It culminated with these words: 'Prison works.' He has since linked the falling crime rate with the rising prison population (itself disputable, as we're not sure whether modern cyber-crime is properly recorded at all). There are, however, undisputed statistics about prisons. This is how they work:

46 per cent of all prisoners released reoffend within a year
60 per cent of those on short sentences reoffend within a year
50 per cent of inmates have numeracy and literacy at primary school levels
24 per cent of those in prison were in care as a child
49 per cent have identifiable mental-health problems[14]
27 per cent was the increase in self-harm incidents in the year to March 2016, rising to 405 per 1,000 prisoners[15]
29 per cent admit to having a drug problem[16]
20 per cent of heroin users first tried the drug in prison[17]

Prisons didn't cause all these social ills. But they caused some of them and exacerbated the rest. If you were born with low levels of the empathy instinct or had it suppressed during your early years, there's a chance you'll end up in prison. There your predicament will markedly worsen.

• • •

Criminology is the scientific study of crime – why we break the law and how effectively it can be prevented. The first professor appointed in the subject was at Cambridge University and when I read Law there in the 1970s we sat a paper in this embryonic subject. We used to joke that you could get an upper second by simply writing, 'Don't blame the individual, blame society.' Society is the nurture bit, to which we might add the element of nature – for instance, psychopaths. But what is the answer to the proposition that all lawbreakers are victims of either their genetic inheritance, their upbringing or both and cannot be blamed for their crimes? Today jurists and philosophers recognise the idea that all individuals have to be held *responsible* for their behaviour, in the vital interests of an ordered society. This doctrine says that even if you are born a psychopath it is not acceptable to infringe the rights of others. You should learn not to do so, or be prevented from doing so in some other way. It also argues that if you are the victim of a broken home, abuse or other deprivation you must understand that, although this can explain why you break the law, it cannot justify it. In this way we uphold our laws and values. But it follows that we should do all we can to assist these victims of nature and nurture, and that's something all prisons should contribute to.

Even in those early days of criminology, we learnt some very useful things, and it was more diverting than the somewhat arid territory of case and statute law (to come clean, it was the only paper in which I achieved better than a third, the lowest possible pass for an honours degree). So I can still recite the six possible reasons for putting someone in prison. In the light of what we now know they deserve renewed scrutiny:

1. *Retribution*: This is the biblical idea of revenge, of an 'eye for an eye, a tooth for a tooth' – that a person deserves to suffer when they've made someone else suffer and that the victim deserves to see that happen. In absolute terms, incarceration is meant to represent an upholding of our moral code.

2. *General deterrence*: When we know there's a real risk of being apprehended and punished, we are less likely to offend.

3. *Deterrence of the offender*: This is the idea that the person punished is less likely to reoffend.

4. *Rehabilitation*: Here the criminal is not merely deterred in future, but reformed, not wishing to offend any longer.

5. *Protection of the public*: While the criminal is behind bars, society is safe from further bad behaviour.

6. *Protection of the offender*: A unilateral attack on the criminal by victims or vigilantes is not possible during confinement.

The trouble with retribution is that revenge is rather out of fashion and is seen as essentially uncivilised. Its logical corollary is the death penalty for murderers ('Let the punishment fit the crime', as the Victorian W. S. Gilbert wrote in *The Mikado*). But we did away with capital punishment more than half a century ago. As a general deterrent, criminal sanctions don't have to involve jail to have some effect. And anyway the evidence has long been clear that if you don't think you'll be caught, you won't be deterred even by harsh sentences imposed on others.[18] It's clear too that general deterrence is not that powerful a force for serial offenders (and that most criminals stop offending around the age of forty anyway). Protection of the public is obviously achieved by locking up criminals. But only until they're let out. At which point, we should observe, if prison more often than not leads to reoffending then that protection is pretty short term. Which leaves us with rehabilitation. This is a fine idea, but if we really cared about it we would change the system so that it lowers our very high reoffending rates. In the light of everything we now know about the empathy instinct, rehabilitation is being rethought on both sides of the Atlantic. It starts in prison.

A 2007 report from the US Department of Justice confirmed what is now blindingly obvious: that the act of incarceration actually increases the likelihood of a felon reoffending. The report said that facilities which incorporate 'Cognitive-behavioral programs rooted in social learning theory are the most effective in reducing recidivism.'[19] (We'll come back to cognitive behavioural therapy – CBT – later.) Unfortunately, many Americans are still of the hang 'em/ shoot 'em/flog 'em school of criminology. Retribution is alive and well as a philosophy in the land of the free (or not so free). They'd do well to study Norway, the country with the lowest recidivism rate in Europe. Firstly, they avoid prison if they possibly can. Per head of population the Norwegians send proportionately one-tenth the number of people to prison that the Americans do. If your express aim was to produce as many offenders as possible, who were most likely to go on and offend again, you would organise your prison system along US lines. And when the Norwegians do resort to prison they've designed them around the idea of rehabilitation. The result is that their rate of reoffending currently stands at around 20 per cent. The American number exceeds 70 per cent. The most often quoted institution in Norway's penal system is Bastøy Prison Island, where the recidivism rate is the lowest of any prison in Europe, at 13 per cent. It has been criticised as 'cushy' and 'luxurious', and journalists like to feature photographs of the inmates sunbathing. But the Governor, Arne Kvernik Nilsen, says:

> being sent to prison is nothing to do with putting you in a terrible prison to suffer. The punishment is that you lose your freedom. If we treat people like animals when they are in prison they are likely to behave like animals. Here we pay attention to you as a human being.[20]

In November 2013 it was announced that prisoners in British jails would no longer automatically be allowed to receive parcels. It was an attempt to introduce a system of privileges to motivate better behaviour from inmates. A public protest, with a nod to Oscar Wilde, was organised, dubbed The Ballad of Not Reading in Gaol. A judge then decided that the order was unlawful and, a year later, it was repealed. What the argument encapsulated nicely was the conflict between authoritarianism and rehabilitation in penal policy. Mark Haddon, the author of *The Curious Incident of the Dog in the Night-Time*, pointed out in the *Guardian* that, apart from the pressing need to encourage literacy, reading books is one of the few solaces in an oppressive place, where inmates are sometimes locked up for twenty-three hours a day. He accused government ministers themselves of lacking empathy.[21]

There have been more promising signals from the government, however. A review of prison education is intended to give control of the budgets to governors, who will be able to bring in new providers.[22] There will also be a fresh social enterprise, similar to Teach First, which encourages bright graduates to go into education. The idea is to get a similar cadre into the prison services.

The former Prime Minister David Cameron was referring to reoffending rates when he said in 2016, 'the failure of our system today is scandalous'. In the same speech he went on: 'So the question must be: wouldn't we be better to focus our scarce resources on preventing crime in the first place and by breaking the cycle of reoffending?'[23] Cameron also called for a system which uses the latest evidence from behavioural insights, something they think about carefully at the Institute of Criminology in Cambridge. In particular, they take the power of empathy very seriously. They've developed a philosophy called Every Contact Matters. The powerful idea is that every interaction in prison has the potential to be rehabilitative. In 2013 this was trialled at Portland Prison in Dorset. In what they called a Five-Minute Intervention, prison officers were trained to talk to inmates in a way that would aid rehabilitation. Here are the four key elements:

1. *Socratic questioning*: Questions are structured to help inmates think through the probable consequences of their actions and think about assumptions they make.

2. *Giving and receiving feedback*: This particularly calls for positive responses to achievements, however small.

3. *Active listening*: Taking time to hear and understand the underlying issues behind a problem an inmate may raise.

4. *Giving hope*: Actively taking opportunities to communicate encouragement, particularly in respect of not reoffending.

This brings to mind the reflective-listening advice for parents, quoted in Chapter 3, particularly the third point about active listening. Once again, this is the conscious practice of theory of mind in order to connect properly with another person. In the Portland Prison trial eight officers were trained in this way and, as a control, eight were not. There were clear advantages reported afterwards for the trained group, both for their charges and for the officers themselves. The prisoners were found to be less impulsive, had better emotion management and were more optimistic about their chances of changing. As a result of the officers' newfound ability to enhance their empathetic skills, they found they had better relationships with inmates and greater job satisfaction.[24] The Five-Minute Intervention is now being rolled out in the Welsh prison service.

SCIENCE AND REHABILITATION

Daniel Reisel started as a doctor and went on to get a PhD in behavioural neuroscience. You can watch a brilliant TED Talk he gave in 2013.[25] Its starting point is his experience working at Wormwood Scrubs prison with inmates who'd been clinically classified as psychopaths. Looking at their brains in an fMRI scanner, Reisel noticed underactivity in their amygdala, one of those areas in our empathy circuit. They couldn't identify with others' emotions, they couldn't empathise. But when I met Reisel for breakfast he encouraged me not to think of psychopathy as a permanent state (though he acknowledged that there are a few, such as the Norwegian mass murderer Anders Breivik, who are irredeemably ill). For Reisel, empathy is an instinct which changes depending on each individual's nature, nurture, culture and state of mind. He pointed to the salmon on top of his scrambled eggs and said, 'I'm eating an animal right now. That could be called psychopathic.' He related how, at the beginning of his medical training, he was dissecting the cadaver of a woman. He suddenly noticed her red-painted nails, became nauseous and had to leave the room. By the end of his studies he'd hardened up and dissections couldn't faze him any more. Reisel drew a parallel between this process of disconnection and those who were able to commit atrocities in the genocides of the twentieth century.

After Wormwood Scrubs, Reisel then went on to conduct experiments with mice. He wanted to help challenge the old conventional wisdom that we cannot grow new brain cells after childhood. New research was showing that human brains can regenerate. The question followed, could conditions such as psychopathy be ameliorated in this way? Like Bruce Alexander and his rats, Reisel compared mice in solitary confinement with mice in a congenial version of the Rat Park – other mice to consort with, ladders and wheels plus places to explore. He found that, while the isolated mice failed to thrive and developed anti-social traits, the fulfilled mice in their own 'park' actually demonstrated *neurogenesis*. That is, they naturally grew new brain cells and were able to perform better on a range of learning and memory tasks. Today it's accepted that human brains can also show neurogenesis, including in the amygdala.[26]

But as with all the latest findings of neuroscience, it's very early days for this research. Just to give a sense of what the possibilities might be, consider a 2008 experiment by neuroscientists at Harvard on an individual with Asperger's Syndrome. They magnetically stimulated the region of his brain responsible for some of our empathetic skills – the dorsomedial prefrontal cortex. Miraculously the subject said that as a result he could, for the first time, understand 'messages in other people's facial expressions'. He had always struggled to read others' emotions until this point.[27]

Reisel imagines a day when we can help offenders with therapies which will help them repair the empathy function of their brain. This would need scientists and clinicians, social workers and policymakers, the courts and the prison authorities all to work together. He says that we now believe the human brain may be capable of extraordinary change in adulthood. But the brain is extremely sensitive to stress. Stress hormones released by the brain suppress the growth of new cells. Here's what he says in his talk:

> This is the interplay between nature and nurture in real time in front of our eyes. When you think about it, it is ironic that our current solution for people with stressed amygdalae is to place them in an environment that actually inhibits any chance of further growth. Of course, imprisonment is a necessary part of the criminal justice system and of protecting society. Our research does not suggest that criminals should submit their MRI scans as evidence in court and get off the hook because they've got a faulty amygdala. The evidence is actually the other way. Because our brains are capable of change, we need to take responsibility for our actions, and they need to take responsibility for their rehabilitation.

• • •

New Approaches to Court

Sir Charles Pollard is a retired Chief Constable and started in the police aged nineteen:

> When I used to go to court as a police officer I used to think, what a hopeless system for trying to reform offenders. The decision was made, guilty or not guilty, and there was no communication with the offender to make them think about what they'd done.[28]

Our courts system is still based on the retributive model of the nineteenth century. There is now a plethora of new approaches being tried around the world, with the accent strongly on rehabilitation instead. The three key principles are that the offender's progress is overseen by the same judge, prison is avoided where possible and justice is transacted speedily. These are based on well-established behavioural insights.

The idea started in Florida, in 1989, where drug offenders were sent to treatment centres rather than prison, and the same judge monitored them, able to send them to jail if they re-offended. This was not only shown to be more effective than prison, it was also cheaper. Today there are thousands of such courts in the US, covering the likes of gun crime, truancy and domestic abuse as well as addiction. More recently Hawaii's Opportunity Probation with Enforcement (HOPE) has excited a lot of interest. Here drug offenders are regularly given drug tests accompanied by a judge-given warning that a positive result will lead to a 'swift and certain' two- or three-day stay in prison. The programme is based on research revealing that a deferred and low probability of *severe* punishment is less of a deterrent than immediate and highly probable *mild* punishment. A study has shown that its participants are 55 per cent less likely to be arrested for a new crime and 72 per cent less likely to continue using drugs.[29]

In the UK, Family Courts have been pioneering this problem-solving approach. A five-year study, published in 2014, looked at mothers with addiction problems who appeared in the London Family Drug and Alcohol Court – which arranges subsequent meetings with the same judge and regular drug testing. It found that 40 per cent of the mothers managed to kick their habit, compared to 25 per cent going through more conventional courts.[30] In New Zealand, Australia and Canada this problem-solving approach has been extended to juvenile courts where family conferences are now the norm.

Early experiments of this sort in the UK proved expensive and cumbersome. Now, because of the international successes, the British government is setting up more problem-solving courts. The judiciary has a reputation for being naturally conservative. But one criminal judge told me that this could work if the sentencing guidelines gave him more latitude to avoid prison sentences and if the statistics-driven parole system didn't encourage the officers to give up on the hardest cases.

Andrew Neilson from the Howard League for Penal Reform says, 'The criminal justice system currently makes sentencing decisions on very little evidence about what works.'[31] When judges are able to see whether their verdicts are having any effect, they might develop a better understanding of offenders.

—————————— • • • ——————————

Criminologists in the US have become very interested in the possibility that neurogenesis might work with juvenile delinquents. This has arisen from an intriguing study carried out by Harvard Medical School. Its starting point was that, despite all the academic debate, there is certainly evidence that a low empathy quotient is a risk factor for youthful offending. This paper has the slightly unprepossessing title 'Mindfulness Practice Leads to Increases in Regional Gray Matter Density'. If you're typically of a sceptical bent, please bear with me as I explain what 'mindfulness' is.

Mindfulness has its roots in Buddhist meditation. It usually involves sitting cross-legged, perhaps on a cushion, with the back straight for periods of ten minutes, at least to begin with. You have to concentrate on the simple act of breathing and on how your body reacts via your abdomen and nostrils. If you notice your mind has wandered you accept it but calmly return to the simple focus. It took a professor at the University of Massachusetts Medical School to apply this ancient technique as a modern therapy. The explanation is in the name of the institution that Jon Kabat-Zinn founded: the Stress Reduction Clinic. As we know, when under stress our bodies release hormones, some of which affect our brain function. Kabat-Zinn's therapies, now being adopted quite widely, are intended to reverse that process, including at Harvard Medical School. They took thirty-three juvenile delinquents and split them into two groups, both of which had fMRI scans at the outset. None had been subjected to mindfulness-based stress reduction (MBSR) before. Sixteen of them then underwent an eight-week programme of MBSR. The other seventeen did not. Comparing the two groups afterwards, again with scans, was fascinating. The sixteen meditators actually showed increases in grey matter in their left hippocampi, compared to the other seventeen, who did not. The different regions in that part of the brain are involved in learning and memory processes, emotion regulation and perspective-taking.[32] It would appear, and this is not surprising, that when you successfully reduce stress in a person's life, and thus the stress hormones in their body, you enable them to function better emotionally.

A relatively early breakthrough in training the brain was

cognitive behavioural therapy (CBT). Although it doesn't work with extreme mental conditions it has been shown to succeed with the more mildly depressed and disturbed, and particularly with offenders. CBT was pioneered in the 1950s and is a recognised psychotherapy technique where patients are gradually guided to take a more positive view of their lives. A survey of more than fifty studies in the US demonstrated that it genuinely assisted the prevention of reoffending, by as much as 25 per cent compared to convicts who had no treatment. One of its practitioners likes to refer to this as 'habilitation' rather than rehabilitation, on the grounds that many of the treated offenders were learning skills and behaviours for the first time. Studies in Europe have been less conclusive, but it would appear there's much to be gained from both pursuing CBT and exploring its effects on the psyche.[33]

To reduce it to its simplest: treat people shrewdly and there's a good chance they'll behave better. What did a future British Prime Minister once say? Was it 'tough on crime, tough on the causes of crime'? The Harvard study and the CBT evidence point to the possibility of requiring offenders to participate in such programmes. It may sound a bit New Age but in fact would be entirely rational and hard headed. One thing we do know is that, whatever other benefits prison may have, consistent rehabilitation is not one of them.

So maybe it's a start that David Cameron's government launched a programme called Transforming Rehabilitation. It was designed to create a National Probation Service to deal with serious offenders and then drive Resettlement Services for the mass of less serious offenders. This was intended to extend formal rehabilitation to the most prolific reoffenders – those released from short custodial sentences – via Community Rehabilitation Companies. The programme has also been setting up what its advocates call 'through-the-prison-gate' services, which will try to bring consistent support to convicts both while they are in prison and after they emerge. It remains to be seen how effective these reforms are. But Britain currently spends £3 billion on prisons and £1 billion on connected services in the community. It's clear if we devoted more to the latter we'd need to spend less on the former.

ARTS, CULTURE AND REHABILITATION

In 1982 James Monahan brutally murdered two men in the space of three months, his only apparent motive being the petty cash he stole from them. He'd been living in a squat in Bethnal Green in east London but evaded arrest by fleeing to France. He eventually gave himself up, was convicted and ended up in Wandsworth Prison. There, during his first Christmas inside, the inmate of the cell above his hanged himself. Sixteen years later, as he continued to serve out his sentence, a journalist called Erwin James started to write a regular column about him in the *Guardian*, revealing what it was like inside Wakefield Prison, to which he'd been transferred. It related how Monahan had come under the influence of a prison psychologist called Joan Branton. She listened to him, not uncritically, but without passing judgement and succeeded in making him feel like an ordinary person. Then she encouraged him to take English O-Level, followed by an Open University degree. These articles in a national newspaper became celebrated, particularly for the insight they gave into life behind bars. As you might already know, James Monahan and Erwin James were one and the same person – after his degree he'd successfully become a journalist. He was released in 2004 and now works for various prison charities, is a fellow of the Royal Society for the Encouragement of the Arts and still contributes pieces to the *Guardian*. An article of his written in 2015 explored the statistic that around half of prisoners in solitary confinement suffer from mental-health problems, more than double the figure for all prisoners.[34]

When he emerged he went to look for Joan Branton, long retired. He located her but before he managed to see her to thank her for completely changing his life, she died. His memoir of 2016 tells the story, ending like this: 'We all need champions, people who believe in us and who want us to succeed, whatever life path we find ourselves on. I found a champion in Joan Branton. She made me believe that I was redeemable.'[35]

Monahan has written about how the gift she gave him was education, in his case in the arts and humanities. These lifted him 'like he'd never been lifted before'.[36] A 2016 Arts and Humanities Research Council (AHRC) report, *Understanding the Value of Arts and Culture*, talks about 'the ability of arts and cultural engagement to help shape reflective individuals, facilitating greater understanding of themselves and their lives, increasing empathy with respect to others . . .'.[37]

That same year the educationist Dame Sally Coates wrote

that education which increases employability is a key to reducing reoffending, and that this should include greater access to high-quality arts. She questions why they're not part of the existing offenders' education service:

> The provision of art, drama and music courses is not a core part of the Offenders' Learning and Skills Service arrangements. Where they do operate, and where there have been one-off projects or performances with visiting arts companies, they are often the first thing that prisoners, staff and Governors tell me about. The arts are one route towards engaging prisoners when they have had negative experience of traditional classroom subjects, or struggle with self-esteem and communication. They can be the first step towards building confidence for more formal learning.[38]

Even though they are not yet core to prison education, the arts are playing a growing role in rehabilitating prisoners and juvenile offenders and there's a swelling evidence base about their effectiveness.

Music

The Irene Taylor Trust funds and develops music projects. Each Music in Prisons project lasts for five days and helps groups of prisoners to form a band, make their own music and professionally record it. A former Lord Chief Justice, Harry Woolf, said that the work helps break the 'vicious circle of offending, imprisonment, release and reoffending resulting in return to prison'. Another of the Trust's programmes, Sounding Out, helps released prisoners get their lives back on track with live performances and paid training placements. Both these programmes have been professionally evaluated, emerging very positively as efficacious and cost-effective.[39]

Literature

The Reader is an organisation based in Liverpool which pioneers the empathetic, healing properties of being read to aloud in groups. Its staff now work in nineteen prisons, as well as all the jails in Northern Ireland. You could call it bedtime stories for troubled adults. One prisoner who takes part regularly said:

> This group is the best thing I do in here. It took me a while to get my head around it – being with so many people in the room all at once was a big adjustment . . . there's an emphasis on great literature and the reading can be quite rich. We read *Frankenstein*, one chapter at a time. It took us a year! It was a deep one – there was so much to talk about and it was quite exciting because you didn't know where the conversation would end up.[40]

Dance

Dance United is an arts company which runs a project called the Academy, in Yorkshire, London and Wessex. It takes young offenders and those at risk of offending and puts them through twelve-week training courses with professional performances at the end. What an evaluation study saw during that time is a 'normalising' effect, calming the participants down and giving them more emotional control, leading to greater maturity. Dance United feel it's particularly effective with those who are not naturally articulate – it gives them an eloquent, alternative mode of expression. The low drop-out rate is impressive and, although it's generally a small sample, the evidence is that there is a significant reduction in re-offending.[41] It costs £7,000 to take one young person through the programme. And an independent report has calculated that for each participant who does not reoffend, the public purse saves £83,000.[42]

Drama

The Clean Break Theatre Company was founded by Jenny Hicks and Jackie Holborough while they were both inmates at Askham Grange prison. They work within prisons and with people after their release. The AHRC report cites a particular prison performance where men convicted of domestic abuse were seated around the stage for a play about violent men and their effect on their female and child victims: 'the art itself had a powerful impact, but so did watching their fellow prisoners watching the art . . . a graphic example of how art can provide the distance and the engagement that together provoke reflection'. This was put on by the Geese Theatre Company which also works in Birmingham with the probation service, youth offending teams and secure hospitals: 'We believe that theatre performance and drama are powerful and effective tools for inviting individuals to examine their own behaviour and acting [sic] as a catalyst for promoting personal development and change.'

Visual Art

Of all the disciplines, visual art has been in prisons the longest. The Koestler Trust has been running a prisoners' art competition for fifty-five years and now offers creative writing as well. The Trust also mentors prisoners after release and says its programmes lead to 'employable skills, high self-esteem, collaboration with others and a feeling of purpose in life'. Dr Leonidas Cheliotis of the London School of Economics carried out a study of Koestler's mentoring scheme in 2014. He found 'long-term, positive effects on the mentored offenders, especially pro-social attitudes that reduce the likelihood of reoffending'.[43]

But it would be wrong to suggest that the use of these therapies has become universal or even widespread. This is something that causes some perplexity among those who take a more enlightened approach to rehabilitation in their own countries. The reaction of some Norwegians at an international conference was summed up by the British delegate like this:

> You mean you don't start rehabilitation as soon as people arrive in prison? How do you manage to fit in education and skills training before they leave? You mean you bang people up for 23 hours without anything to do? Why do you do that? You get no (or little) core funding from the state? Don't they know it works? We know it works.[44]

Where they're happening, the success of these arts interventions is down to a combination of the inspiring work itself and the personal attention and care from all the arts professionals engaging with troubled individuals. In some cases they'll never have had such an intense, personal and positive experience before in their lives. This can be the path to desistance (ceasing to offend). The AHRC report cites an Ohio study, listing four key steps towards desistance: openness to change, exposure to 'hooks' for change, imagining and believing in a replacement self, and changing the way offending is viewed.[45] It's thought that, although the arts can help several of these stages, its significant effect is on the third – imagining and believing in a different self. This requires improved confidence, motivation and self-esteem. It needs an ability to form more open and positive relationships and becoming someone who's willing to go through a learning process to achieve an alternative future. But it also demands a different attitude from all of us towards offenders. Perhaps the most exacting of us, for good reason, are the victims of crime. In 2010 the Koestler Trust boldly and imaginatively asked crime victims to curate an exhibition of offenders' art. One of them, Vanessa Pearson, said afterwards, 'I used to believe offenders should not be given any privileges – as they didn't deserve it. Now I believe activities like art can make a big difference to offenders in a good way.'[46]

Bringing victims and offenders together is the basis of so-called 'restorative justice'. It's one of the clearest expressions of all of the empathy instinct.

RESTORATIVE JUSTICE

Laura Coel was sexually abused by her stepfather between the ages of four and fourteen at their home in Morpeth, Northumbria. In 2014, at the age of thirty, she decided she wanted to meet him again. By this time, he'd served four years in prison for indecent assault and gross indecency. As part of the growing trend towards restorative justice (RJ), a victim liaison officer referred her to the National Probation Service in Northumbria. They set up the session and she supplied her questions in advance. It took eleven months to arrange and Laura even visited the location so that she could decide where everyone would sit. She had suffered from mental-health problems since the abuse, including anorexia. So she also had appointments with her community health nurse before and afterwards. She was able to ask her stepfather why he had picked her from the siblings in the family and whether he'd originally got together with her mother with child abuse in mind. She could tell him that he was the cause of her lifelong mental-health problems:

> He got very emotional and had to leave the room – he said he couldn't understand why I'd want to forgive him . . . I told him it was because I didn't want to carry around what he'd done to me any more. I'd moved on, and was forgiving him for me, not for him . . . I wanted an apology, and I got one . . . I'm not as angry any more – that's lifted. And hearing him say that it was all his fault was massive . . . Without restorative justice I'd have struggled to move on with my life.

I also had the chance to say goodbye to him, which was what
I wanted.[47]

In 2011 in Warrington David Rogers came face to face with
the man who'd killed his teenage son in a pub, an innocent
bystander to a pub brawl. William Upton had been convicted
of this manslaughter and, after two years, agreed to meet the
father of his victim. Contrary to his evidence at the trial, he
confirmed that there had been no provocation whatsoever
from Rogers' son. Rogers said afterwards that although it
hadn't healed his sense of loss, the confession had put an
end to his anger.[48]

In 2013 in Berkshire Charlotte Hooper confronted the
woman who'd burgled her house while high on drugs. This
time it was the offender who'd initially requested the
encounter. At the end she confessed that Hooper reminded
her of her mum, a 'normal person' who didn't deserve to be
burgled, and she said sorry. In the same year a mugger met
the student he had assaulted in Manchester. He was moved
by hearing that the victim's mother had subsequently feared
constantly for him and needed up to five reassuring phone
calls a day.[49]

These encounters are the product of work by victim
support, the probation service and RJ charities. They're most
often applied to crimes against the person and can be
time-consuming and costly to set up. But allowing victims
to meet perpetrators is a powerful influence on offenders and
gives victims some closure. Restorative justice allows offenders
to make amends to victims, often face to face. For this to
work the criminal has to apply, or learn to apply, empathy:

to understand the emotions of the victim and to experience them – that is, the cognitive and the affective.

The first country to apply RJ widely was New Zealand in the 1980s. Many young Maoris did not trust or believe in the country's courts and prisons, and here was an alternative. With the full involvement of tribal elders it was found both to encourage remorse and to discourage reoffending.[50] RJ has been championed in the US by Howard Zehr, a criminologist. He argues that the philosophy of retribution is to regard crime as something perpetrated against the state. RJ, by contrast, treats crime as a violation of people and relationships: 'Restorative justice requires, at minimum, that we address victims' harms and needs, hold offenders accountable to put right those harms, and involve victims, offenders, and communities in this process.'[51]

The pioneer of RJ in the UK was the former Chief Constable of Thames Valley, Sir Charles Pollard. I've already quoted his dissatisfaction with the courts system. In 1997 he decided to try RJ out with two sixteen-year-old joyriders. They had written off an elderly woman's car and severely shaken her up. Worse, they took the spilled contents of her car and threw them over a hedge. At a meeting between them she emotionally described how that had included a precious rug, given to her by her recently deceased husband, but now lost for ever. Once face to face, Pollard says, the power of the meeting will take over. The joyriders were appalled and this became a 'eureka moment' for him: 'In simple humanitarian terms it's a chance for victims to find out what, why and how. Forgiveness does occur, but it's a bonus if it does.'[52]

Scaling Up Restorative Justice

Most attempts to try out restorative justice in Britain have been small scale. But in Surrey, since 2011, they've had a county-wide scheme dealing with young offenders.

Instead of going to court, the majority of youth crimes are referred to a panel of police and youth workers. They decide whether the appropriate response is a caution, referral to the courts or Youth Restorative Intervention (YRI). Such an intervention would typically be some form of community service, in addition to meeting the victim. Only a few, more serious crimes go through to a criminal court. The panel can take the offender's background into account in terms of previous convictions, whether in care and so on.

Victims are always consulted to check they're happy with the proposed approach. Critically, this will happen within three days, compared to the average of eight months waiting for a court case. When victims meet offenders, the latter get the chance to make amends in person. But if victims prefer not to come face to face with them, the system still works well because they are involved and consulted.

In its first three years YRI dealt with 3,000 cases, comprising more than 70 per cent of youth crimes in Surrey. Youth crime itself fell by 18 per cent and 1,160 fewer young people had criminal records. In this case it was also cheaper, saving the local criminal justice system several million pounds. But, perhaps most important of all, it had an extremely high satisfaction rate among victims.[53]

• • •

Because restorative justice is increasingly seen to be beneficial, the Ministry of Justice provided £29 million of dedicated funding for projects between 2013 and 2016. Now they've come up with a plan for the future. Its basis is that victims get good and equal access to RJ, that we all develop an awareness and understanding of RJ in terms of how it works and what its benefits are, and that the schemes are well run and delivered by trained facilitators.[54] There's now a not-for-profit organisation called the Restorative Justice Council which works with the government to further the RJ cause. It has its own definition of RJ:

> Restorative justice gives victims the chance to meet or communicate with their offender to explain the real impact of the crime. It empowers victims by giving them a voice. It also holds offenders to account for what they have done and helps them take responsibility and make amends. During a restorative justice process, the offender and victim will often agree on certain actions that the offender can undertake to repair the harm they have caused.[55]

The Council's response to the Ministry of Justice's plan is to call for exemplary RJ projects, such as the successful services operating in Surrey and Northern Ireland for young offenders, to be replicated elsewhere. To assist this, they've developed a set of standards and a quality mark which can be awarded to well-run RJ schemes. The idea has now spread to prisons where offenders can also be brought together with victims – Leeds Prison was the first to receive the quality mark.[56] The idea that the plight of a victim can make a difference to the future behaviour of an offender is catching on. Now the definitions and objectives of RJ should more explicitly acknowledge the power and value of empathy.

— • • • —

Jobs Friends Houses

'I love it. It gives people in recovery an opportunity to move on with their lives, doesn't it?'

Terry is an ex-offender and heroin addict who's part of a revolutionary experiment in Blackpool, now two years old. Steve Hodgkins, a former policeman fed up with the endless cycle of catching and convicting, set up a restorative-justice project. Jobs Friends Houses (JFH) buys and restores derelict houses, training their teams of addicts and ex-offenders in all the necessary skills. It was evaluated by the Professor of Criminology at Sheffield Hallam University, David Best, at the end of its first year and was, astoundingly, found to reduce reoffending by 94 per cent. That is, it almost eliminated it. Even if the participants were selected as individuals more likely to respond to the programme, that's still a startling statistic.

One of the principles Hodgkins based JFH on is 'the social cure'. This is the idea that better social connections have been shown to create happier, healthier people – that's the 'friends' bit in JFH. They can also show you how the participants' social connections palpably grow by tracking their Facebook activity over the months. And as their network expands so their language becomes more positive.

JFH also has high-visibility uniforms and boards outside their houses, helping to emphasise the positive contribution they make to restoring Blackpool, one of many seaside towns which have suffered from deprivation and crime. Once ex-offenders and addicts are accepted rather than shunned by the community their rehabilitation speeds up. Harnessing their infectious *esprit de corps*, the participants are encouraged to engage with townsfolk as often as possible. The townsfolk in turn then understand how the JFH team are engaged in an act of restoration, in every sense.

As a bonus, Hodgkins expects JFH to break even quite soon, benefiting from charging for its services and receiving rents on its restored properties. It looks like becoming a profitable social enterprise. Paul is another addict and ex-offender who does JFH's books while training in accountancy: 'It's surreal sometimes. In a shirt and tie, doing stuff like this, it's brilliant.'[57]

——————————— • • • ———————————

This chapter is partly about reducing crime by getting offenders to understand the effect their misdemeanours have on their victims. There's a long-running project at Sheffield University called Sheffield Pathways out of Crime. This has looked at what the most reliable predictors are of a change in offenders' behaviour – how likely they are to 'desist'. Key elements are an offender's own analysis of the challenges they face, as well as other, objective assessments, such as the likelihood of employment or the probability of resorting to a drug habit. But also featuring on the list is a measurement of the offender's empathy levels. Where it's seen to rise over time among those beginning to desist, the study says, there will be a developing awareness of the importance of others' needs and feelings.[58] As we now know, this is called the empathy instinct. And when it's deployed with families, to nurture young children at risk, it can genuinely prevent the criminals of the future from developing. For them, for all of us, this must be the most important priority of all.

────────────── • • • ──────────────

More Civil Justice

Roman Krznaric, the author of *Empathy: Why It Matters, and How to Get It*, has been hired by the Ministry of Justice to train Employment Tribunal judges in empathy. He gives them a two-hour workshop which covers how to read and understand emotions, empathetic listening and the science of empathy. ('It's important to ground them in this so they don't think the concept is wishy-washy.')

Among the different kinds of exercises Krznaric does in his various empathy workshops is one where participants are given a piece of card with four words on it, such as anger and jealousy. They then hold it over their face, just revealing their eyes, and adopt the emotional expression of each word, while another person tries to guess the correct emotion just by looking at the eyes. Our eyes are enormously informative, if you can read them.

Good, disciplined, empathetic listening helps judges manage courtroom proceedings more effectively and people are calmer when they think they're being listened to properly. Getting into the habit of cognitive perspective-taking means that judges can elicit and understand more evidence and make better judgements. It also assists impartiality and fairness. Krznaric has now trained over 100 judges.[59]

• • •

6

IN SICKNESS AND IN HEALTH

Kate Granger was a doctor specialising in geriatrics. When she herself was diagnosed with cancer she was shocked at how casually and impersonally she'd be referred to in hospital as 'Bed Number 7' or 'the girl with cancer'. Her lowest point was when a junior doctor whom she'd not met before, without even introducing himself, simply announced, 'Your cancer has spread.' Kate launched a Twitter campaign with the hashtag #hellomynameis, echoing the words of a hospital porter who had treated her humanely. The hashtag had been used more than a billion times by the time Kate died.

We all rely on health and social care services. The majority of our experiences are positive, despite the fact that, when using such services, we're ill and probably anxious too. There's abundant evidence that happy, confident, secure patients recover more quickly. But I've personally learnt from my own occasional brushes with the medics that there are modern pressures endangering the empathetic bond which should exist between patient and carer. I had an infection in my elbow and found myself in a public ward of a London teaching hospital. It was dominated by elderly men with dementia. They shouted and swore at all times of the day and night. They threatened the nurses with violence and they frequently trashed the toilets. With a fairly high temperature I was slightly out of it, but I felt the nurses had an appalling time of it and behaved with restraint. Visitors of mine, however, were critical of how perfunctory the nursing was. This was one small example of how the rapid growth of an ageing population is clogging and pressurising the system. Around one pound in six of public expenditure already goes on health and social care – we cannot afford to increase it much more. Demand is infinite and each novel drug and breakthrough therapy adds to the spiralling costs. Resources are finite. All new treatments rightly now have to demonstrate value. But the growing need for ruthless efficiency and uncompromising systems is in danger of obscuring the purpose of the whole exercise: people's well-being.

Some years previously a specialist had found a growth in my bladder. I'll spare you the details but he was adept at deploying all his superb state-of-the-art equipment to identify the problem and remove it with surgery. The obvious question was whether it was cancerous. While the surgeon manipulated his technical toys with dexterity and relish, he was hopeless at either understanding what my anxiety might be or explaining the eventual diagnosis clearly. In fact, for some months I thought I had cancer when in fact I did not. I only eventually cleared it up by visiting another specialist who was both sympathetic and clear. So here's another trend: as medicine gets more technical it's in danger of becoming less human. Indeed, the training required for these high-tech applications not only omits the 'care' bit, it means that more dispassionate, systematising types may be attracted into the profession in the first place.

Have you tried to get an appointment with your GP recently? So high is the demand, from elderly patients in particular, I've often been offered a time a month away. And when you finally get into the surgery you'll usually be talking to a different doctor from the one you saw before, making the whole experience much less personal, less empathetic. It is a wonderful thing that we have publicly funded health services to care for us. Studies suggest most of us are still satisfied with our treatment.[1] But there are some worrying trends.

THE EMPATHY DEFICIT

In September 2007 Bella Bailey, aged eighty-six, was admitted to Stafford Hospital with an enlarged hernia. This fairly routine admission was eventually to lead to the uncovering of a major scandal and a reorganisation of how hospitals are run and inspected. Her daughter Julie Bailey, who owned a local café, visited her mother soon afterwards. She found that Bella had been left without her oxygen supply and had collapsed. She was so nervous about the quality of care that she moved in and stayed with her mother till she died eight weeks later. What Julie saw during that time led her to start a nationwide campaign, Cure the NHS. There was a chaotic shortage of staff, with receptionists sometimes attempting to assess arriving patients. Patients were ignored, soiled their beds and were left in their own excrement and urine. Others were stranded for hours on commodes without attention. One of the most shocking details was dehydrated inmates drinking water out of flower vases. Julie was joined by the families of other elderly patients who had died in the hospital and they plastered their photographs around the town to make their point. There was a succession of private, internal inquiries into the state of Stafford Hospital, but Cure the NHS believed that only a public inquiry would change things.[2]

An unusually high number of deaths occurred at Stafford Hospital between 2005 and 2009 and this added to the clamour. A public inquiry was set up and chaired by Robert Francis QC. In 2013 he published his final report, concluding that 'for many patients the most basic elements of care were neglected'. He reported that those needing pain relief were getting it late or not all. Some patients were left unwashed for a month. Food and drink were put out of the reach of those bedridden and many were fed by families or not at all. Discharge of some patients was premature so they ended up back in hospital soon afterwards. Amid awful standards of hygiene, relatives found themselves removing used bandages and dressings from public areas and cleaning the toilets. While some staff did their best, many showed 'a disturbing lack of compassion towards their patients'. Francis blamed a chronic shortage of staff, particularly of nurses, for the substandard care. Morale was low, staff who spoke out felt ignored and there was a culture of fear and bullying. The report condemned the health trust's board for not taking patients' complaints seriously and singled out their 2006 decision to save £10 million in order to apply for foundation trust status:

'The board decided this saving could only be achieved through cutting staff levels, which were already insufficient.'

The Francis Report made a number of recommendations, several of which related to how the staff cared for the patients: there should be a common culture shared by all, putting the patient first; all carers should be properly accountable and the public should be protected from those not fit to provide services; in improving education and training, those in nursing and leadership positions should be able to integrate essential shared values into everything they do. And the report said this:

> An . . . argument was used sometimes to justify inaction or a lack of response . . . mortality rates, concerns about governance, and staffing issues, could be found at many places and therefore were justifiably regarded as not being of particular significance or of requiring exceptional action . . . It is an attitude which would be unlikely to be persisted in if those adopting it were constantly to place an empathy for the predicament of patients at the forefront of their mind.[3]

The Health Secretary, Jeremy Hunt, responded by saying 'high quality care and compassion' must be at the heart of the health and care system. Professor Sir Denis Pereira Gray was Chair of the Academy of Medical Royal Colleges and is Patron of the National Association for Patient Participation. His analysis was that the Francis Report 'revealed a serious loss of empathy by both doctors and nurses over several years and a management system that prioritised accountancy over clinical care'.[4]

As a result of the scandal the government decided to appoint a Chief Inspector of Hospitals, and the first person to fill the role was Professor Sir Mike Richards, working through the Care Quality Commission (CQC). Richards says, very simply, patients should be safe, made better and treated with dignity and compassion. The other essential ingredient he points to is good leadership with high emotional intelligence. He remains worried by staff shortages and their effects in NHS hospitals.[5] But the fear that health is becoming more impersonal, less personalised, is not confined to Britain. In the US a 2011 study of 800 hospital patients found that only half of them thought their doctors were empathetic or caring.[6] Before that a North Carolina project videotaped hundreds of encounters between cancer sufferers and their oncologists, talking about the most frightening disease of all. The researchers found that the specialists often overlooked or dismissed signs of distress displayed by patients and demonstrated empathetic responses only around 20 per cent of the time.[7]

Also in 2011 a team at the University of Witten/Herdecke in Germany reviewed a number of studies of medical students. They found that empathy declined among the would-be medics during their courses and early internships in hospitals, threatening healthcare quality. Dr Melanie Neumann, who headed the review, wrote about medics who were naively and overly open to empathy to begin with, and then suffered from distress themselves when faced with real, critical cases for the first time. They then protected themselves by 'dehumanising' their patients (this is the disconnection we looked at in Chapter 2, which can switch empathy off). To support this, she pointed to a study which showed that experienced doctors have a lower than normal perception of pain in other people. And Neumann also cited a study that won't surprise us: anxiety, tension and stress have been shown to reduce the signal rate of mirror neurons in our brains, adversely affecting the ability to understand others and empathise.[8]

These findings were echoed by a study of medical students in Philadelphia whose empathy levels decreased during their course, particularly in the third year when they first came into contact with patients.[9] There's evidence that some mentors specifically recommend detachment as a way of surviving the medical traumas they will encounter.[10] As we'll see, there is another way.

As well as the training, the environment can also be a problem. The need to create ever larger and more efficient hospitals can add to the sheer impersonality of healthcare. Steve Hilton, the former adviser to David Cameron, in his 2015 book *More Human* writes about the rise of 'factory hospitals':

> Go to a hospital today and it's an ordeal: navigating the large car park, walking what feels like miles through corridors, travelling in giant lifts before finally reaching a soulless waiting room where you have to wait endlessly to be called . . .[11]

Large hospitals are undoubtedly more economic, a clear benefit in an era of cash-strapped public funding. But Hilton quotes a number of care experts who argue that in these major health centres the person can get squeezed out, patients and their families don't know who's in charge to ask questions of, and this 'failure to see the person in the patient' can be dehumanising. In Melanie Neumann's German study the same trends were identified. Even the proponents of modern 'polyclinics' accept that they're at risk of becoming soulless machines dedicated to efficiency rather than nurture. They argue that the answer lies in organising them into small, delegated units with good leadership. In this way you can replicate the benefits of small hospitals. There is also a necessary trend towards short hospital stays but this too can fragment the patient–physician relationship, reducing the number of bedside interactions.

However, hospitals are highly funded, scrutinised and managed compared to care homes. And if you add care homes to nursing homes (where a qualified nurse is in attendance) Britain now has half a million residents being looked after in this way. The problems of their inadequate care are also mounting. Here are some incidents that have all happened since 2013. In Braintree, Essex, elderly residents of an adult care home were taunted, slapped and roughly handled by their carers. In Beverley, East Yorkshire, a care worker mocked an elderly inmate with Alzheimer's, asking, 'Are you a witch?' In Northampton residents were left unattended for thirteen hours. In Fareham, Hampshire, serious complaints by relatives of their loved ones' treatment were ignored. In Banstead, Surrey, dementia sufferers were mistreated. And in Haringey, London, hidden cameras revealed that staff turned up late, falsified time logs, left elderly clients dirty and failed to administer medicines properly.[12] In the cases of Banstead and Haringey Angela Sutcliffe, the Chief Inspector of Adult Social

Care at the CQC, took swift action and closed both homes. Sutcliffe said the goings-on at the Haringey home were 'completely unacceptable'.[13]

• • •

Awakenings

Many of the elderly residents of care homes suffer from one form of dementia or another. One of the common symptoms of the condition is getting agitated and frustrated, and the easy, quick way to deal with this is to dole out anti-psychotic drugs, originally developed for conditions such as schizophrenia. It's reported that 300,000 care-home residents are given these drugs every year in the US. In many ways, such prescriptions are both lazy and a counsel of despair, the idea being that a better, more dignified quality of life for dementia sufferers is not possible. At the Pathstone Living nursing home in Minnesota, they do things differently.

A psychiatrist who works with Pathstone, Dr Tracy Tomac, decided to see if they could reduce the amount of drugs they gave to their dementia patients and create more activities, such as cooking and listening to music, that would connect with them and reduce their agitation. She targeted reducing their drug intake by 20 per cent in the first year, but they were in fact able to cut it by a dramatic 97 per cent. The company which runs the home is now rolling the policy out across all its homes.

One of the team says that residents whose personalities had virtually disappeared started interacting with their fellows. People who hadn't been speaking began speaking, they came alive and engaged. And now, if any resident is acting up, Pathstone carers have properly to investigate why. It's all about treating elderly people as human beings. They call the programme Awakenings.[14]

───────────── • • • ─────────────

We know that nurses are relatively lowly paid compared to other professions. But care workers are the worst paid of all. The PayScale website in May 2016 revealed that the average hourly rate for care workers was £6.97, amounting to an annual salary of just over £13,000. The National Living Wage will raise this to £9 by 2020, but most care is funded by local authorities which are themselves under considerable financial pressure as their central government funding reduces and the number of elderly increases. The CQC's 2014/15 report on the state of adult social care in England said that services have been 'asked to deliver more with less'. They found 60 per cent of services to be good or outstanding, but 7 per cent were inadequate, meaning 'care is so poor that urgent improvements are needed'.[15] So one of the biggest challenges is how to engender more compassionate care for patients when staff are very lowly paid and their organisations are facing budgetary challenges.

Another acute challenge is the interface between hospital and care in the community. In 2016 the Parliamentary and Health Service Ombudsman reported that large numbers of elderly patients, particularly those with dementia, were being discharged from hospitals before they were ready.[16] This represents a double dose of funding challenges. Hospitals are desperately trying to clear beds to improve efficiency and service the growing demand, while care services cannot cope with the demand either, with local authorities under considerable financial pressure themselves. In this complex, organisational game of chess the individual patient can be forgotten. This is where the deficit in empathy often occurs.

EMPATHY AND HEALING – THE EVIDENCE

'Every patient wants their doctor to be academically prepared . . . But equally important, they want their doctors to have personal attributes that contribute to their professionalism – what a patient might call their "bedside manner".'[17]

That's the view of Darrell Kirch, the President of the Association of American Medical Colleges. We know that if you feel happy and secure during your treatment, you'll recover more quickly from illness and operations. But because such vast sums of money are expended on medicine we cannot proceed on a hunch – everything must be researched and proved. And there's a growing body of studies which demonstrate that our common sense happens to be on the right track. Dr Neumann, whom we quoted earlier, points to evidence that empathetic relations between patients and doctors not only are beneficial for quality of life and anxiety but can also reduce symptoms such as high blood pressure and blood glucose levels.[18] And a 2010 paper in the US entitled 'Empathy in Medicine – A Neurobiological Perspective' stated: 'Evidence supports the physiological benefits of empathic relationships, including better immune function, shorter post-surgery hospital stays, fewer asthma attacks . . . and shorter duration of colds.'[19]

Let's look at some of the worldwide evidence in more detail. In 2004 a South Korean study of 550 outpatients suggested that patients who feel their doctors have listened to them and understood their concerns are more likely to adhere to their treatment and thus get better more quickly.[20] A 2011 research project in the US looked at 719 patients just beginning a cold. They split them into three groups, one with no medical attention, one looked after by physicians who displayed standard empathy, and one with super-empathetic doctors (they even developed a way of measuring this which they called CARE, for Consultation and Relational Empathy). The people in the third group actually got over their colds more quickly.[21] CARE was later employed in another US study where they assessed medics in trauma units (Accident and Emergency departments) and then charted how the patients felt about the procedure afterwards. Those who rated their surgeons as highly caring were twenty times more likely to deem the outcome of their treatment a success.[22] That study, while significant, had an element of subjectivity about it. In Italy in 2012 there was an even more startling publication, looking at more than 20,000 diabetes sufferers and the 240 doctors tending to them. Again the doctors were all measured for empathy and the researchers found that the patients who'd been looked after by physicians with high empathy scores suffered significantly lower rates of acute complications. This could be mainly down to a positive frame of mind aiding their recovery, or to their trust in their doctors making them more likely to follow the prescribed course of treatment. Either way it points to the importance of the bedside manner.[23]

These intriguing studies were carried out in hospitals. Considerably more of us enter GP surgeries than attend a hospital. Eighty per cent of all contact with the NHS, for example, is with GPs. So our relationship with our family doctor is just as important. In 2013 a Dutch paper was published entitled 'Effectiveness of Empathy in General Practice: A Systematic Review'. Its authors looked at almost a thousand studies of empathy and general practice and rigorously narrowed them down to just seven that they thought the most valid. They defined empathy as 'The competence of a physician to understand the patient's situation, perspective, and feelings; to communicate that understanding and check its accuracy; and to act on that understanding in a helpful, therapeutic way'.

Their conclusion, covering outcomes and 'enablement' (how well patients understand and cope with their health issues), was remarkably similar to the hospital studies: 'There is a good correlation between physician empathy and patient satisfaction and a direct positive relationship with strengthening patient enablement. Empathy lowers patients' anxiety and distress and delivers significantly better clinical outcomes.'[24]

Ten years earlier a team at Exeter University had looked at all the worldwide, English-language studies about 'continuity of care' in GP practices. Many countries had become concerned that patients who rarely saw the same doctor did not fare as well as those who did. The researchers found this to be the case, because of a number of benefits derived from continuity of care: some people, adolescents in particular, are more likely to reveal problems to a familiar figure they feel comfortable with; such doctors hold a more comprehensive picture of not just the patient but also their family; they are more likely to get their patients to adhere to treatment and heed advice; and patient satisfaction grows with all the benefits that flow from that.[25] There's also evidence from the US that continuity of care can make primary medicine more effective, thus reducing referrals to hospitals, where treatment is much more expensive. The Exeter team are working on a further major review of continuity of care as I write, which is expected to reaffirm its importance. This will be timely because Sir Denis Pereira Gray believes things in the UK are getting worse:

> The one branch of the medical profession where people ought to be known as individuals and be treated with empathy is general practice. The evidence is patients are experiencing increasing difficulties in even seeing the GP of choice and continuity of care is deteriorating.[26]

Jean Decety, the neuroscientist at the University of Chicago, has been taking a close interest in empathy in the medical profession. He gave questionnaires to 7,500 doctors and found that those who reported feeling more empathetic concern for their patients also reported higher job satisfaction. And those who felt the need to disengage from their patients, because they were the least able to regulate their emotions, were also more likely to suffer burn-out.[27] So when physicians work with intelligent regard for their emotions, the empathy instinct works for both them and their patients. What can be done to enhance it and to tackle the empathy deficit?

SOLUTIONS TO THE EMPATHY DEFICIT

In Philadelphia, at the Thomas Jefferson University, they've been carrying out a longitudinal study of medical education. It's headed by Mohammadreza Hojat. It was he who discovered that empathy levels of medical students tend to decrease during their course, particularly when they start meeting patients in their third year. Hojat's conclusion is that these would-be doctors need training in cognitive empathy to develop a better understanding of the experiences, concerns and perspectives of a patient.[28] One of Hojat's own studies, echoing the Italian one I quoted earlier, showed that diabetes sufferers have better control over their illness and fewer admissions to hospital if their physician scores highly on empathy.[29]

Hojat makes the distinction between cognitive and emotional empathy. Too much emotion can interfere with performance or clinical decision-making: 'Physicians should not become too emotionally involved in the patients' suffering. If they are too sympathetic, at the end of the day they'll be exhausted and burnt out.'[30]

We should remember how recent our neurological understanding of empathy is, and how it's still developing. Hojat's work is valuable and instructive, but he may not be entirely right with his rigid approval of the cognitive and disapproval of the emotional where doctors are concerned. Jean Decety agrees about the importance of cognitive empathy in health-care, but takes a more nuanced approach. He argues that if doctors entirely tune out of their emotional responses they'll feel and display less concern for their patients, something patients will miss: 'The most critical aspect of healthcare is that patients perceive that their doctors care about them . . . Doctors should not be afraid of their emotions.'[31]

However, you cannot have doctors breaking down in floods of sympathetic tears every time they're confronted by a case of cancer. In their 2011 book *Intelligent Kindness: Reforming the Culture of Healthcare*, John Ballatt and Penelope Campling report how a hospital chaplain had to work this out and deal with it:

Peter Speck, used to working with death and the dying, described the tragic death of a thirteen-year-old boy who had run in front of a lorry because he was late for school. Speck describes candidly how the level of his own distress prevented him from being of much support to the parents and his over-identification was such that he even mixed up the name of the dying boy, John, with his own son, David. Once Speck had been helped to reflect on the level of his upset and work out what was going on in his mind, he was able to resume his role and be emotionally available to the suffering parents.[32]

So the key is not to turn off emotional empathy, but to learn how to regulate it. This is supported by a paper from a professor of medical humanities at the University of California. Jodi Halpern wrote *From Detached Concern to Empathy: Humanizing Medical Practice*. In it she argued that total emotional detachment prevents doctors from understanding their patients and getting important clues about the care they need. 'Not feeling' is more likely to make them act in ways that impair proper listening and thus good judgement.[33]

In 2016 the government appointed a National Guardian for the NHS, to encourage higher standards and better reporting of failure. Henrietta Hughes said, 'Wouldn't it be better if oxytocin was the predominant neurotransmitter in the NHS?' And whereas even as recently as the mid-1990s doctor–patient relationships were virtually ignored, there are now a number of initiatives to try to enhance them: courses in mindfulness, contemplation of the nature of suffering when ill, reductions in workloads, regularity of contact and so on. Let's look at some of them.

Doctors

The 2011 book *Intelligent Kindness* calls for attentive kindness to become a central and valued professional skill, a pre-eminent quality of the 'duty of care'. The authors say that this will require changes to recruitment, education and training. They argue that the capacity to make and sustain attentive relationships with patients is as important as any technical or theoretical education. And they point to a proliferation of well-meaning statutory and mandatory training schemes which produce rigid and indiscriminate systems, calling instead for a learning environment which nourishes kindness. At Harvard Medical School, Helen Reiss has developed a module for training doctors called Empathetics. Undergoing a course based firmly on our developing knowledge of neuroscience, students are taught how to read emotional cues in their patients in order to respond better to their needs. But the modules also involve students recognising their own emotional responses and regulating them with breathing exercises and other mindfulness techniques. A recent assessment of the course was promising: trainee doctors who had been through it received better ratings from patients on how empathetic they were.[34]

$$\cdots$$

Circle of Care

Performing Medicine is an offshoot of the Clod Ensemble Theatre Company and it's been working with doctors since 2001. After the watershed of the Francis Report on Mid-Staffs the producers developed Circle of Care together with the Simulation and Interactive Learning Centre of Guy's and St Thomas' Hospitals. The big idea was to get medical students to see compassion not as something in a bucket which gets depleted during the day, but as a 'flow'. They say if everyone has it for everyone else then compassion becomes a constant – it's sustainable.

Through a series of theatre-led skills, such as voice development and movement-based classes, they aim to hone nine skills: self-care, verbal communications, non-verbal communications, appreciation of the person, spatial and situational awareness, learning from success and error, decision-making, leadership and teamwork. 'Appreciation of the person' is defined as understanding difficult perspectives, appreciating personal narratives (of the patient) and recognising unconscious bias. This has become part of the compulsory Year Four course and this is how a student doctor judged it:

Just by changing certain things about yourself, your posture
. . . people react to you differently . . . the patients, the
doctors. I'm sure I'm a lot better in how I come across
now . . . for the first time I had [the following feedback],
this patient would definitely want to see this doctor again.

Ian Abbs is the Medical Director at Guy's and St Thomas'
NHS Foundation Trust. He believes this is just the beginning:
'In the future healthcare will be less about diagnosis and the
technical side – as robots will increasingly take care of that
– and more about making sense of things for patients. That's
why initiatives like Circle of Care are so important.'[35]

IBM's Watson computer, famous for winning at chess and
TV game shows, is already focusing on cancer diagnosis. It's
claimed that Watson, working with a medical centre in New
York, has a successful diagnosis rate with lung cancer of 90
per cent, compared to 50 per cent for human specialists. But
empathetic doctors and nurses are what's needed to deliver the
bad news to patients, and to help them through the treatment.

––––––––––––––––––––– • • • –––––––––––––––––––––

The King's Fund is a charitable research body dedicated to
improving health and care. In 2008 it brought out *Seeing the
Person in the Patient – The Point of Care Review Paper*, about
how to nurture and promote compassionate care. It points
to the importance of getting close to patients when teaching
compassion and it recommends that medics get trained in
the same way as psychiatric professionals – encountering
real patients' stories and even being placed with families
coping with chronic disabilities and disorders. A second

recommendation concerns how to deal with a tendency for doctors to develop, shall we say, a God-like complex.

Anyone my age (I'm in my sixties) will remember a series of hugely popular and pretty lame film comedies in the 1950s and 1960s: *Doctor in the House, Doctor at Sea, Doctor at Large* and so on. These black and white comedies were dominated by the actor James Robertson Justice, playing the bombastic, aggressive, megalomaniacal surgeon Sir Lancelot Spratt (even a biography of the actor was called *What's the Bleeding Time?*). Spratt harassed the nurses, terrified the junior doctors and treated the patients like unfortunate serfs. This parody, though, had more than a hint of truth in it. And the *Point of Care Review* addresses this tendency in doctors towards grandiosity and omnipotence. It suggests that some doctors, quite early on, adopt these sort of mannerisms to protect themselves from painful anxiety, a sort of trauma armour. As well as warning about such bad role models, the report points to the power of good, empathetic exemplars that junior doctors can emulate.

The person behind the Point of Care programme at the King's Fund was Jocelyn Cornwell. Following the final Mid-Staffs report she set up a Point of Care Foundation to further the ideas that had emerged. Their first publication, in 2014, highlighted how caring about people who work in healthcare is one of the keys to developing a compassionate service. Cornwell points out that patient satisfaction is consistently higher in hospital trusts with better levels of staff health and well-being. There's even a discernible link between higher staff satisfaction and lower rates of mortality. Stress and burn-out are more frequent in the NHS than in other areas of the public sector: 30 per cent of sickness absence by healthcare professionals is due to stress. But there are hospitals where good leadership and management, despite the pressures, have delivered higher rates of staff satisfaction and more empathetic regimes.[36]

Growing attention is now also being given to 'therapeutic alliances'.[37] This is a term commonly used in psychotherapy to describe the quality and strength of the relationship between therapist and client. When the patient believes that the therapist has their best interests at heart there's evidence that outcomes are more positive. All of this is easier said than done, of course. Not to get too starry-eyed, we've seen that the pressures in many hospitals are extreme. Mike Richards points out that in some acute hospitals as many as one in four of the staff report being harassed and bullied.[38] That's why simple, focused interventions can be very beneficial. At Yale School of Medicine they've developed a disciplined, five-minute intervention for emergency treatment of drug addicts and behavioural disorders. It's based on an approach known as SBIRT – Screening, Brief Intervention and Referral to Treatment. It includes counselling techniques which rely on reflective listening and empathy.[39] In Chapter 5 we looked at the same approach now being used in the equally pressured environment of prisons.

How is it possible, in such a workplace, to provide a little bit of breathing space in order for staff to top up their empathy reserves? One solution that's taking off rapidly is Schwartz Rounds, pioneered at the Massachusetts General Hospital. The Rounds are monthly, one-hour sessions for caregivers from multiple disciplines to come together and discuss difficult emotional and social issues of patient care as they arise. The Schwartz Center, which developed the programme, exists to 'advance compassionate health care'. Its staff based the idea on the evidence we've looked at about better listening, more accurate diagnoses through better clinical judgement, happier patients who recover more quickly, and less stressed clinicians who can manage their emotional responses. Schwartz Rounds are proving very popular – not only are they now in operation in twenty-nine US states, they're also being used at more than 140 different healthcare sites in the UK.[40] One particular advantage is that they create a 'safe space' to discuss challenges and dilemmas. The growing number of legal actions against doctors and hospitals is creating an atmosphere of blame in which it's difficult openly to share problems.

Another new idea from the US is to try anchoring medical students in a particular ward. Denis Pereira Gray is enthusiastic about the idea of giving them a 'home'. He cites work done at Harvard where it was concluded that medical students are moved around so often, without stable work relationships, that they become cynical and dehumanised. They've developed a way of managing medical students' placements so that they stay in a department for longer periods of time and build real working relationships.[41] In France hospitals also manage to make medical students feel more part of a team and this approach is now going to be tried at Exeter and Leicester Medical Schools to see if it works in the UK.

There's a wealth of good ideas and solutions emerging to address the empathy deficit in healthcare. And there's no doubt the issue is beginning to be taken seriously. I spoke to a recently qualified doctor in London – let's call him Philip:

We had what they call 'Threads' in our course, which covers compassionate care. We were warned about possibly becoming less empathetic as we trained. We met real patients and learnt about how to talk to them about their ideas, concerns and expectations. The importance of listening without making assumptions, and silence, which allows people to talk. They brought actors to help us with role-playing, to simulate things like angry patients so we could learn how to deal with them.

Philip thinks that as yet the field is embryonic: it doesn't have enough of an evidence base and is still led by what we feel 'might be good'. He believes that this sort of training is most critical for doctors who are going to become GPs. Shrewd medical schools already look at the emotional intelligence of their students, but Philip wouldn't rule out assessing all entry-level medical students for their EQ. This might help decide which direction they go in: 'for palliative care it's critical, but not so important for a pathologist'. Finally, Philip points to older doctors he's met and worked with who've not had the benefit of more modern training: 'Some of them have a lot to learn.'

Nurses

The *Intelligent Kindness* book points to the current vogue for more academic 'competencies'. This has a value, but simply learning about technical and practical elements of nursing doesn't necessarily nurture compassion. Its authors want to see clinical educators build a culture of reflection and self-awareness to develop a capacity for empathy, often in difficult circumstances:

An important element of kindness that comes up frequently in patient narratives is that kind behaviour is usually about very ordinary, day-to-day things such as speaking clearly when someone's a bit deaf, remembering someone's special diet, taking the time to help someone brush their hair or bothering to clean someone's spectacles. One of the commonest complaints . . . is that call bells are left out of reach: surely something that a bit more caring attentiveness could easily remedy, and something that should naturally follow from empathising with the sense of powerlessness experienced by people in a state of vulnerability.[42]

The King's Fund *Point of Care Review* quotes evidence from the US which shows that higher ratios of nurses to patients and of qualified to unqualified has an effect on quality of care, unsurprisingly. But investing in more nurses wouldn't help if they spent their time unproductively. The review quotes the NHS Institute for Innovation and Improvement and its evidence gathered from acute hospitals, that nurses now spend up to 40 per cent of their time on activities such as paperwork, shift handovers and searching for missing items.[43] With focus, the time nurses spend on this 'non-productive' work could be reduced, freeing them up for their primary role as caregivers.

Professor Jane Cummings is NHS England's Chief Nursing Officer. In 2012 she issued a policy document entitled *Compassion in Practice: Nursing, Midwifery and Care Staff*. She promoted 'the 6Cs – care, compassion, competence, communication, courage, commitment'. You'll note that she put compassion second on her list and defined it as: 'how care is given through relationships based on empathy, respect and dignity – it can also be described as intelligent kindness, and is central to how people perceive their care'.

Cummings defined a number of 'action areas' for nurses, the second of which covers working with people to provide a positive experience of care. As well as dignity, empathy and respect, their feedback needs to be listened to and acted upon. These 6C values are being extended to all staff at NHS England and they're also reflected in a new code of professional standards published in 2015 by the Nursing and Midwifery Council. The Royal College of Nursing has now taken to publishing the stories of nurses experiencing the challenges and rewards of patient care.[44]

Care Workers

We saw earlier how many people are now looked after in care homes and how badly paid their carers are. After the Mid-Staffs inquiry the government commissioned a report from the journalist Camilla Cavendish into care workers. She established that there are 1.3 million front-line NHS staff who are not registered nurses. When she published her findings in 2013, there was no minimum standard of training for healthcare assistants before they were able to work unsupervised. Cavendish recommended that care workers should get at least two weeks of training to prepare them for the provision of basic care in hospitals, residential homes and private houses.[45] And three years later the National Care Certificate emerged, gained after an obligatory twelve weeks of training for all care workers, covering fifteen standards which include person-centred working and communication:

The learner must . . . describe the importance of finding out the history, preferences, wishes and needs of the individual; explain how individual identity and self-esteem are linked to emotional and spiritual wellbeing; list a range of communication methods and styles that could help meet an individual's communication [style]; demonstrate the use of appropriate verbal and non-verbal communication.[46]

The UK National Institute for Health and Care Excellence (NICE) also issued a set of recommendations for delivering personal care to older people living in their own homes. It includes a section about 'Ensuring care is person-centred'. It urges carers to treat older people with 'empathy, courtesy, respect' and it recommends 'continuity of care by ensuring the person is supported by the same home care workers so they can become familiar with them'.[47] Of course, it's one thing to write a report and quite another to change a system, but the empathy instinct is now very much on the agenda.

* * *

The Arts and Empathetic Care Homes

Many older people in care homes are physically infirm and often suffering from dementia. There's a dystopian view of these places, which is sadly sometimes a reality, of elderly residents drugged up to the eyeballs to keep them sedentary and quiet. These are people whose own circle of friends are probably dead and whose relatives might rarely visit them. And yet some care homes are demonstrating that it is possible to achieve a decent quality of life for their residents, however challenging their conditions.

The Baring Foundation and Arts Council England have been funding arts and culture in homes in four areas, based on the conviction that these activities entertain, inspire and simply enliven the most humdrum of existences. Abbeyfield care homes in Nottingham have been experimenting with an Armchair Art Gallery. They persuaded the Duke and Duchess of Devonshire to video an exclusive guide to the treasures in Chatsworth, which was then shown to Abbeyfielders on iPads. They were also treated to live digital transmissions of concerts from the city's Theatre Royal. In Hereford they've recruited poets, dancers and actors to organise sessions in those three art forms and trained care-home staff to act as activity managers to keep the programmes going in the future.

One of the stated aims is to help care-home staff towards a better awareness and appreciation of individuality and a greater empathy for their charges. Lesley Garrett, who runs Abbeyfield in the East Midlands, says it has all been enormously beneficial:

> For the residents they're more relaxed, it taps into what they can do and enjoy. For those with dementia they don't need to recall how to do something or initiate an activity, both of which they find difficult. Often, though, it resurrects talents we didn't know they had. For the staff it's hugely rewarding and enjoyable, compared to the more difficult aspects of care. It assists them to be compassionate and makes the residents easier to care for.[48]

National Museums Liverpool has pioneered a wonderful project for dementia sufferers called House of Memories. This helps participants collect personal mementos so as to capture their disappearing memories. Now the museums offer one-day training events for carers too. The Storybox project in Manchester also helps carers see dementia patients as 'real, distinct people', via theatre performance. And the Creative Carers Programme in Suffolk, which set out to develop the creative skills of the carers themselves, was judged to have assisted them to 'imagine themselves in residents' shoes'. Classic empathy.

———————————————— • • • ————————————————

In the era after Mid-Staffs there's a new mantra in British healthcare, mentioned in the NICE guidelines: *person-centred care*. The umbrella organisation for patient charities, National Voices, has issued a manifesto, *Policy and Person Centred Care 2020*. The manifesto defines it as making people partners in decisions about their health and care, helping patients to retain control and independence and continuing to achieve a good quality of life. National Voices says that high-profile failures to provide compassionate care serve to demonstrate that we're still too far from achieving this goal. It is fundamentally an empathetic approach to healthcare that they want: 'Make people the priority, not the system . . . create people-powered services.' National Voices promotes the 'I Statement' – what the patient wants and what 'good' looks like for them, rather than treatment defined by waiting times, bed clearance and other important but defocusing efficiency measures. One piece of good practice, echoed by Philip above, is 'No Assumptions' – ask the patient rather than decide for them.

It's easy to write these words but we shouldn't underestimate the huge challenges that health staff face. Not least, the modern patient, empowered by the internet, is increasingly informed and opinionated. But this underlines the necessity for a dialogue delivering patient-centred care.

7

RACE, RELIGION AND CONFLICT RESOLUTION

'Donald J. Trump is calling for a total and complete shutdown of Muslims entering the United States until our country's representatives can figure out what is going on.' (Press release for a speech delivered in December 2015.)

'Several hundred Roma in this town are a foul-smelling presence.' (Jean-Marie Le Pen, founder of the French National Front, speaking in Nice in 2013.)

'I got the train the other night . . . It wasn't until we got past Grove Park that I could actually hear English being audibly spoken in the carriage. Does that make me feel awkward? Yes. I wonder what's really going on.' (Nigel Farage, leader of UKIP, speaking in 2014.)

Three white politicians publicly articulating their xenophobia. The third of them, Nigel Farage, is the least incendiary and perhaps the most honest.

A few hours after the victory for 'Brexit' in the UK's 2016 referendum, flyers were distributed in Huntingdon, Cambridgeshire, reading, 'Go home Polish scum' and 'No more Polish vermin'. That is not just concern about jobs or crowded GP surgeries, it's plain, old-fashioned racism of a sort that lurks somewhere within all of us. It seemed that in the days after the vote people thought it was permissible to behave in public in a way that has not been acceptable for several decades. A black colleague of mine, British born and bred, was asked in the street when she was going home. Three British doctors of Asian extraction from St Mary's, Paddington were shouted at from a car and told that they should go back to their own countries. A primary school head told me she had to try to explain to a six-year-old black boy (British born and bred, as were his parents) why they had been abused as a family in a south London street. And a driver of a car was asked by a group at traffic lights what language he spoke. When told, 'English', they replied, 'That's all right then.' The police revealed that incidents of hate crime rose fivefold in the week after the referendum,[1] and the think tank Demos registered more than 5,000 xenophobic or racist tweets.[2] Perhaps we shouldn't be surprised: another Demos study, over nine 'normal' days in 2012, found around 10,000 racist terms being tweeted every day, of which 500–2,000 were directed at individuals.[3]

In Chapter 1 I quoted Frans de Waal, the primatologist whose work has given him such insights into humans, observing that we become different animals in our treatment of strangers. The same empathy that renders us loyal to our own kind can make us hostile to others. And we noted that even babies have been shown to prefer faces of people from their own race or who speak in their native tongue. The genocides of the twentieth century had their roots in this instinct for our own kind, and occurred when malign extremists skilfully exploited it.

Racism is so summarily condemned in many societies today that we're in danger of failing to understand where it comes from and how best to tackle it. We all have racist instincts within us. What was it that possessed me and some friends, aged about six, verbally to abuse some gypsies coming up the road selling bunches of heather? We shouted 'Dirty gypsies, go away!' out of a top-floor window. My mother was appalled and went out to apologise to them with a tray of tea. By contrast, how much I now appreciate those parents of my Jewish friends at school who invited me into their houses on Friday night for Shabbat. Their parents had, to me, strange central European accents, they ate foreign dishes and their ceremonies were a long way from the tepid Anglicanism of my youth. I was nervous of it all, but ultimately won over by their warmth and openness.

In this chapter we'll see how tribalism is not merely a question of race or religion, but crucially one of group identification, whatever the common bond. We'll meet some brilliant psychologists and sociologists who've dispassionately investigated our tribal behaviour and come up with shrewd ways of breaking it down. And we'll consider what their findings mean for conflict resolution around the world. De Waal has stressed how important conflict resolution can be within groups as well as between them. He's often seen chimpanzees from the same troupe kiss and embrace each other after fighting. This, and the death he witnessed of a beaten and castrated chimpanzee, Luit, at the zoo where he worked, had a big effect on him: 'The tragic end of Luit opened my eyes to the value of peace-making and played a major part in my decision to focus on what holds societies together.'[4]

THE TRIBE

On 4 April 1968 Martin Luther King was shot and killed. That evening a television reporter asked a local black leader, 'When President Kennedy was shot, his widow held us together. Who's going to control *your* people?' Watching the interview was a junior school teacher in the little town of Riceville in Iowa. Jane Elliott was horrified that the reporter assumed Kennedy and the First Lady represented only white people. She resolved to conduct a bold experiment the very next day with her class of eight- and nine-year-olds. A repeat of the exercise was filmed by ABC two years later, billed as an experiment in the anatomy of prejudice. You can watch it on YouTube, entitled 'The Eye of the Storm'.

The all-white class sing 'God Bless America' and note that it's 'National Brotherhood Week'. Elliott leads them to think about treating everyone as a brother and asks whether there are any people not treated as brothers. 'Black people. Indians', they offer. 'Do you know how it would feel to be treated differently according to the colour of your skin?' she counters, and then asks whether those of them in the class are different in any way. Eventually one child obligingly offers eye colour as a differentiator. Elliott then tells them that they're going to organise themselves for a day governed by whether their eyes are brown or blue: 'Sounds like fun?' she asks.

There's a boy who'd complained that his father kicked him and it turns out his father's eyes are brown. Blue-eyed dads wouldn't have done that, would they? George Washington's eyes were blue, of course. Elliott then lies that melanin is linked to higher intelligence. 'Blue-eyed kids are smarter, cleaner, more civilised', she instructs them. A hierarchy is quickly established in which the blue-eyed sit in the favoured seats at the front of the class, get five minutes extra at break and have the exclusive use of the drinking fountain. In the most sinister note, the brown-eyed kids are made to wear a special collar to identify them. The classmates are perplexed and hesitant to begin with, but soon enter into the spirit of the discrimination wholeheartedly, suggesting that brown-eyed rule-breakers should be treated especially harshly, simply on account of the colour of their irises. And Raymond, a member of the superior blue-eyed caste, says afterwards: 'I felt . . . like I was better than them, happy.'

The story of the original experiment was picked up rapidly by the media and Jane Elliott appeared on the top-rated Johnny Carson show to be interviewed about it. There was a huge reaction, including this letter:

> How dare you try this cruel experiment out on white children? Black children grow up accustomed to such behaviour, but white children, there's no way they would possibly understand it. It's cruel to white children and will cause them great psychological damage.[5]

In the years since, Jane Elliott has become a well-known campaigner for equality, running courses based on her 1968 class. The work has remained controversial, and not just with the naive and ignorant who so resented it at the time. Some education professionals have disputed its validity too. But just watch the video and see how quickly the children descend into tribalism, notwithstanding the strong influence of an authority figure like Elliott pulling the strings.

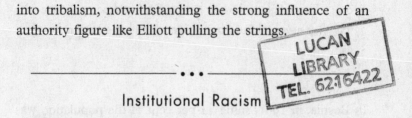

———— • • • ————

Institutional Racism

'How many racists does it take to change a light bulb? None, they're all in the dark.'

'What word starts with N and ends with R and can be used to describe a black person? Neighbour.'

It's 9.30 in the morning and I'm visiting the Museum of Tolerance in New York at the same time as a posse of police. We're all listening to a retired black policewoman who's conducting a mandatory course for New York public servants covering racism and criminal profiling. The Museum of Tolerance, an offshoot of the original institution in Los Angeles, uses the story of the Holocaust to show what can happen when the forces of law and order subvert a justice system, all in the name of a creed of hatred.

The Los Angeles museum began the courses for the LA Police Department after the 1992 riots, provoked by the acquittal of four white policemen who had beaten a black motorist, Rodney King. The courses were then extended to prison officers and other municipal employees. In all they've trained hundreds of thousands of public servants. As well as New York, similar courses are now provided at the Washington Holocaust Memorial too.

The training does more than simply warn about racism and tribalism. It attempts to get police to understand the anxiety a black driver in a white area may feel, for instance, when pulled over. 'They taught us how to hold a gun,' said one policeman, 'but they never told us how to interact with the person facing us.'

— • • • —

In Bosnia, in 1991, some 44 per cent of the population was Muslim, 31 per cent Serbian/Orthodox and 17 per cent Croatian/Catholic. This mix of faiths had lived peacefully side by side since the 1870s, except during the upheavals of the two world wars. When the Soviet Union dissolved in December 1991 and with it Yugoslavia, a third dangerous catalyst had occurred late in the century. Bosnia, led by a Muslim leader, declared independence. The Serb minority wished instead to be part of a contiguous 'Greater Serbia'. They armed themselves, and civil war broke out. It culminated in the acts of barbarity by the Serb army in 1995, at Srebrenica, where 8,000 civilian Muslim men were exterminated. In all, 100,000 Bosnians died in the conflict and, twenty years later, the Serb leader in Bosnia, Radovan Karadžić, was convicted of war crimes.[6] What astonished many Bosnians was the speed with which neighbour turned on neighbour, as old tribal enmities percolated up to the surface. Just as in Armenia or Rwanda, people found themselves shunned or, worse, tortured by those who'd previously been their friends, neighbours or teachers.

Perhaps the cruellest, most rapid phase of the Holocaust was in Hungary in the summer of 1944 when this German ally was finally occupied by the Nazis. Around a quarter of the population of Budapest was identified as Jewish and many others had Jewish antecedents. Forced deportations to the concentration camps began in earnest. I know a little about this because a friend of mine was a first-hand witness – the gastronome and food critic Egon Ronay. Before he died in London in 2010, aged ninety-four, he told me what had happened to his uncle. Ronay was brought up as a Catholic but his wealthy hotelier father came from a Jewish family. Neighbours of Ronay's uncle, people he regarded as friends, outed him as Jewish, even though that is not how he regarded himself. He was taken away and held in a transit camp for deportation by train the following day. Ronay had to dig up a gold cigarette box, hidden in his garden, to bribe a German colonel to go with him and get his uncle released. Leaving the transit camp in style, in a German staff car, his uncle was taken into hiding and survived the war. But fifty years later Ronay would still express amazement and horror at the rapidity with which incipient anti-Semitism poisoned the relations of neighbours and friends and drove many Jews to their rounding-up and death.

• • •

Hostile Media Effect

In 1954 there was a particularly brutal American football game between the old rivals Princeton and Dartmouth College. Some enterprising researchers then showed a film recording of the match to two groups of students – first those from Princeton and then those from Dartmouth. Each said they saw many more wrong refereeing decisions against their own side than against their opponents. The researchers pointed out that partisanship, based on personal values or a strong sense of affiliation, is universal. It applies to football, presidential candidates, Communism or even spinach (for which we might read Marmite).

In 1982 a team at Stanford University showed the same news coverage of the Sabra and Shatila massacre of Palestinian refugees by Christian Lebanese militia (abetted by the Israeli army) to two groups of students, one pro-Israeli and the other pro-Palestinian. The news reports were from channels which attempt to be impartial. Both groups said the reports were biased in favour of the other side. The researchers dubbed this the 'hostile media effect'. Veterans of arguments about whether BBC News is politically impartial or not will know that the Corporation is probably doing its job properly when both the left and right are complaining simultaneously, which they normally are.

In 2012 Dan Kahan and colleagues at Stanford came up with a further idea to test tribal inclinations in relation to the media. Kahan showed participants a video of a demonstration by the Westboro Church from Kansas. This small group, who describe themselves as 'Primitive Baptists', had a track record for vociferous protests at the funerals of AIDS victims, at entertainment shows featuring gay stars and at high-profile gay-rights court cases. They'd sport banners declaring 'God Hates Fags' and similar. (They were even filmed picketing a hardware store because it sold vacuum cleaners from Sweden, a country they regarded as over-tolerant of homosexuality.) Kahan and his colleagues showed fairly wide, unspecific shots of the demo to two groups, disguising its origin. The task for the participants was to decide whether the protesters were fairly exercising their right to free speech, or whether they had crossed the line into illegality. One group was told they were watching an anti-abortion picket. The other was informed it was a protest against the military's 'don't-ask, don't-tell' policy for tolerating gays in the forces. They'd gauged the participants' attitudes to the two issues in advance. It turned out that the subjects who were unsympathetic to the protesters' cause – be that anti-abortion or pro-gay rights – were more likely to say that the protesters had broken the law and overstepped the mark during their demonstration. In the video it was ambiguous, and the viewers capitalised on this to apply their own pre-existing bias, while always believing they were making balanced judgements.[7]

The hostile media effect is one of the best demonstrations of the tribal mindset in action.

─────────────── • • • ───────────────

In 2013 a Harvard professor of psychology, Joshua Greene, published *Moral Tribes: Emotion, Reason, and the Gap between Us and Them.* In this book he observed that tribes are so prone to 'biased fairness' that they allow the interests of the group to distort their sense of justice. He cites Dan Kahan's Stanford experiment and concludes that tribal beliefs are easily biased and that once such a belief becomes a cultural 'identity badge', it can perpetuate itself. Greene's conclusion chimes with de Waal's:

> Our moral brains, which do a reasonably good job of enabling cooperation *within* groups (Me vs Us), are not nearly as good at enabling cooperation *between* groups (Us vs Them). From a biological perspective, this is no surprise, because . . . our brains were designed for within-group cooperation and between-group competition . . .[8]

Philosophy and religion have been engaged in an age-old struggle to articulate the moral arguments for cooperation between groups, tribes, countries. The word *pact* is derived from the Latin *pactum*, meaning agreement, and is etymologically related to *pax*, or peace. It is not a sentiment that finds much favour in many of the books of the Old Testament, which include extraordinary catalogues of rape, torture, slaughter, internecine conflict and general brutality. That is probably an accurate reflection of tribal conflict in the Middle East 3,000 years ago.[9] Contrast this with the New Testament, not a walk in the park either, but where you find 'Blessed are the peacemakers' in the Gospel of St Matthew, and the story of the Good Samaritan in Luke. Jesus is asked, 'Who is my neighbour?' And in reply he tells the story of a man who has been mugged and left injured on the ground. The man ignored by both a priest and a Levite. In other words, his own kind pass by on the other side when confronted by the calamity, preferring not to get involved. But a Samaritan, from another sect, helps the stricken man: 'Which now of these three, thinkest thou, was neighbour unto him that fell among the thieves? And he said, He that shewed mercy on him. Then said Jesus unto him, Go, and do likewise' (Luke 10:36–7).

Despite these enlightened sentiments, religion has remained perhaps the most powerful definer of tribe, after race and nationality, of the past 2,000 years. And during all that time it has more often been an instrument of repression and in-group behaviour than of tolerance. In other words, despite the Good Samaritan, we sometimes still find ourselves in an Old Testament world. The conflict between the modern, inclusive liberality of British civil society and the beliefs of its three million Muslims was highlighted in a 2016 poll commissioned by Channel 4. More than one in five think sharia law should replace British laws in their community. More than one in three think wives should always obey their husbands. And just over half think homosexuality should once again be outlawed in the UK.[10] But we should reflect that the standard British, Anglican marriage service had the word 'obey' in it until 2000. And homosexuality was a crime in the UK until 1967, with civil partnerships and gay marriage enacted only in the past decade. All these liberalisations were attempts by society to understand the sentiments of others, reach out beyond the tyranny of the majority view and break down unjust, tribal divides.

* * *

Homophobia

'Queer bashing' was quite common in Britain in the 1950s. Gangs of youths would set upon gay men, or suspected gay men, in public pick-up locations. Today 'gay bashing' refers to any bullying of perceived homosexuals, most often among school children picking on classmates who are different. But this sort of prejudice is generally in decline in Western societies where 'coming out' is more and more accepted. Post-puberty, the origins of this aggression probably lie in the strength of our sexual passions. The majority are strongly attracted to the opposite sex and, it seems, many of them are also instinctively disgusted by a minority with different sexual habits.

Culture has had a big part to play in defining attitudes.

While discrimination has been the norm, the pendulum has sometimes swung the other way. The ancient Greeks famously accepted sexual love between men as well as between women. The Romans tolerated male homosexuality, but only if the younger, passive partners were slaves. Two thousand years ago, Chinese societies accepted gay relationships too. We can thank Christianity for much oppression through the ages and, in this case, the Old Testament codified the disgust felt by its authors into a supposedly God-given edict: 'If a man also lie with mankind, as he lieth with a woman, both of them have committed an abomination: they shall surely be put to death; their blood shall be upon them' (Leviticus 20:13).

The Pew Research Center surveyed international attitudes to homosexuality in 2013. A majority in the EU, much of Latin America and North America are relaxed about it (the US only just – but in the McCarthy era, as recently as the 1950s, Americans had their 'Lavender Scare' where gays were hounded out of government employment on the grounds that they were part of a clandestine Communist conspiracy). At the time of writing seventy countries still outlaw homosexuality, and it continues to carry the death penalty in places like Saudi Arabia, Northern Nigeria and Iran (where 4,000 homosexuals have been put to death since the 1979 revolution). Here a strict interpretation of sharia law is just as harsh and cruel as the Christian Old Testament. And we should never forget that in Nazi Germany, that ultimate society without empathy, homosexuals were put to death in concentration camps, along with Jews, Roma and the disabled.

The advances in tolerance towards lesbian, gay and transgender people in Western cultures have their roots in the

Enlightenment. Voltaire was one of the first to argue for decriminalisation of homosexuality, which first happened in France after the revolution in 1789. Jeremy Bentham expounded the idea that if it was consensual and harmed no one else then it should be allowed. Because of the malign influence of religious shibboleths, recognition by society of civil partnerships and gay marriage has been relatively recent in Britain (it was only in 2014 that a UKIP councillor informed us that floods in Somerset were God's punishment for legalising gay marriage). We now know that homosexual inclinations are involuntary and quite possibly accounted for by hormonal influences in the mother's womb. The influence of genes and early aspects of nurture, also, have yet to be ruled out as contributors. What matters is that it's a natural occurrence in up to 10 per cent of the population. Contemporary films and books have helped nudge attitudes to homosexuality beyond tolerance towards celebration.[11]

Empathy, as the capacity to understand unfamiliar perspectives, helps eradicate homophobia. It's hard to hate a group of people for where they direct their affections once you've taken a moment to understand the strength and validity of those feelings.

———————————— • • • ————————————

The progress mankind has made generally owes much to the eighteenth-century philosophers of the Enlightenment and their later followers. Jeremy Bentham's formula 'the greatest happiness of the greatest number', John Locke's call for the separation of the Church and state, John Stuart Mill and Richard Cobden's support for more trade between nations – these were all attacks on narrow tribalism. The ideas of the Enlightenment inspired the American Declaration of Independence with its 'life, liberty and the pursuit of happiness'. Thomas Jefferson even produced a version of the New Testament with all the miracles (including the resurrection) removed, in order to concentrate on its moral code. Though let's not get carried away: most of the authors of the Declaration of Independence were slave owners.

Despite the depredations of the twentieth century – the genocides we looked at in Chapter 1, two world wars, continuing conflicts today – there's a view that mankind is gradually improving. I was recently addressing the sixth form of a state school in North Norfolk – it was for a charity which encourages speakers to raise the ambitions of children from poorer backgrounds. There were 120 students in the room and, since this was during the run-up to the 2016 referendum on Britain's European Union membership, the subject of 'Brexit' came up. One hundred and seventeen of them were in favour of staying in the EU. When I questioned them, they were extraordinarily attracted by what the EU (with all its manifest imperfections) represents in terms of continental peace since 1945. And the voting in the referendum itself bore out the suggestion that older voters tended to be more alienated by the EU while younger voters were more idealistic about it. Often the source of the alienation was the open-border agreement which allows immigration from EU countries. Beyond the concern at pressure on housing and health services lay a familiar instinct: tribalism.

A cynic might observe that the United Nations Charter is more 'honoured in the breach than the observance'. But the UN Assembly, the peacekeeping forces and the global humanitarian initiatives are quite unlike anything the world has ever seen before. It's worth quoting, in full, the first three articles of the 1948 Universal Declaration of Human Rights, passed soon after the UN was set up. They summarise what we might call 'the new enlightenment' and represent the most powerful assault on tribalism ever written:

Article One: All human beings are born free and equal in dignity and rights. They are endowed with reason and conscience and should act towards one another in a spirit of brotherhood.

Article Two: Everyone is entitled to all the rights and freedoms set forth in this Declaration, without distinction of any kind, such as race, colour, sex, language, religion, political or other opinion, national or social origin, property, birth or other status. Furthermore, no distinction shall be made on the basis of the political, jurisdictional or institutional status of the country or territory to which a person belongs . . .

Article Three: Everyone has the right to life, liberty, and security of person.

Domestic laws, such as anti-discrimination legislation, and international laws, such as the growing body of human rights charters, are playing their part in gradually establishing a new order of mutuality. But laws alone cannot change human attitudes; it requires a change in our ethics too. We have to believe it's right and necessary to transcend our baser instincts and to reach out beyond our tribes. In *The Better Angels of Our Nature*, Steven Pinker describes how this has already been happening – people alive today are less likely to be killed violently than in any previous century:

Humans are not innately good (just as they are not innately evil), but they come equipped with motives that can orient them away from violence and toward cooperation and altruism. *Empathy* (particularly in the sense of sympathetic concern) prompts us to feel the pain of others and to align their interests with our own . . .[12]

As we know, the empathy instinct can exacerbate tribal behaviour. But if Pinker is right to say it can also break it down, how can this be achieved?

BEYOND THE TRIBE

Mehmed Jelal, Josef Placzek, Zofia Kossak, Gabriel Mvunganyi, Sula Karuhimbi . . . these were the individuals we met in Chapter 1 who, at great risk to their lives, showed kindness to those beyond their tribe in the genocides of the twentieth century. To these we might add the Bosnian Muslim Dr Nedret Mujkanović, who ensured that injured Bosnian Serb soldiers got the same treatment as their enemy in his makeshift hospital in Srebrenica, shared the same food together and lived, at least temporarily, without strife.[13] And witness this act of extreme and extraordinary bravery shown during the time of sectarian killings in Northern Ireland: the poet Seamus Heaney set down what happened when a group of predominantly Protestant workmen were on their way home one evening. They were held up at gunpoint by masked men who asked any Catholics to step forward. The workmen thus assumed these were Protestant paramilitaries who would therefore be targeting the Catholic man in their party:

> in the relative cover of the winter evening darkness, he felt the hand of the Protestant worker next to him take his hand and squeeze it in a signal that said no, don't move, we'll not betray you, nobody need know what faith or party you belong to. All in vain, however, for the man stepped out of the line; but instead of finding a gun at his temple, he was thrown backward and away as the gunmen opened fire on those remaining in the line, for these were not Protestant terrorists, but members, presumably, of the Provisional IRA.[14]

The noble gesture of solidarity, beyond the sectarian divide, was the last, mortal act of that Protestant worker. For he and the rest of the party were gunned down by the armed group, leaving only the Catholic he had helped to relate the episode. The story is included in *Humanity: A Moral History of the Twentieth Century* by Jonathan Glover, a book which includes a chapter on 'The Capacity to Unchain Ourselves'. Glover borrowed that phrase from the Middle East hostage Brian Keenan. This Northern Irish member of the working class spent many months shackled to his fellow captive John McCarthy, a middle-class Englishman. Keenan said that while he and McCarthy were chained together they unchained themselves from what they had known and been. Yet Glover believes tribalism runs so deep in us that it may be impossible to eliminate. In a nod to how neuroscience is revealing the nature of our deep-seated instincts, he writes:

the only realistic option is to accept our tribal psychology as a fact of life. But there is also a long, slow strategy which goes deeper. Perhaps we need not abandon the Enlightenment hope that eventually these tribal loyalties may take second place to a more general humanism. Greater self-consciousness about our psychology may mean that these simple-minded commitments grow into something more complex. A more sophisticated awareness of how tribal narratives are constructed may slowly erode uncritical acceptance of them. And seeing how modern plural nations differ from tribal nations may weaken the grip of old narratives. Belief in such ideas as 'Greater Serbia' depends on myths which are unlikely to survive a more critical outlook.[15]

We're now developing that more critical outlook, thanks in part to the work of many social psychologists. Four decades ago Henri Tajfel conducted a seminal experiment which showed how easily we slip into tribal behaviour, underlining that it doesn't even need conflict over land, as with the Israelis and Palestinians, or over wealth, as with the Tutsis and the Hutus. At Bristol University Tajfel showed 48 boys various paintings by Paul Klee and Wassily Kandinsky. He asked them which ones they liked and which they hated. He didn't tell them who had authorerd each painting. Then he split the boys into two, the 'Klees' and the 'Kandinskys', and informed them that they were in a group with people who admired the same painter as them. In fact he had assigned their group at random. Next he gave each boy a small amount of money to distribute as he wished between one Klee group member and one Kandinsky group member. Even though the boys had no names to go on, only ID numbers, they tended to give significantly more money to the boy in their group. Subsequently the researchers saw a potential problem with this demonstration of in-group favouritism: perhaps some of the boys had already felt strongly that Klee was a genius and Kandinsky a fraud? So they slimmed down the experiment even further, arbitrarily assigning participants into a Group X or a Group Y, with no other differentiation. Just the same in-group favouritism resulted.

These experiments have parallels with Jane Elliot's blue-eyed/brown-eyed one. In the absence of any other loyalties or dispute, mere categorisation can create group bias. And in the right circumstances loyalty to in-group members can lead to hostility towards out-groups. Think of football supporters, playground gangs in schools, the friction between West Africans and people of Caribbean origin within our black communities, and even the passionate academics in the past divided by the nurture-versus-nature debate. They're all behaving according to type.

How can these insights be deployed to resolve conflicts? In the 1950s an American psychologist, Gordon Allport, came up with his 'contact hypothesis'. This suggested that bringing two opposing groups together successfully depended on four necessary conditions: equal status during the contact period, a common goal, intergroup cooperation and the sanction or support of authority figures.[16] As we'll see, it's been established since then that conflict resolution is simpler still and doesn't require all these conditions. But they can all help. For instance, Daniel Barenboim's West–Eastern Divan Orchestra, containing many Palestinian as well as Israeli musicians, follows these principles. The world-famous conductor set it up as a peace initiative in 1999 with a clear intention:

> The only way out of this tragedy . . . is to . . . force everybody to talk to one another. [There's] a need for a mutual feeling of empathy, or compassion . . . In my opinion compassion is not merely a psychological understanding of a person's need, but it is a moral obligation. Only through trying to understand the other side's plight can we take a step towards each other.[17]

* * *

Group Identities

Miles Hewstone originally studied psychology under Professor Henri Tajfel. He's now a professor of social psychology himself, at Oxford University, where he also heads the Oxford Centre for the Study of Intergroup Conflict.

One of Hewstone's most discussed insights came from an early study he carried out. He wanted to know how many of Allport's conditions for successful contact between hostile groups were really essential. So he recruited two Germans to meet a group of British men and women. One of the Germans was straight from central casting. He was reassuringly named Heinrich, he was an engineer by profession (of course) and his personal characteristics matched our stereotype. The other was altogether a bit of an oddball, by the name of Anthony, who had esoteric interests such as the study of Chinese literature.

Hewstone asked his participants to carry out various tasks with Heinrich and Anthony. After contact and cooperation with

Heinrich their general view of Germans improved. But after working just as harmoniously with Anthony their slightly prejudiced attitude to Germans in general had not changed. Hewstone concluded that the contact hypothesis works best when people are allowed to maintain their group, or tribal, identity. It may seem counter-intuitive, but otherwise people are prone to putting their positive experience down to an individual rather than the wider group to which the individual belongs.[18]

Another way to defeat prejudice is through integration and cultural homogenisation. But Emile Bruneau (see below) has found that this can isolate the least integrable people in a negative way. He's studied prejudice against Roma in Europe. Outside Hungary many Roma can pass as non-Roma and become integrated.

--- • • • ---

At a conference in London in 2016, 'Empathy Neuroscience: Translational Relevance for Conflict Resolution', there was a presentation by an organisation called Seeds of Peace. It pursues peace in the Middle East and one of its projects was to set up a peace camp in the US state of Maine, far away from the conflict. Ninety-five Palestinian and Israeli teenagers joined a similar number from other countries and took part in three weeks of team-building challenges and small, facilitated-dialogue groups. A seventeen-year-old Israeli boy, on the verge of conscription into his national army, said at the end: 'The other side is also a people. They have a face, a personality.'[19]

But there's different thinking about which is the best

approach to take when coaxing entrenched members of tribes to see the other side's point of view. The debate revolves around the twin elements of empathy: the cognitive and the emotional (affective) and how to balance them. In 2015 Ruth Feldman, a professor of psychology, wanted to apply our growing neuroscientific understanding of empathy to a group of a hundred Palestinian and Israeli teenagers. She arranged eight group sessions in which participants learnt about the similarity of their two cultures and explored their personal experiences of the conflict, as well as its history. The aim was to see if this cognitive perspective-taking would create a greater understanding between them. She also had a 'control' cohort who did not experience this intervention, so she could compare the two after the exercise. Those who took part in the reciprocal dialogues had brain scans, both before and afterwards, to see if they responded sympathetically to the expressed pain and suffering of the other side, the 'out-group'. She also tested them for levels of hormones such as oxytocin, the so-called cuddle hormone we looked at in Chapter 2. The initial results were disappointing. The participants did not appear to be less hostile to their counterparts, nor did they individually express greater acknowledgement or understanding of the other side's perspective. And their hormonal levels did not markedly change. However, when scrutinising some of the evidence of emotional empathy – shared gaze, greater social comfort in the presence of the 'enemy' and other signs of non-verbal bonding – she found these did increase. Nevertheless, after an initial response to the pain of both the in-group and out-group, Feldman saw the sensory-motor area of the brain intervene and suppress the response to the suffering of the out-group. It killed off the beginnings of a sympathetic reaction. (This is the disconnection we examined in Chapter 2.) Her tentative conclusion was that working on emotional empathy via our more primitive, non-verbal social behaviours, may be a better route for conflict resolution than targeting our higher, cognitive processes. Peace-promoting exercises might be most effective, allowing humane, person-to-person exchanges without too many complex history lessons.[20]

But others emphasise the importance of cognitive perspective-taking as well as emotional empathy. Jean Decety says: 'Perspective-taking . . . has been linked to social competence and social reasoning and can be used as a strategy for reducing group biases.'[21]

Decety cites a study carried out in the early 2000s in the then strife-filled island of Sri Lanka, where the minority Tamils resented being ruled by the majority Sinhalese. The former are mostly Hindus while the latter are predominantly Buddhists. The bloody civil war ended in 2009 during which it was estimated 65,000 had died and ten million people had been made homeless. At one point the Norwegian government funded the establishment of a series of peace camps for forty Sri Lankans aged eighteen to twenty-one. Along with Sinhalese and Tamils, a number of Muslims also participated. The four days of activities included lectures, peace workshops, experience of the creative arts and tours of multi-ethnic villages. There was also intense socialisation, with all the boys sharing a large dormitory and the girls another. There was a particularly interesting follow-up done with one class a year after their gathering. First their residual attitudes were tested. Participants, from all the ethnicities, still showed significantly greater empathy for the out-groups than some other young people who'd not attended a camp. And their behaviour was also assessed. The study used the same method that Tajfel had used with his two art tribes, asking them to divide up and donate monies to groups of needy children of the three Sri Lankan tribes. They gave almost 40 per cent more to the children belonging to the two out-groups than they did to those of their own in-group, an apparently very encouraging result for the benefits of perspective-taking. But, of course, emotional empathy was also being exercised. So there's more work to be done on the alchemy between these two elements of the empathy instinct. Overall, the authors of the study conclude:

> Empathy may play a crucial role in reconciliation between groups in conflict . . . [it] is likely to increase the willingness to make concessions and to accept agreements that involve between-group interaction, mutual cooperation, and coexistence. Empathy may even lead to the development of trust.[22]

There's an important qualification to how empathy may develop trust. A Palestinian who took part in a programme run by the United States Institute of Peace said that the process had helped him understand the other side (the Israelis) and that they had been humanised in his eyes. But he also said his new understanding of the Israeli perspective meant that he now doubted peace would ever be possible. He did not believe the Israeli government would ever make the necessary compromises.[23] So if empathy can also be a limiting factor, it's important to be very thoughtful about what works.

Two American academics decided to draw on 515 studies of peace-building initiatives, such as the ones in Sri Lanka and the Middle East, to see which kinds are the most effective. The studies had been conducted across thirty-eight countries involving a quarter of a million participants. The three most important ways in which the initiatives helped reduce prejudice were: increasing knowledge of the other group so as to help people realise how similar they really are; reduction in anxiety after spending time with members of another group; and the deployment of empathy (both cognitive and emotional) drawing out-group members into people's circle of concern. Anxiety-reduction and empathy are the stronger of the three factors. The authors concluded:

> We do not have enough studies to detach the effects of empathy from those of the closely related variable of perspective-taking – which represents a more cognitive dimension of empathy. But these results are consistent with much of the developing literature on the robust effects of empathy and perspective taking.[24]

Research such as this, pinning down precisely the best ways to win friends and influence people mired in conflicts, is not just an academic exercise. Such insights are sorely needed in the Middle East, in the Horn of Africa, in the Ukraine and in many other places. Intervening is one thing, intervening effectively is quite another.

Empathetic Mediation

The law of Kanun governs the ancient Albanian custom of blood feuds. In the past quarter-century there are thought to have been at least 12,000 instances where families have settled grudges by killing each other. Sometimes teenage boys carry out the assassinations but then have to be hidden away and thereafter often suffer from depression. Gjin Marku, who worked in state intelligence in the Communist era, now volunteers at and runs the Committee of Nationwide Reconciliation in Albania. They mediate to bring blood feuds to an end. Marku says: 'I prepare carefully, gathering the facts of the incident and putting myself in their shoes – as if I myself was their grieving relative.'[25]

Matt Waldman and his Center for Empathy in International Affairs has gathered together experts for conferences around the world. They have discussed instances when empathy has been crucial, such as during peace talks in the Caucasus in the 1990s. There the Armenian delegation wanted the Azerbaijanis to apologise for their role in the Armenian genocide of 1915–17. But, not being Turkish, the Azerbaijanis could not understand why. It transpired that for years the Armenians had felt themselves to be unfairly cast as villains for appropriating two-fifths of Azerbaijan, and inadequately recognised as the victims of genocide. Once Azerbaijan had shown a degree of empathy for the Armenians' position, the peace talks could move forward.[26]

Mediators need to have high levels of empathy, instinctively or acquired, to succeed. They have to be able to understand the emotions and motives even of people who may have done terrible things. And because mediation teams often work under great pressure there needs to be good communication within a team too. Waldman himself has mediated in conflicts in places such as Afghanistan and Syria. He says mediators should seek to get inside the minds of the conflict parties, while maintaining discipline and rigour by remaining impartial and non-judgemental. James Duffy, an Australian academic, believes that 'mediator empathy' is an essential skill for communicating to a party that their feelings have been heard and understood. But he agrees with Waldman that there are dangers. If empathy becomes sympathy, he warns, then that might be seen to compromise mediator neutrality.[27]

The answer would appear to be that cognitive empathy is the key to good mediation but too much emotional empathy, leading to over-involvement, is a mistake. Since mediation now plays an important part in the law and family policy as well as international relations, there are now training courses for mediators. In the UK the Centre for Effective Dispute Resolution offers these, as does Peaceworks. The latter has a specific module on active listening.

In the future Matt Waldman would like to see training in empathy provided to all those who work in international affairs, including mediators, diplomats and NGO practitioners. He also believes universities should offer courses in empathy.[28]

——————————— • • • ———————————

Steven Pinker agrees with Decety on the value of perspective-taking. He writes about experiments carried out by the social psychologist Daniel Batson with some American college students. Batson wanted to test whether perspective-taking might induce sympathy not only for that individual but also for the wider group to which they belong. He asked two sets of participants to listen to a radio documentary about a young woman who'd accidentally contracted AIDS from a blood transfusion, necessitated by a car accident. One group was asked objectively to evaluate the radio report for its technical merits – for instance, whether it was good journalism. The other was instructed to imagine how the AIDS victim felt. When they all filled out a questionnaire later, it was the perspective-takers who recorded more sympathetic attitudes to all AIDS sufferers. Their sympathy had spread from the individual to the wider class she belonged to. By contrast the technical evaluators were less sympathetic.[29]

As our understanding of the empathy instinct grows we'll get a better fix on the best way to resolve conflicts and encourage pro-social behaviour. We can see that these many studies show that real improvements do occur. We're still working hard on precisely how those improvements are driven. But in the future they could all contribute to a new Enlightenment, because it seems likely that the best results occur when both emotional and cognitive empathy are married to a reasoned respect for justice and human rights.

EMPATHY WITHOUT BORDERS

We've looked at a number of studies involving small numbers of people which indicate that clever, informed interventions can make a real difference in situations of conflict. But how can you scale up the empathy instinct? There are some people thinking very hard about this.

Miles Hewstone has spent four years researching an educational experiment which has been attempting to integrate two hostile communities in a British city. It's a test of the contact hypothesis writ large.

In May 2001 a white teenager threw a brick at two Asian boys. It happened in a street which divides the white and Asian communities of Oldham in Lancashire. The white boy took refuge in a nearby house which was then attacked by Asians. Rioting broke out in the town and continued for three nights. The local newspaper was attacked by Asian gangs and a petrol bomb was thrown at a school. The shocking violence then spread to Bradford and Burnley, which also have sizeable Asian populations. It was a national story and a political crisis for the government of the day.[30] The debate was heated and followed other incidents. One had occurred in Oldham itself, when a septuagenarian had been beaten up by an Asian youth leading to the *Mirror* headline 'Beaten For Being White' and the *Mail on Sunday*'s 'Whites Beware'.

Oldham's population was 80 per cent white and 20 per cent Pakistani and Bangladeshi. Over the years the minority communities had ended up living together in very defined parts of the city. Two reviews were commissioned by the government in the aftermath of the riots. The Cantle Report observed that the white and Asian communities were living 'polarised lives'. The Ritchie Report, about Oldham specifically, said the town's 'major issue . . . is the segregated nature of society'. In response, in 2007, a plan came together to merge two schools: Breeze Hill, almost entirely Asian, and Counthill, almost entirely white. They started building on the site of an old cotton mill and a new school, Waterhead

Academy, began to take shape. Between 2010 and 2012 they brought classes from Breeze Hill and Counthill together. And then they all started on the new site in the autumn of 2012. Everything was carefully and sensitively planned, with separate sports activities for boys and girls, assemblies incorporating a range of faiths and menus which included both halal meat and bacon sarnies.

Hewstone and colleagues have been able to monitor whether and by how much attitudes between the communities changed once they were thrust together. Observational data from the cafeteria shows that the children continued to eat in their own ethnic groups but that, very slowly, a thaw occurred. At the outset, only 2.5 per cent of the friends of the white children were Asian, but by the end of the first year that figure was 7.5 per cent, still very low but improving. Detailed surveys of the pupils' attitudes have shown more encouraging results, with carefully measured, negative sentiments between the two groups markedly declining year by year.

Hewstone told the *Guardian* that he had been 'blown away' by the results, pointing out that the positive trends should be compared to the possibility of growing antagonism or even total failure which might have resulted from the merger. He also optimistically quoted the eighteenth-century radical Thomas Paine: 'The mind once enlightened cannot again become dark.'

How much attention the Waterhead Academy garners, and how likely it is to be replicated elsewhere, depends partly on other factors. The two schools it was formed from had plenty of problems coping with children from disadvantaged backgrounds, including drug issues and low educational attainment.

Many of those challenges persist in the new school and there's currently pressure on it from Ofsted, the schools inspectorate: because of its below-average academic outcomes it has been put into 'special measures'. Nevertheless it would appear that Hewstone has demonstrated a powerful strategy for bringing communities together in many divided cities across the country.[31]

———————————— • • • ————————————

Faith Schools: For and Against

Faith schools teach a general curriculum but have a religious ethos and formal links to their chosen faith. Most are state funded. They're allowed to give priority to applicants of their religion and are excluded from equality legislation to allow them to discriminate in this way (the same exclusion has been used to justify gender segregation in Muslim faith schools). Astonishingly one-third of British schools are faith schools.[32]

There's a big debate over whether or not these schools perpetuate divisions and prejudice. The 2015 Commission on Religion and Belief in British Public Life found that there's more segregation by religion among school-age children than there is among those aged eighteen to thirty-four. In an increasingly secular society public opinion has been shifting against these schools. In 2012 it was found that 71 per cent of respondents opposed their selection freedoms and two years later 58 per cent said they disapproved of the idea of faith schools. The commission recommended that, while preserving their ethos, the schools' right to purely religious selection should be abolished and that they should all develop clear plans to mix children of different faiths and ethnicities. Already a special inspectorate for faith schools has been disbanded for paying too much attention to faith and not enough to general scholastic standards. And some Muslim schools in the Midlands have been closed because their ethos has been condemned as unacceptably extreme.[33]

Those who wish to keep the current system and maintain the privileges of faith schools point firstly to often high academic standards – though a spokesperson for Ofsted said: 'Selection, even on religious grounds, is likely to attract well-behaved children from stable backgrounds.'[34]

Then the Archbishop of Canterbury defended both their popularity and their public merit: 'People seem to choose these schools in large numbers. They are often in the poorest parts of the country, we seek to love and serve people, as we should, through these schools – and have done for hundreds of years.'[35]

Others defend them simply on grounds of freedom of choice, much as they'd defend the right of parents to send their children to private schools. To abolish them, it's argued, would be illiberal and intolerant.[36]

One of the most telling perspectives is that of Jamie Martin, a former special adviser to the Department for Education, who deploys the intolerance argument on the other side. He's very concerned that faith schools do not have to teach about other religions. He believes they should be made to abide by the same admissions code, curriculum requirements and equality laws as other state schools:

I profoundly wish we had been bolder [at the Department for Education] . . . Bringing communities together should be the aim of every school and an education that promotes tolerance and inclusivity should be the birthright of every child. These are not British values, but universal ones. They are our most important weapon in the fight against extremism.[37]

Perhaps the way ahead lies in Northern Ireland, where the education system was specifically designed to help end the sectarian hostility which fed the Troubles for so many years. There schools are obliged to put children of different faiths together.

————————————— • • • —————————————

Emile Bruneau is a psychologist at the Brain and Cognitive Sciences Department at the Massachusetts Institute of Technology (MIT). He's highly influenced by an experience at the age of twenty-four, when he volunteered at a peace camp for young Protestants and Catholics in Northern Ireland. After three weeks of bonding and well-meant corporate activity, on the last day the mother of all fights broke out between the two groups. What it's taught him is that scepticism, rigour and proof are all incredibly important in order to identify the interventions which really work. He believes that the money they receive is too often a product of their intuitive appeal. His hunch is that 10 per cent are effective, 10 per cent are counter-productive and 80 per cent are useless. He wants them to be evaluated properly so that 'we can drop 90 per cent of them, and massively increase our use of the remaining 10 per cent'.[38]

Much of his research has been into how best to resolve 'asymmetric' conflicts (in which one side has more power than the other). He's worked with white and Mexican Americans, with white and Roma Hungarians and with Palestinians and Israelis. His greatest ambition now is to explore how the most effective interventions can be best scaled up, so that we can make real advances in conflict resolution.

In 2012 Bruneau did some very instructive research on 'perspective-taking' (listening) and 'perspective-giving' (talking) between in-groups and out-groups. He found important differences in what works best for each side. So for white Americans perspective-taking, that is being in listening mode, had the most positive effect on their attitudes to Mexicans. And the same holds for Israelis towards Palestinians. Whereas it was perspective-giving that brought about the biggest positive shift in the Mexican and Palestinian views of the opposing groups they face. It says a lot about the power of empathetic listening that a group who feel oppressed can have their perceptions improved simply by being heard.[39]

Bruneau is using empathy know-how in his work on the relations between white Hungarian and Roma communities in Budapest. He's been deploying mimicry to help white Hungarian children develop a more positive attitude to their Roma counterparts. They watch a music video of Roma kids and they're asked to copy them. The activity is based on research showing a clear link between mimicry and pro-social behaviour: it seems that simply to copy someone is to be in sympathy with them and to want to do something about that.[40] This takes us back to the debate around the cognitive versus the emotional: mimicry is very much a mechanism of emotional empathy, and interventions like Bruneau's and Ruth Feldman's remind us of emotional empathy's importance.

Yet much of Bruneau's research also shows the importance of cognitive empathy. When he asked people in a brain scanner to watch the Pixar short *Partly Cloudy*, he got some fascinating results. The animation contains different scenes in which characters sometimes experience physical pain and sometimes emotional pain. The two different kinds lit up two distinct networks in the viewers' brains. This finding tallied with other research of his demonstrating that the physical pain of an out-group member can merely make people distressed, whereas when they are party to the emotional pain of an out-group member they are much more likely to feel sympathy. In one study which demonstrates this he gave two groups a short story about Melanie, who had been out one day when a stranger threw up all over her. The first group felt no sympathy at all with the stranger. Things were different for the second group. Before hearing the story, they had been told about the stranger's character and state of mind – 'She is always forgetful', 'She was down that day because . . .' This group of participants felt empathy and sympathy towards the sick woman.[41]

Bruneau believes that the digital age offers the best chance of scaling up conflict resolution. He wants to explore whether popular television soap operas in Hungary might be able to write in positive Roma characters, perhaps bonding with the viewers before revealing their ethnicity. Those apparently very effective but small peace camps in Sri Lanka took place in 2001. The worst and most brutal part of the civil war was still to come. Might it have been different if mass media had been deployed to help break down tribal barriers for a much larger number? In Chapter 8 we'll see how a radio soap opera became a national weapon in helping to make peace between the Tutsis and Hutus in Rwanda. This is the direction in which Bruneau is now taking his work. But, as we saw earlier, simple knowledge of others needs to be enhanced and powered by active empathy too.

In this chapter we've looked at the many ingenious studies which point the way ahead to preventing tribalism, most often fuelled by race and religion, from causing conflict. There are two final points to add. You often hear politicians say, 'We don't talk to terrorists.' But Jonathan Powell, who helped bring peace to Northern Ireland for the Blair government and has now founded an NGO called Inter Mediate, says you always have to talk to make peace. In his book about ending armed conflicts he quotes the past Labour leader Hugh Gaitskell: 'All terrorists, at the invitation of the government, end up with drinks in the Dorchester.'[42]

The second point is that peace is only ever achieved with intelligent, brave and empathetic leadership. Nelson Mandela had to negotiate with the white South African Prime Minister F. W. de Klerk to end apartheid. De Klerk said he 'got to know him as a good listener'.[43] As Jonathan Glover pursues the idea of our capacity to 'unchain ourselves' in his book, he says this about Mandela's towering achievement:

The only escape from the trap of vendetta is awareness of how stories on both sides were constructed. There has to be some recognition of how things have gone wrong and that showing mutual respect is the only way out. In post-apartheid

South Africa the fact that Nelson Mandela . . . resisted the temptation . . . to humiliate the white minority gave all groups a chance to escape the cycle of revenge. Symbolism matters. The once all-white Springboks were a symbol of apartheid. When President Mandela wore their rugby shirt, a new version of an old story was starting to be written.[44]

8

THE ART OF EMPATHY

And one day Julie sat down at a desk next to me and put a tube of Smarties on the desk, and she said, 'Christopher, what do you think is in here?' And I said, 'Smarties.' Then she took the top off the Smarties tube and turned it upside down and a little red pencil came out and she laughed and I said, 'It's not Smarties, it's a pencil.' Then she put the little red pencil back inside the Smarties tube and she put the top back on. Then she said, 'If your Mummy came in now, and we asked her what was inside the Smarties tube, what do you think she would say?' . . . And I said, 'A pencil.'[1]

Christopher is the central character in Mark Haddon's hugely successful novel, *The Curious Incident of the Dog in the Night-Time*. Though Haddon deliberately doesn't mention the term, if Christopher were to receive a diagnosis, it would be Asperger's. He appears good at maths but he struggles to identify emotions and has difficulty reading other people or imagining their state of mind; he thinks that if he knows a tube of Smarties unexpectedly contains not sweets but a pencil, then everyone else would know that too. Christopher suffers from what psychologists call, as we've seen, a theory-of-mind (or cognitive empathy) deficit, which can now be identified by means of the Sally–Anne test implemented in 1985 by Simon Baron-Cohen, Alan Leslie and Uta Frith and considered a reliable indicator of this deficit. Christopher can't interpret the emotions on another person's face and he can't think himself into someone else's shoes. He lacks empathy for people due to this deficit but though he may know when they're unhappy or suffering, it is not instinctive for him and his recognition of it is unreliable. Like many people on the autistic spectrum, however, he can show compassion, such as concern for his pet dog.

• • •

The Asperger's Paradox

Jon Adams is a Fellow of the Royal Society of Arts and artist-in-residence at Portsmouth University. He's an illustrator by profession and in 2016 was creating *Democracy Street*, a map of the UK based on patterns of user-generated content found online. What this shows is that Adams has a gift – he can find meaning and symbolism in lots of random information. He's brilliant at systematising and has been diagnosed as Asperger's by no less an authority than Simon Baron-Cohen. 'It's not true we don't have empathy', he says. 'Music can overwhelm me, I have a high sense of justice. We do feel, we do care.'[2]

Here's the Asperger's paradox: someone who has difficulty interpreting human emotions can produce creative art that plumbs the depths of human experience. It's now thought a vast number of great artists in the past, judging by their known behaviour, might have been diagnosed as Asperger's had we had such knowledge at the time. In music: Bruckner, Bartók, Satie, Mahler, Beethoven, Richard Strauss, Mozart. In art and design: Charles Rennie Mackintosh, Michelangelo, Van Gogh, Warhol, Lowry. In literature: Emily Dickinson, Kafka, George Bernard Shaw, Austen, Twain, Virginia Woolf. If they were all indeed Asperger's, it is an extraordinary list and shows there are more than a few aspects of autism we should celebrate. They would have had difficulty comprehending the instant interplay of everyday relations, but they could think deeply about the human condition on their own, in a more controlled setting.

Jon Adams: 'We're neurodivergent, and it needs to be recognised. It's more about hidden ability than hidden disability. We can make a really positive contribution to the arts.'

• • •

Mark Haddon makes us love his subject, Christopher, and the novel has resonated with all age groups. It has sold more than five million copies and become a hit play, which in 2015 was running simultaneously in London's West End and on Broadway in New York.[3] So Haddon's book succeeds in making us identify strongly with a boy suffering from severe behavioural problems. Paradoxically, and triumphantly, Haddon gets us to empathise with a character who has difficulty doing that himself. *The Curious Incident of the Dog in the Night-Time* has undoubtedly helped many of us understand those who are low in emotional intelligence, whereas as recently as the 1990s few of us would have understood the condition or have heard of autism. Witness the power of a good book or, indeed, of any work of art. This chapter is about how arts and culture, by their very essence, tell us stories about the human condition and help us to understand and live with our fellow citizens. It's a demonstrably powerful and positive force. As one critic put it: 'A work of art . . . is a bridge between one mind and another . . . it's a primary way in which people create and exchange meaning.'[4]

That is the function of all art. But recently some artists have decided to make the principle explicit. One group set up the Empathy Museum, what they call 'an experiential arts space dedicated to helping us all look at the world through other people's eyes'. It included an exhibition entitled *Walk a Mile in My Shoes*, which has been mounted in Britain and Australia so far. Its creator, Clare Patey, records audio interviews with people and borrows their shoes. Visitors are asked to put on headphones and listen to these life stories while actually walking in their shoes: the man whose marriage is in trouble and his only solace is to swim in very cold water, the sex worker who gave up a career in finance to bring tenderness to lonely men, and the lorry driver jailed for smuggling heroin who became a prolific artist in prison. One visitor said: 'I found myself gazing at the shoes as I walked and feeling an eerily close identification with the guy. It was powerful.'

And there are countless other less explicit explorations of empathy in art. Marcelo Vallejo is an Argentinian ex-soldier who fought in the Falklands War. He's subsequently been a drug addict and has attempted suicide. All these years he has reviled the British to such an extent he would not allow his son to speak a word of English in his presence. David Jackson fought on the British side in the same conflict, suffering badly from post-traumatic stress and depression in the years afterwards. Later he qualified as a psychologist. Marcelo and David are sitting opposite each other asking searching questions about how their war service affected them both. Marcelo, perhaps ironically, asks David how much he charges for professional counselling services: 'Fifty pounds a session. But for you, Marcelo, it's free.' Their encounter is taking place on a stage in front of an audience, because it's part of a play put on at the London International Festival of Theatre in the summer of 2016. *Minefield* was written by the Argentinian artist Lola Arias and required three British veterans and three Argentinian veterans to rehearse and develop the show over several months. This dramatic experiment, the deliberate building of a bridge between former enemies, culminated in the cast performing in a band together, with a rousing Beatles song. Reviews called it 'a cathartic reunion' and 'a work of extraordinary compassion'.[5] It had the overt purpose of creating an understanding between former foes and clearly succeeded, for the audience as well as the participants. But the arts have always been expected to deliver something much more than entertainment.

PITY, FEAR AND EMPATHY

There's always been a debate around whether 'good' art should have a positive moral or ethical purpose. This needn't detain us long since we'll see that work which resonates does so because it connects us to those around us and uplifts us in the process. Most of us find pure negativity disturbing and ultimately empty. When the video game, *Call of Duty*

Modern Warfare 2, came out in 2009 users were asked to play a terrorist who has to walk through an airport shooting unarmed civilians to prove their commitment. Only a designer of low emotional intelligence could have created that scene. It has echoes of Nietzsche's 'will to power' which emphasises the individual over society. Some of us might naturally recoil from such cold egoism, but not its fans.

Plato is often quoted as wanting to ban poets from his ideal society, but that's not strictly accurate. He actually wanted to ban the wrong sort of poet, mere entertainers, in favour of those with a more positive purpose: 'Good speech, good accord, good grace, and good rhythm follow upon goodness of character.'[6]

Some leading critics have since argued that not only should the artist display morality but the critic too. For the Victorian John Ruskin this depended on contemplation, imagination and, in the case of artists, once again, good character. Whose version of morality? we might ask. Well, 'decency' did it for Plato and 'God and nature' were essential to Ruskin. But for the purposes of empathy, a positive quality in its own right, an artist's work needs only to employ imagination so as to help the audience put themselves in the shoes of others. For the poet Shelley this was enough:

A man, to be greatly good, must imagine intensely and comprehensively . . . the pains and pleasures of his species must become his own. The great instrument of the moral good is the imagination; and poetry administers to the effect by acting upon the cause.[7]

William Shakespeare

A few critics — Voltaire, Shaw, Tolstoy, Wittgenstein — have attacked Shakespeare for the ambiguity and moral confusion of his plays. But those works remain the greatest cultural gift which Britain has given the world, in any art form. Why are they performed in more than eighty countries 400 years after his death? Because the plays capture the complexity and contradictions of the human condition so sympathetically and so completely, like no other writer. Let's take ten of his thirty-seven dramas — histories, tragedies, comedies — and from each select just one of the many universal themes which they contain:

All's Well That Ends Well . . . unrequited love
As You Like It . . . . sibling rivalry
Coriolanus . . . . the arrogance of power
Hamlet . . . . troubled adolescence
Julius Caesar . . . . loyalty and treachery
King Lear . . . . inter-generational angst
Measure for Measure . . . . . . morality and lust
The Merchant of Venice. . . . . racism
Othello. . . . . psychopathic malice
Romeo and Juliet . . . . gang warfare

These are all things which we recognise and understand. Watching the plays reminds us of the complexity of our society and our relationships. And they make us experience profound emotions such as pity and fear, both of which require us to imagine the feelings of the characters.

• • •

It was Aristotle who defined tragedy as evoking *pity* and *fear* in us (leading to *catharsis*, a sense of cleansing resolution). Pity for the characters caught up in the drama and fear as to what might happen to them. This is, in itself, an act of empathy on the part of the audience, sparked by the playwright. It seems Aristotle had worked out what neuroscientists have now proved: that to experience or perceive no fear is to be less human and, in extreme cases, to be psychopathic. A perfect representation of this is the libretto written for Mozart by Lorenzo Da Ponte, *Don Giovanni*. He based the story on the legendary philanderer Don Juan, and we see the central figure manipulate, cheat, seduce and murder before he descends into hell. In Act Two he sings: 'I'll not be called a coward. I've never been afraid.'

In his book, *Empathy: Why It Matters, and How to Get It*, Roman Krznaric talks about the trick pulled off by Aeschylus more than a hundred years before Aristotle with his Greek tragedy *The Persians*. The Persians were the great enemy of the Greek city-states whom they had recently defeated. But Aeschylus chose to tell a story from the Persians' point of view, asking his audience to sympathise with the enemy's wives who had lost their husbands in battle. Krznaric says:

> The Greeks believed that drama could have a transformative effect on the audience . . . Greek theatre was a deeply communal activity where the experience of weeping together in response to the characters' personal suffering and moral dilemmas helped to strengthen the bonds of citizenship.[8]

In the second half of the twentieth century our television soap operas performed a similar role, highlighting live social issues and holding millions of us in thrall to the everyday lives of the characters. So strong was their pull that some had difficulty in remembering that it was actually fiction, sending the various characters birthday cards, heartfelt condolences and outraged complaints about their behaviour. The tabloid newspapers aided and abetted the conspiracy, reporting the dramas and crises as though they were real events. Now that media channels have fragmented, the soaps, while still relatively popular, have less influence. But many pressing social issues continue to be aired in the plotlines of *Coronation Street* (ITV), *Emmerdale* (ITV), *EastEnders* (BBC) and *Hollyoaks* (Channel 4), all seen through the empathetic prism of fictional communities.

ARTS, CULTURE AND BRAIN POWER

You could argue it's plain common sense that the arts broaden our minds and help us understand people. But what actually happens in our brains when we become empathetic? And does it really translate into more socially positive behaviour? In Simon Baron-Cohen's view empathy is 'the drive to identify another person's emotions and thoughts, and to respond to them with an appropriate emotion'.[9]

As we saw in Chapter 2, neuroscientists have now demonstrated that when we see people in pain it stimulates the neurons in our brains to fire in the same way as if we ourselves were in pain. And other parts of our brain interact with this process, partly prompted by hormones such as oxytocin. So most of us are conditioned to recognise others' feelings and empathise with them.

The particularly sophisticated trick we've also mastered with the arts is that we've developed the ability to *imagine* a fictional person is in pain, and still empathise. This extraordinary feat is performed by children from an early age, which tends to make us take it for granted. But some people don't have the ability: Lewy Body Dementia severely impairs our cognitive functions. The result can be that sufferers often think a TV show or film is real and that the characters are with them in the house. This is described as a 'hallucination'. Fantasy, essential to fiction, is by comparison a conscious act of imagination.

As neuroscience develops rapidly, more is discovered all the time. There's now research which demonstrates that both storytellers and listeners have the same regions of their brain active. Other work shows that it's not only the language-processing parts of the brain which are deployed, but also the areas which deal with the various emotions evoked by the story. In his book *The Storytelling Animal*, Jonathan Gottschall writes: 'The constant firing of our neurons in response to fictional stimuli strengthens and redefines the neural pathways that lead to skilful navigation of life's problems.'[10]

The evolutionary biologist Robert Trivers even argues that because of humanity's original need to cooperate, our cognitive abilities and language skills specifically evolved to manage larger networks of reciprocity (this makes Shakespeare the literal as well as the literary vehicle for empathy). And according to Professor Martha Nussbaum, enjoying stories is an essential step to being responsive to others' needs, to moral interaction. She sees it as a habitual practice in the service of citizenship and community. Nussbaum is actually a professor of law at the University of Chicago Law School. Her interest is in what it takes to make societies work, with cooperative, law-abiding citizens.

When we tell and listen to stories, we rehearse our human responses. So the bedtime story, read by a parent to a child, is not just a demonstration of love and security or a comforting way to bring on sleepiness. It is a fundamental exercise in empathy, between parent and offspring and in terms of sharing the pity and fear inherent in the story. *Alice in Wonderland, Peter Pan, Winnie the Pooh, Paddington, The Tiger Who Came to Tea* – all have been used by different generations but for the same purpose. Now consider children in deprived circumstances who do not regularly enjoy this bonding moment with a parent. And think how much more difficult it is for them to empathise and what effect that might have on their lives and those around them. Worse still, what if you cannot read at all? The illiterate in our society are not only deprived of a basic skill but are also excluded from the extraordinarily positive stimulus of storytelling via the written word. Is it a coincidence that 60 per cent of US prisoners are functionally illiterate, or that one-third of those jailed in the UK have a reading age of ten or worse? Perhaps more worrying is the statistic quoted by the American writer Michele Borba, showing the decline of the bedtime story in the US. In 1999 children between the ages of two and seven were read to for an average of forty-five minutes a day. By 2013 that had fallen to thirty minutes.[11] Digitally distracted parents are losing this precious contact time with their offspring. Could we set up the NSPBS – the National Society for the Preservation of the Bedtime Story?

Someone who's set up a local chapter of this yet-to-be-founded organisation is Jane Davis, founder of The Reader organisation in Liverpool. They work with the city council to take shared reading aloud to the homes of vulnerable children. Trained volunteers have so far made regular visits to seventy children at home, many of whom had never been read to before. This is what a Family Support Worker said about it: 'Something changed after The Reader. My manager said recently, "What do they do?" I don't know what they do exactly at The Reader, but it works!'[12]

In fact, participants have shown improved behaviour, reduced offending and improved school attendance. How much of this is specifically down to the reading as compared to the one-to-one nurture from another person? Does it matter? Here's ten-year-old Daisy:

> I feel so happy when I read with Joyce. Sometimes when you're closing your eyes and Joyce is reading, and you're just feeling comfortable and there's a pillow behind your back, breathing in and breathing out, and it takes all the bad memories away and brings all the good memories.[13]

The great insight here is that almost all of us have the capacity for empathy but we need to learn to exercise it. The arts help us do that. Both evolutionary biologists and neuroscientists now believe it's possible to train our brains to be more empathetic. The arts provide some of the equipment in this mental gymnasium. We need to connect our children with this precious gift at an early age. In Chapter 3 we saw how crucial the early years are in the formation of the brain and its empathetic functions. I've quoted scientists and academics on this. Now let's hear from Keith Oatley, who's not only a cognitive psychologist but also a novelist: 'the process of entering imagined worlds of fiction builds empathy and improves your ability to take another person's point of view'.[14]

And here's the Canadian novelist Margaret Atwood: 'What really hits people is the story because it's not an intellectual thing and it's not just a scream. It's not pure emotion, it's a melding of those two things, which is where we exist as human beings.'[15]

THE POSITIVE FORCE OF ART AND EMPATHY

We make our claims for the power of the arts, but the question arises: do they merely give us a gratifying emotional experience or does our future behaviour actually alter? We've seen Simon Baron-Cohen writes about the difference between cognitive empathy, which gives us an understanding of another, and affective (or emotional) empathy, which allows us to feel another's state and can generate compassion and positive action. We've spoken of Iago in *Othello*. He's brilliant at the cognitive bit, but he uses it destructively to exploit others' weaknesses. We could add Richard III ('Conscience is but a word that cowards use').[16] One thing these characters definitively don't have is affective empathy, the quality that can lead to pro-social behaviour. This is how the educationist

Sir Ken Robinson puts it: 'I think of compassion as applied empathy, so to speak, the executive wing of empathy. It's one thing to empathise . . . something else to do something about it . . . Compassion is the . . . cultural glue that holds us together as communities.'[17]

Raymond Williams, a leading post-war literary critic, was concerned about whether literature could goad us into action in this way. He argued that nineteenth-century novelists like Charles Dickens exposed the cruelties of a new industrialising, urban society. But he was critical of their inhibition, their reluctance to go beyond recognising evil by proposing a better-organised society. He believed that in their novels 'sympathy was transformed not into action but withdrawal'.[18] There's a parallel with news media today. When we see yet another humanitarian catastrophe featured in the news, we might empathise but feel hopeless because there's nothing we can personally do to help. Worse, we might find the repetition of such events exhausts – burns out – our ability to empathise. We know we can disconnect, switch empathy on and off. And yet the British public's continued and generous response to charity appeals shows how quickly the on-switch can be activated again. Normally this is because news outlets feature the stories of individual victims – people with whom we can connect – to exemplify the wider phenomenon.

The narratives offered by arts and culture, so appealing and so carefully wrought, are arguably much more powerful and engrossing than short news reports from faraway places. And despite Williams' misgivings, they *can* lead us to action. Indeed, some classic works have gone on to help change our society. In 1862 Charles Kingsley revealed the first instalment of a new story in *Macmillan's Magazine*: *The Water-Babies (A Fairy Tale for a Land Baby)*. When published in book form the following year it quickly became a classic. It's a surreal tale featuring Tom, a boy who's obliged to squeeze up chimneys to clean them. Oppressive child labour of this sort was permitted in the early and mid-Victorian era. When Tom later drowns he's transformed into a mythical underwater creature and his moral education begins. The book had an enormous influence as a tract against the evils of child labour, assisting the political movements campaigning to outlaw it. The Chimney Sweepers Regulation Act was passed by Parliament in 1864, followed by the Chimney Sweepers Act in 1875. Both of these were consolidated into the Factory Act of 1878, by which time child labour was genuinely being stamped out. It seems that society was taking the lesson Kingsley intended from one of his submarine characters, Mrs Doasyouwouldbedoneby. Do unto others as you would have them do unto you, originally a biblical precept intended to promote compassion for others, was known by the Victorians as 'The Golden Rule'.

That demonstrates the force of literature. *Cathy Come Home* was one of the most powerful television dramas of the last century. It was about the plight of homeless families. The writer, Jeremy Sandford, created the story of Cathy and her husband Reg. Reg is injured and loses his job, after which they and their children are evicted by bailiffs from their home. They then camp in illegal squats and, finally, Cathy has her children taken away from her by the social services. Ken Loach directed the play in a fresh, documentary style. Twelve million people watched the broadcast on BBC1 in 1966 and so powerfully did viewers identify with Cathy's predicament that it provoked a national debate about homelessness. The charity Crisis was formed as a direct result the following year and the film greatly assisted another new charity, Shelter, to gain more supporters.

Cathy Come Home was commissioned and funded by the BBC. It, in turn, is financed by a compulsory levy on British viewers, the licence fee. One way of regarding these payments is that of a society deciding to invest in its sense of community. This idea of 'public service broadcasting' was invented in Britain in the 1920s with high ambition, famously to 'educate, inform and entertain'. To that its founder, Lord Reith, might have added 'to empathise'. Because with its radio dramas and comedies up to the 1950s and its huge television output thereafter that is what the BBC has achieved, via news, documentaries, fiction and sport. It's all about us, what we think and how we interact as citizens. The BBC, funded in the same way today, continues to play a dominant role, even in a digital age of media plenty. It still invests around £1.5 billion a year in original programming which defines our culture and contributes to our national conversation. It often leads the political debate on issues that exercise us, such as health, immigration and racism. To this are added the sizeable programme productions of ITV and Channel 4, not to mention the more recent intervention of Sky, Netflix and Amazon. All this pervasive news, documentary and entertainment enriches our social discourse and tops up our empathy reserves.

Today we consider racism to be one of our biggest societal challenges. You'll remember how Professor de Waal encapsulates the problem:

We've evolved to hate our enemies, to ignore people we barely know, and to distrust anybody who doesn't look like us. Even if we are largely cooperative within our communities, we become almost a different animal in our treatment of strangers.[19]

Uncle Tom's Cabin (Life among the Lowly) by Harriet Beecher Stowe was extraordinarily the bestselling book in the US in the nineteenth century after the Bible. It was originally published in instalments from June 1851 in an abolitionist magazine, the *National Era*. Many find it sentimental, but it was one of the first books to treat slaves as human beings rather than property. It was a work of fiction which touched a chord with millions of people. And historians believe it had a significant effect in persuading Americans of the justice of abolishing slavery. This helped make the cause of the North in the Civil War, ostensibly waged by Abraham Lincoln on the issue, supportable and eventually winnable. But the abolition of slavery did not end the persecution of black people.

One of the most influential books of the twentieth century was *To Kill a Mockingbird*. It won the Pulitzer Prize, became a classic movie and remains on most school syllabuses today. The author, Harper Lee, chose fiction to expose the racism woven through her upbringing in the 1930s. The central figure, the unyielding lawyer Atticus Finch, has been described as an example of 'racial heroism'. The practical use of the book today is in the essential task of advocating not merely justice for all races, but empathy for all races. In other words, it's the antithesis of the tribalism we looked at in Chapter 7. The publication by an elderly Harper Lee of a prequel (*Go Set a*

Watchman) in 2015 disappointed some of her admirers. In it Finch is seen to display some racial prejudice as a younger man. But this merely reflects the truth, that we all have racist instincts within us. Many argue that the episode actually makes his eventual conduct more human, more believable and more noble. This complex treatment of character, typically Shakespearean, lifts fiction above monochrome sentimentality. This was what the commissioner of a recent play in the UK intended.

Indhu Rubasingham is Artistic Director of the Tricycle Theatre in north London. She came across the story of an American black actor, Ira Aldridge, working in Europe in the 1820s and 1830s. She asked Lolita Chakrabarti to write a play about Aldridge's experiences in England. In 2012 this became *Red Velvet*, in which Adrian Lester played Aldridge. The core episode of the play was when Aldridge was asked to take over the part of Othello from the famous tragedian Edmund Kean, who had become unwell. So, on the Covent Garden stage, a black actor was taking over the most famous black character in theatre – from a white actor. There were immediately public complaints from those who were outraged by this. Within a week the play's promoter had bowed to the hostility and removed Aldridge from the show. There's some ambiguity in the story as to how much Aldridge's own personality contributed to his difficulties. But, memorably and cruelly, the play ends with Aldridge putting on white make-up to play a European for another production. He couldn't get work as a black actor in a black part, only as a black actor pretending to be white. Indhu Rubasingham explains: 'I couldn't believe I'd never heard of him. Who controls history and whose perspective is it? Who's allowed access to the main stage? This is really important.'[20]

The play had an electrifying effect on its audience, whether black or white. It garnered many awards and was quickly revived and later transferred to the West End. It achieved everything Rubasingham had hoped, and more: 'Theatre is powerful because it emotionally engages you with character. I feel strongly that you can't change society unless you can walk in someone else's shoes, understand a different point of view.'[21]

Street theatre is arguably even more powerful than that performed the other side of the proscenium arch, because it's direct and immersive. In the summer of 2016 the Turner Prize-winning artist Jeremy Deller conceived a remarkable public event to mark the hundredth anniversary of the Battle of the Somme. Young men clad in the army uniforms of the time marched into and occupied thirty public spaces (they had all been carefully rehearsed by the directors at the National Theatre and the Birmingham Rep). As they stood silently, for example, in Waterloo Station in London, members of the public came up to them and asked them why they were there. Silently they'd take a card out of their jerkins. Researched by the Imperial War Museum, each card had the name, rank and time of death of a real soldier who had fought and perished on the Somme. When commuters looked them in the eye and then read the card some burst into tears. They'd understood and identified with an individual tragedy previously lost in the bank of terrible statistics.

Beyond the Tribes

Thomas Aikenhead, an Edinburgh student aged twenty, was the last person in Britain to be executed for blasphemy. In 1696 he was indicted for 'maintain[ing], in conversation, that theology was a rhapsody of ill-invented nonsense, patched up partly of the moral doctrines of philosophers, and partly of poetical fictions and extravagant chimeras . . .'. Having been tried, found guilty and sentenced to hang he was going to be reprieved only if the Church of Scotland interceded. Their response? They urged vigorous execution to curb 'the abounding of impiety and profanity in this land'. The historian Thomas Babington Macaulay called the preachers who attended the execution 'murderers' and said they'd 'insulted heaven with prayers more blasphemous than anything [Aikenhead] had uttered'.[22]

In 2016 the theatre production company Told by an Idiot performed a musical play about Thomas Aikenhead: *I Am Thomas: A Brutal Comedy with Songs*. Told by an Idiot say they explore the human condition by celebrating and revelling in a style of theatre that is bigger than life. They announce in their programme that they aim to tell universal stories that are accessible to all. One spring evening at Wilton's Music Hall in London's East End they certainly lived up to their manifesto with a riotous musical. But they did something else too.

The cast was three women and five men, of whom two were black. During the performance each of the actors took the part of Thomas in turn. I doubted the audience even noticed, as they were swept along by the pungent gallows humour of the piece. But, in its way, it was a positive sign of the times. Nothing happens by accident on stage. The casting, the allotting of the lines and roles, all of this was quite deliberate. And what the writer and the director were saying was: 'We can all share this story and we can all represent this story. Everyone – male or female, black or white – can bring their perspective to the fate of young Thomas Aikenhead.' In this way, subliminally, we in the audience that night subscribed to the breaking down of tribal boundaries in the quest for a broader, more humane understanding.

That is the role of the arts. The 2016 AHRC report, *Understanding the Value of Arts and Culture*, surveyed the current worldwide evidence on this critical role of the arts and concluded:

> The enlarged experiences associated with cultural engagement can be unpacked in various ways: an improved understanding of oneself, an ability to reflect on different aspects of one's own life, an enhanced sense of empathy which need not mean sympathy for others, but an empathetic appreciation of their difference, and a sense of the diversity of human experience and cultures.

• • •

We've seen how arts and culture can capture the human condition in an emotionally powerful way. This enables us to empathise with others, even those different to us. Via our imagination we produce a 'theory of their mind'. This is an instinctive brain function for most of us and is potentially beneficial in society, but only if we go beyond the cognitive. It needs to produce actively positive behaviour, and the arts can promote this. In fact, there's now a swelling body of academic and other evidence which demonstrates that there are such positive outcomes, across the different art forms and media.

THE GROWING EVIDENCE FOR EMPATHETIC ARTS

Literature

Keith Oatley and colleagues have published a paper entitled 'On Being Moved By Art: How Reading Fiction Transforms the Self'. Having studied people reading novels they concluded that the activity demonstrably develops empathy if done regularly, and makes us more adept at reading the emotions of others.[23] Oatley argues elsewhere that our propensity to identify with characters is actually a remarkable demonstration of our ability to empathise. He believes literature affords a 'safe space' in which to 'practise' empathy. He also points to the universality of the phenomenon: Indian poetry promotes the idea of fictional characters being created in our minds by a process of suggestion. The Sanskrit word for this is *dhvani*. This gives rise to special, empathetic literary emotions called *rasas*.[24]

In 2013, *Science Express* reported on a new study: 'Reading Literary Fiction Improves Theory of Mind'. Researchers had taken eighty-six people and tested their empathy levels. Next they asked them to read literary fiction, popular fiction and non-fiction books. They then tested them again and concluded that literary fiction, more complex and challenging as it is, enhanced their theory-of-mind abilities, at least in the short term. That literary fiction has a more refined role to play has been met with a certain scepticism by those who see an ulterior motive in devotees of the genre. But it certainly aspires to profound exploration of human emotion, as we saw with George Eliot in Chapter 2. An endorsement of this activity came from the unlikely source of the *Lancet* in 2015. It argued that doctors need to embrace ambiguity and uncertainty: 'books offer the opportunity to see the world from a different perspective, through the vicarious experiences of other people, places and times . . . Thoughtful reading helps develop the observation, analysis and reflection that are fundamental to delivering good care'.[25]

In the summer of 2016, researchers at Yale University published their exhaustive analysis of eleven years' worth of data on the health and reading habits of thousands of men and women over the age of fifty. They had found that the longer people spent reading books each day, the longer they lived – by an average of two years. (And this was so even after stripping out other factors, such as the healthier lifestyles of the middle classes.) They reasoned that the mental effort of reading keeps the brain active and sharpens 'empathy, social perception and emotional intelligence', which have all been linked in previous studies to longer lifespans, possibly because they curb stress.[26] So it seems a chapter a day might just keep the doctor, or the shrink, away.

Theatre

In 2014 a University of Arkansas team, concerned about the narrowing of syllabuses to exclude the liberal arts, tested a group of 670 students. Their paper, 'Learning from Live

Theater', reported the outcome. Half the participants had to attend a performance of either *Hamlet* or *A Christmas Carol*, and the other half attended neither. Testing the students before and afterwards, they discovered in the theatregoers a greater sense of tolerance and an improved ability to read the minds of others.

Every year the Shakespeare Schools Festival helps thousands of students from primary, secondary and special schools perform thirty-minute versions of Shakespeare plays in professional theatres. Its most recent evaluation had around seven out of ten teachers judging that, as a result, the participating school children were better able to empathise with their peers and with adults.[27] Granted that is anecdotal, but common sense tells us that communal activities of this sort increase confidence, reduce shyness and thus connect individuals – and that's before you add in the extraordinary insights Shakespeare gives us into the human condition.

Dance

Until 2016 Kenneth Tharp led the Place, a contemporary dance academy in London. A professional dancer himself, he personally attests to how dance, for the performers, involves connectivity to everything around you. And how this forms a bond with audiences who are often visibly very moved by dance performances. His experience is borne out by an intriguing research project, a collaboration between four universities funded by the Arts and Humanities Research Council. Dee Reynolds and Matthew Reason, academics specialising in literature, theatre and dance, published a book about the project in 2012. They explained that audiences at dance performances were able empathetically to 'step into the dancers' shoes'. This 'kinesthetic empathy' allowed those watching to experience the dancers' movements more than just mentally.[28]

Music

In 2012 the journal *Psychology of Music* published a Cambridge University study which took fifty girls and boys aged eight to eleven and divided them into two groups. One participated in musical exercises, the other in different communal activities. They then showed them a series of film clips and questioned them carefully on their emotional reactions, testing their relative empathy. They concluded that interacting with a group through music makes us more emotionally attuned to others, even beyond the immediate musical setting. Just an hour a week of musical activity, conducted over the long term, had increased the emotional empathy of these children. If you've ever sung in a choir or played in an orchestra you'll know how wonderful the experience can be. Choirmaster Gareth Malone's many life-changing series for the BBC has shown the effect. But the Cambridge study tied this down in terms of our relationships.[29]

• • •

Musical Taste

David Greenberg is a jazz saxophonist and a psychologist. He'd spoken to many great jazz performers and become intrigued by the way they 'play a crowd', how they intuitively know which songs produce which emotional reactions in audiences. At the same time, he wanted to know why one person might react so differently to another upon hearing a piece of music.

In 2015 he persuaded a sample of Facebook users to do an EQ (Empathy Quotient) test and then answer how they felt about different songs. People with high empathy levels (Type E) tended to prefer mellow music like R&B, Soul and Soft Rock. Whereas people with lower empathy, the systematisers we met in Chapter 2 (Type S), preferred a strong beat and music like Hard Rock. On average, Type E preferred low-energy music with negative emotions and emotional depth, while Type S preferred the opposite: high-energy music with positive emotions and intellectual depth. Of course not everyone fitted neatly into one category or the other, and some people (Type B for Balanced) had taste which straddled the genres. Greenberg published a paper with Simon Baron-Cohen and others revealing his results.[30]

We know how music stirs us. There's speculation that sad music releases prolactin, the hormone that we generate when crying with happiness or sadness and also after sexual intercourse. It makes us calm and is consoling. But research carried out among patients recovering from open-heart surgery also suggests oxytocin may play a part. By listening to soothing music, their oxytocin levels increased.

Greenberg recently created the Musical Universe project, which at the time of writing has collected data from over 100,000 people about the way they use and are affected by music in everyday life. One aim of the project is to identify how music can prime different character traits such as empathy.

Greenberg wants to know 'What are the sonic and emotional characteristics in music that can increase empathy levels and how long does this increase last for?' On top of this, Greenberg is looking at Israeli–Palestinian orchestras to see how music, dialogue and empathy work together to increase group bonding and mutual understanding.[31]

• • •

Art

In 2007 an American art historian and an Italian neuroscientist jointly published a paper exploring how paintings can provoke empathy in us. They'd been working in the relatively new field of 'neuroaesthetics' which is based on the discovery of mirror neurons in our brains, enabling us actually to experience the emotion and movement found in works of art. They cite common reactions to the elevating sculpture by Michelangelo, *Prisoners*, and the horrifying series of prints by Goya, *Los Desastres de la Guerra*. People who view the art 'find themselves automatically simulating the emotional expression, the movement or even implied movement within the representation'.[32] These automatic empathetic responses, which we're just beginning to learn about, give a new meaning to the phrase 'the power of art'.

Museums

In rural Nottinghamshire, near Newark, is the National Holocaust Centre. This museum was set up by the Smith family in their own house and gradually grew over time. It now attracts some 20,000 visitors a year, and one of the most popular elements is 'The Journey'. Here children and adults are able to enter the life of Leo, a young Jewish boy suffering increasing prejudice and exclusion in the Germany of the 1930s, including being shunned by his classmates at school. Eventually he escapes and joins the *Kindertransport* to London. The Holocaust, as we've seen, demonstrates what terrible events can take place in a society without empathy. And study of the Holocaust can teach us many critical lessons about human rights, racism and bullying.

Between 2012 and 2015 the Centre operated an outreach programme for schools in the county, combining trips to the Centre with work in class. The programme (In Our Hands) was then independently evaluated, producing a very positive verdict, particularly for its effect in those communities which had seen recent influxes of immigrants. The report said that In Our Hands helped pupils make meaningful connections between the study of the Holocaust and the day-to-day lives of contemporary families and the changes they were experiencing in their communities. The conclusion was that it positively influenced the attitudes of children and young people towards those who were different to them. And here are some of their quoted reactions: 'Their clothes are different, their food is different, but they're still children like us.' 'I've discovered that each person has their own story that you can learn from and should respect.' 'Other people are not different to us. They're still people, but with different religions and opinions.'[33]

Television

We explored the influence *Cathy Come Home* had in the 1960s. We remember how Michael Buerk's 1984 BBC News report on the Ethiopian famine led to an outpouring of active compassion and fundraising, particularly via the Band Aid single and Live Aid concerts in London and Philadelphia. When television news reports even the most technical economic or health story, it will always include how it affects individuals, the better to engage our emotions as well as our intellect. Pictures, of course, enable us to see close-ups of people's faces and thus engage our empathy equipment.

Although visual media have digitally fragmented since the 1980s, with the addition of hundreds of satellite channels and the video explosions represented by YouTube and Facebook, television still commands a mass audience. The popular soap operas can engage millions in social issues, promoting an empathetic understanding in us. In 2011, ITV's *Coronation Street* had the character Carla raped by her fiancé Frank. Rape was seen as something mostly perpetrated by strangers. But the truth is that 90 per cent of rape victims know their attackers. The national helpline Rape Crisis saw an 800 per cent increase in calls following the transmission, as people who had been raped by their partners understood that they would be listened to.[34] In 2015, ITV's *Emmerdale* ran a story in which the local Vicar, Ashley, was diagnosed with young-onset vascular dementia. He even forgot his own wedding day. The Alzheimer's Society said that the plot helped many more people understand the impact of dementia, which almost a million Britons now suffer from.[35]

So-called 'reality television', which thrusts members of the public into social situations and then follows the results, has followed the soaps in reflecting our society and relationships back to us. There's a proliferation of such shows, many tabloid in nature. One of the first was *Big Brother*.

Big Brother

This popular TV reality show had a surprising and revealing effect on its audience. At its simplest the Dutch format is defined as twelve members of the public who agree to live together for two or three months under the twenty-four-hour surveillance of television cameras. The public then vote them out, one by one. Today it's an unremarkable, mainstream piece of entertainment in the countries where it's still broadcast. At the turn of the century, when I produced the British version, it was detested and demonised by as many viewers as it was loved by. Hotly debated issues of privacy and good taste swirled around the heads of the amorous and occasionally aggressive housemates. It provoked a constitutional crisis in Malawi, a fatwa in Bahrain, an advertising boycott in Mexico and was temporarily banned in Germany. And plenty of money was made by the owners and broadcasters of this highly commercial popularity contest.

But beneath the ballyhoo something else was happening. In the very first series in Britain, in 2000, a public school contestant, Nick Bateman, was unmasked as cheating in the house nominations for eviction. His accuser was a semi-literate, working-class builder from Liverpool, Craig Phillips. Millions of viewing fans had got caught up in this real-life soap opera and the tabloid newspapers fed greedily on its twists and turns. Posh 'Nasty' Nick became a pantomime villain and Craig a national hero, going on to win the entire competition. What became clear was that the many who were following the show and voting were looking for characters who displayed authenticity with whom they could empathise. Craig emerged as a person of determination with leadership qualities and a keen sense of fairness. He was rewarded accordingly. In subsequent series, in Britain and around the world, heroes and heroines emerged where the strength of their personalities confounded the stereotypes by which they were originally portrayed. And the fan base empathised with them very strongly.

The runner-up to Craig Phillips that year was Anna Nolan, an openly gay woman and the following year the winner was the gay man Brian Dowling. Long before civil partnerships were legalised, and at a time when some still found homosexuality abhorrent, this TV show was demonstrating that these were people like anyone else (though often rather more agreeable). It was even more dramatic when gay housemates were cast in some of the heavily Catholic countries of Latin America, where homosexuality could be frowned upon and was largely underground. Colombia launched the show in 2003 and a gay contestant, who helped the women with their hair and make-up and did all the laundry, became known as Burbujita ('little bubbles'). When he was allowed to propose to his boyfriend via the camera one night (he said yes in a flood of tears) liberal Colombians believed it was a major step forwards for gay emancipation. Everyone could see and sympathise with the humanity behind the sexual predilection.

In 2004 one of the British housemates was a post-operative transsexual, Nadia Almada. She wanted to enter the house and be accepted as a woman, which she achieved. But she also became the runaway winner when British viewers took her to their hearts. Many understood for the first time the challenges that people like her have had to overcome and empathised strongly. Two years later Pete Bennett, who had Tourette's

Syndrome, triumphed. This was perhaps the most startling of all. Here was someone prone to sudden and regular outbursts of bad language discovered by the public to be, behind his condition, not wicked but an absolute and genuine charmer. Tourette's is now much better understood. Some will never like such shows or their commercial origins, but they arguably have some redeeming outcomes.

• • •

Radio

We've looked at the abundant research showing how our natural empathy is much stronger within our own groups, whether familial, racial or sporting. We've seen that hostility can replace empathy when we face those who are different. The arts have the power to stretch our imagination and sympathy beyond those boundaries. Since the 1920s, radio has been doing this. It's been described as 'having the best pictures'. This is a reference to the peculiar process by which the medium demands a feat of imagination from us, to characterise the voices we hear in drama, news and documentary. That challenge, or stimulus, to our imagination invites empathy. This is why *The Archers*, Radio 4's soap opera, has remained so popular since its inception in 1950. One of its most influential storylines recently has been an exploration of violence within a marriage.

And here's one more telling example: in Chapter 1 I described how the Rwandan government attempted to wipe out the Tutsi minority in the most shocking genocide ever recorded in Africa. In three horrific months in 1994 the Hutu majority killed 70 per cent of the Tutsis, more than half a million people. One of the most terrible catalysts of the slaughter was the inflammatory radio broadcasts. But in efforts since to heal this country, one of the most potent community forces has been a radio soap opera, *Musekeweya* (New Dawn). It's been on air since 2004 and reaches an estimated 85 per cent of the population. The honest storylines are widely believed to have contributed strongly to the new Rwanda, and a research study published in 2012 found the human narratives far more effective at promoting harmony than more factual, talk-based programmes.[36]

Film

Because it's widely believed that movies promote empathy in us, educational charities are now promoting the best examples. In the US, the non-profit organisation Common Sense Media lists its viewing recommendations. The educational movement Ashoka has set up Start.Empathy.org asking us to vote for the most empathetic films (*To Kill a Mockingbird* headed the list in 2015), and the Empathy Library set up online by Roman Krznaric also asks us to nominate our favourites. A body of evidence is now beginning to emerge to back up what many of us believe is the power of movies.

In 2012 *Scientific World* published an article headed 'Human Empathy through the Lens of Social Neuroscience'. It reported that viewers of that year's hit film *The Hunger Games* came out of the cinema with changed thought processes: that the movie had enhanced their empathetic ability to make tough ethical or moral choices.[37] And *Wired* has more recently reported the work of a neuroscientist at Tel Aviv University, Talma Hendler. She had carried out brain scans of subjects watching the psychological thriller *Black Swan*, with interesting results. The central figure is Nina, a ballet dancer involved in a terrible career struggle with another dancer. In one scary scene Nina hallucinates that the black feathers of her costume are actually growing out of her back. The brain scans of the audience at that moment showed a disturbed pattern similar to that of schizophrenia. Hendler also reported scanning people watching *The Stepmom* with Susan Sarandon. Sarandon plays a mother explaining to her son that she is going to die of cancer, and again Hendler's scans demonstrate a recognisable neurological pattern of empathy in the audience.[38]

Photography

On 8 June 1972 a jet of the South Vietnamese air force swooped on some villagers escaping their homes. Mistaking them for enemy Vietcong the pilot dropped napalm, burning them alive. One severely injured girl, Kim Phuc, tore off her clothes in agony and ran screaming down the road. That is where a photographer of the Associated Press, Nick Ut, was standing. His picture of this girl – her extreme anguish and her naked vulnerability – became one of the most famous war photographs ever taken. It won a Pulitzer Prize and was the subject of much discussion in President Nixon's White House. The image is accepted as having been of great assistance to the anti-war movement, hastening the end of the Vietnam conflict. This is because millions of people identified with the pain and suffering of Kim Phuc.

On 3 September 2015 newspapers published the photograph of the body of a three-year-old boy washed up on a Turkish beach. Alan Kurdi was like anyone's toddler, with curly hair, casual clothes and neat trainers. But he was dead and alone on the shore. He, his brother and his mother had all drowned in their desperate attempt to get away from the devastation of Syria to a safe haven in Europe. Within hours, communities across Britain, which had been saying their country should not receive any more immigrants, were offering to take Syrian refugees. Individuals were offering their holiday properties to house them. And, perhaps most dramatically, the British government's policy of not accepting more than a few refugees was reversed the next day. The power of two pictures, the power of empathy.

Games

Many acres of newsprint have been expended on the alleged anti-social nature of some video and computer games. Which family has not tut-tutted at the constant chatter of digital machine-gun fire coming from teenage boys' bedrooms as they refight the Second World War and kick-start the Third World War? It's difficult to come by comprehensive evidence of the damage these games might be doing to the attitudes of our children. They certainly involve much online cooperation between players, thus demonstrating empathy within a group and hostility to a rival group. No surprise there. One American study found that really hostile activity in a game (such as *Call of Duty* I mentioned earlier) might even reinforce the moral compass of the participants via feelings of guilt for their anti-social excesses.[39] The jury's out on that.

But there is another genre of games, known as 'pro-social', which emphasise empathy, interpersonal skills and the building of harmonious societies. The most widely known and bestselling of these (200 million and counting) is *The Sims*, published by Electronic Arts. Players create virtual people, place them in houses, help direct their moods and satisfy their desires. It came out of *Simcity*, an earlier game which challenged users to develop a stable city, maintaining the happiness of the citizens. The enormous, worldwide success of *The Sims* has spawned many competitors and established a popular genre. *Harvest Moon* requires players to 'tend to crops, animals and friendships and reap the rewards'. *Animal Crossing* is all about running the economy and society of a town, finding goods to buy and sell, while new residents turn up randomly to be integrated into the community. *Tomodachi Life* is a so-called 'ant farm' game where you can create a cast of neighbours on an island and then see them interact. And *Magician's Quest: Mysterious Times* presents a faux Harry Potter scenario in which you're a new student in a magic school and you have to make yourself a useful member of the community, completing quests for classmates and staff.

What effect do pro-social games have on their fans? Can they make us more empathetic and do they reduce anti-social instincts such as *Schadenfreude*? Those are the questions two German academics set out to answer in 2010 with two studies. Tobias Greitemeyer and Silvia Osswald took around sixty students and got half of them to play pro-social video games and the other half 'neutral' games (ones that challenged them but were neither pro- nor anti-social). They then tested them all immediately afterwards, by reading them real-life stories of misfortunes which had befallen celebrities and getting their reactions. They accept that their results tested the students' reactions only in the short term. But, intriguingly, they found that those who had played the pro-social games had enhanced interpersonal empathy and diminished feelings of *Schadenfreude*.[40] Other work by Swiss psychologists investigated the aspect of games that offers both 'real' and 'fictional' experiences at the same time. They found that players of *Trauma Center* (in which you can perform life-saving but rather bloody surgery) were more likely to help others in real life.[41] Several studies have shown similar beneficial effects of playing pro-social games.[42] And a recent American one illustrated that cooperative games – where you play *with others* as opposed to against them or by yourself – can have widespread benefits by making players think helpful behaviours are valuable and commonplace.[43]

ARTS AND CULTURE AS PART OF AN EMPATHETIC EDUCATION

I've argued that the power of arts and culture to cultivate empathy means they should be a fundamental part of education and training for people of all ages. But the truth is that the arts are being marginalised in our schools and only a few have so far experimented with harnessing their benefits in the training of professionals.

In our state schools much effort has rightly been poured into raising basic standards of literacy and numeracy. There has also been a strong accent on STEM subjects – science, technology, engineering and mathematics. Recently the

EBACC syllabus, while it includes English, excludes the visual and performing arts. They used to be a standard part of our education. Art rooms are closing in some areas and music education, which is patchy, now has to rely on special consortia for its proper provision (the Music Hubs, funded by the Department of Education, now doing so much to help young people discover music). The take-up of arts GCSEs is declining every year. But if you were among the 7 per cent of British children who attend private schools, you would still receive a rich, full arts education. In the US, meanwhile, there's a similar diminution under way. The Common Core State Standards Initiative, adopted by forty-six states, actually calls for less emphasis on fiction in secondary education. This represents an attack on the arts and civic society: starve our imaginations and you impoverish our human relations.

There is another way. We saw in Chapter 4 how some educationists are trialling empathetic techniques in British primary schools. Ashoka is an international education movement which also talks about the cultivation of empathy, teamwork, leadership and changemaking in school students. Ashoka is seeking to establish a network of affiliated 'Changemaker' schools, of which thirty will be in the UK. In due course the effectiveness of all such initiatives will need to be evaluated. But one of the schools which has already applied for changemaker status is the Spinney Primary School in Cambridge. 'Teamwork and Community' is one of their seven stated values and it's no coincidence that the Head gives arts education great importance in the school. Rachel Snape frequently asks poets and artists to join the children:

The ethos of collaboration and reciprocity comes from doing lots of creative activities . . . The children can play with ideas and make them grow. It's transformative. Empathy is an outcome, of course, but it's the compassion that flows from it which really matters.[44]

For one project the school got the help of a local agency, Cambridge Curiosity and Imagination, to bring artists in to inspire the children.

There's now growing evidence of the benefits of an arts education beyond the purely academic. A recent worldwide review carried out by Arts Council England highlighted a number of intriguing studies. In the US, students who engage in the arts were twice as likely to volunteer as others, and 20 per cent more likely to vote as young adults.[45] And a separate study in the UK of ten- to fifteen-year-olds found that those who had built up 'cultural capital' (that is, immersed themselves in cultural activities) were again more likely to volunteer.[46] All these chart individuals in essence connecting with the societies in which they live.

Among professionals who deal with and care for the public, such as doctors and nurses, lack of empathy is now a recognised problem, as we saw in Chapter 6. Suzanne Peloquin investigated whether the arts have the potential to train occupational therapists to be more empathetic, and her conclusion was that they could: 'Empathy requires a growing from inside the self. A person who hopes to be empathetic must pursue an experience that awakens the sense of fellowship. Artists and art philosophers suggest that such an awakening can occur through art.'[47]

In the US the George Washington University School of

Medicine has now had a medical humanities programme for eight years, including art history, poetry and fiction. The Columbia University College of Physicians and Surgeons has a Narrative Medicine course because Professor Rita Charon realised that doctors need to understand and connect with the stories patients tell. Literature can deliver this narrative training, and Charon now lectures on how this helps increase empathy and reflection in health professionals. A study by the Cleveland Clinic showed how doctors who had undertaken creative writing displayed greater empathy skills than their peers who had not. The conclusion was that their reflective and narrative skills helped them develop the emotional resonance and self-awareness they needed in their jobs.[48] And two Brazilian doctors now use clips from movies such as *Nurse Betty*, *Blood Diamond* and *Amistad* to teach their medical students how to empathise effectively: 'Arts and Humanities, because they enhance the understanding of the human condition, are a useful resource when incorporated into the educational process and help in building a humanitarian perspective of doctoring.'[49]

A chapter in the AHRC's *Understanding the Value of Arts and Culture*, 'The Reflective Individual', states that an ability to reflect about oneself and others is an important basis for empathy. Reflective capacity, it says, is integral to the competencies defined by the General Medical Council: 'Arts engagement has emerged not as an alternative to formal systems of training, but as being able to play a significant role within that training and in the more fluid care environment.'

We began this chapter with Christopher from *The Curious Incident of the Dog in the Night-Time*. He found it difficult to empathise because his ability to think himself into someone else's shoes was unreliable. Hence the author, Mark Haddon, also has him shying away from the arts: 'I don't like proper novels because they are lies about things which didn't happen and they make me feel shaky and scared.'[50]

Thankfully, for most of us, fiction and its effect on our imaginations is profoundly enriching, inspiring and intensely human. In conclusion, here's a great novelist Christopher would certainly have disapproved of. Leo Tolstoy understood that storytelling is just the beginning: 'The task for art to accomplish is to make that feeling of brotherhood and love of one's neighbour, now attained only by the best members of society, the customary feeling and instinct of all men.'[51]

It's clear that if we ensure each generation immerses itself in arts and culture, in all its many manifestations, we'll build better citizens who understand each other's feelings and needs. This is what it is to be human.

9

A CHARTER FOR EMPATHY

'I have great empathy for Chris . . .' So said Roy Hodgson about a rival when his England football team snatched a rare late winner in the 2016 European Championships. 'Neuroscience shows us the pivotal importance of the first few years of life . . .' That's David Cameron in a 2016 speech about the life chances of children from deprived back-grounds. 'He is . . . incapable of empathy . . .' The charge levelled at Donald Trump by the 2016 Democratic Convention, arguing that he was unfit for leadership.[1] When the national football manager, the Prime Minister and the US presidential election all reference the empathy instinct, something is stirring. Sitting at my desk on a summer's day in 2016 a cursory search online yields 'Empathy for the Devil' (a television review in the *New Yorker*); 'Beware the empathy-washing of self-proclaimed caring capital' (a *Guardian* article on the environment); 'Rats feel empathy for other rats . . .' (a science report); 'Companies Try a New Strategy: Empathy Training' (*Wall Street Journal*); and 'Finding Dory's Cute, Annoying Empathy Play' (a headline in an online movie review). The idea is out there and entering the general consciousness.

I quoted Barack Obama on the subject in the Introduction. In fact, it was in the 1940s that the frequency of the word 'empathy' greatly increased. For instance, as a term of popular psychology it overtook 'will power' in 1961, and then outstripped 'self-control' in the 1980s.[2] And we've seen that leading thinkers in family policy, education, health and the arts are now all picking up on the discoveries and new thinking about empathy emerging from the science community. The empathy instinct has truly entered the public realm. But can we harness it to the benefit of us all in order to create a more civil society? And if we do, how different could things be in the future, in thirty years' time? We now need to ensure that the science of empathy leads and informs public policy.

So the purpose of a Charter for Empathy is twofold. First, to set out an ambitious vision for that more empathetic future. Second, to define some of the incremental first steps we should take to get there.

THE CHARTER

1. The further mapping, as a priority, of the brain's empathy circuit.

2. A culture in which every young child gets the one-to-one nurture and stimulation they need to give them their own functioning empathy circuit.

3. An education which assesses and cultivates the emotional intelligence of every pupil.

4. Special help for the empathetically challenged, especially in their early years.

5. An internet which protects children and educates parents.

6. Doctors, nurses and carers trained in and committed to empathetic practice.

7. A justice system truly dedicated to rehabilitation, in which the only people incarcerated are those who represent a danger to others.

8. Sustained programmes that curb prejudice and integrate different groups.

9. Public promotion of the arts and popular culture that help us understand the perspectives of others.

10. At the threshold of the artificial intelligence age, the reaffirmation of the empathy instinct and the supremacy of the human spirit.

1. The continued mapping of the brain's empathy circuit

There are parallels with the mapping of the human genome, but they only go so far. The brain is infinitely more complex, with up to 100 billion neurons and 100 trillion synapses, all of them in constantly and rapidly changing interaction. But an enhanced knowledge of the basic neurological functions of empathy will assist better therapies, more effective child-rearing and education, and the tackling of racial and religious conflicts.

In 2015 the US federal government and private industry started funding the BRAIN Initiative. Its intention is to marshal the latest technology to identify the underlying causes of such conditions as Alzheimer's, epilepsy, schizophrenia, depression and autism. The results may have a profound impact on the prevention and cure of empathy-related disorders, and shine further light on the complexity of how a healthy brain empathises. It's very important that this and similar projects focus significant resources on empathy. In the area of conflict resolution alone, I quoted above Emile Bruneau's recounting of how much there is still to be learned:

> We still need to map a host of other empathy-related tasks – like judging the reasonableness of people's arguments and sympathising with their mental and emotional states – to specific brain regions. And then we need to figure out how these neural flashes translate into actual behaviour. Why does understanding what someone else feels not always translate to being concerned for their welfare? Why is empathising across groups so much more difficult?[3]

Progress is being made all the time. For example, in the summer of 2016 scientists produced the most comprehensive map of the brain to date, by asking 210 healthy young volunteers to lie in an fMRI scanner and do things like listen to stories, solve maths problems and simply chill out. By combining the thousands of resulting images – indicative of function, structure and connectivity – the scientists discovered ninety-seven new brain regions to add to the eighty-three already known. Timothy Behrens, a professor of neuroscience at Oxford University, said of the new map, 'It will lead to a profound change in how people think about the brain, and become the default way of describing human brain activity for years to come.'[4] Our rapidly developing knowledge of genetics will also play a crucial role in our mapping of the mind.

This is critical research which needs rich funding, worldwide cooperation and dissemination for humanity's benefit.

2. One-to-one nurture for young children

Every parent needs to understand the inestimable value of intimate encounters, eye contact and bedtime stories. They should appreciate the corrosion of healthy, emotional development that comes from the always-on distraction of the mobile device. Baby and childcare manuals should incorporate the latest learning from the science of empathy. The Early Years Foundation Stage Profile, which our schools follow, equally needs to reflect the empathy instinct and school behaviour codes should be built on its principles.

The Troubled Families programme attempts to target the limited resources of the state at those most in need. As it and its successors are rolled out, they should be designed to give as much support to young children as to parents. The one-to-one nurturing by an adult, as we've seen, is the clear route to endowing people for their lifetime with Baron-Cohen's internal pot of gold. So the clear conclusion is that every child in care and therefore at risk must have a consistently designated adult who can nurture their development. These children have a legal right to an 'independent mentor', but in practice the system's delivery is patchy. We need to remember the statistic: one-quarter of our prison inmates were once in care.

3. An education for emotional intelligence

Whether it's learning about sex, cooking or participation in democracy, you'll find campaigners saying that the schools have to do it. As each social objective is added, another groan goes up from the teaching profession, which feels over-regimented and under-resourced. But with empathy all we're really asking is for schools to do what they're already doing, just more cleverly. The Holocaust is already a mandatory part of the syllabus, but many students aren't getting a proper grasp of it or other genocides by the time they leave school.[5] (University College London's Centre for Holocaust Education has been helping thousands of teachers here.)

The subject which could be beneficially expanded to cover more empathy is the Personal, Social, Health and Economic Education (PSHE). Our school inspectorate, Ofsted, already assesses each school's 'social, moral, spiritual, cultural' development. This is another opportunity to promote empathetic practice without any onerous new obligations.

The classroom exercises which EmpathyLab and Roots of Empathy have developed could be rolled out at minimal cost too. If many head teachers gave these the backing they deserve it would constitute a massively beneficial social influence.

4. Special help for the empathetically challenged

For children who display signs of autism, psychopathy or post-traumatic stress (many teachers are already adept at spotting them), there's a strong argument for proper diagnosis. Then the correct social-skills intervention can be prescribed. Some are concerned about children's rights and about their being labelled criminals, or potential criminals, at a tender age. But I'm not proposing universal screening (which would be an abuse) – only in clear cases of need. And is it not better to help children early than to allow their lives to unravel?

Troubled children can be saved. It's been demonstrated, for example, that many autistic children and adults can learn to read facial expressions. And we've seen how abused children can recover, given the right nurturing. We have only begun to apply the science of empathy in the service of effective therapies.

5. An internet which protects children and educates parents

The technology which has afforded us extraordinary benefits is also profoundly challenging. We're only a few years into a new digital era and we urgently need to develop pro-social strategies to cope with this often anti-social phenomenon. Even greater use of apps like FaceTime (for video calls) over purely textual communication would restore elements of the empathy instinct to our interpersonal relations.

In addition to the way we must expand education to cope

with the explosion of porn, hate crime, cyber-bullying and radicalisation, there will have to be better tools for users to protect their families. The principle of opting in to pornography should be extended beyond the current few internet service providers to cover all of them.

We're witnessing the coarsening of our political discourse and terrible public displays of racism. The police are neither trained nor resourced to deal with this tsunami of digital abuse. Prevention may be better than cure – that's where education comes in. But the remorseless policing and prosecution of this new wild west is also essential. To that end the rationalisation and modernisation of the many relevant laws should be a priority.

But an intelligent attitude to modern communication needs to inform all our relationships at home and at work. Should we text our relatives when we're in the same house and could talk to them face to face? We often do. Should we any longer design workplaces with separate offices and personal compartments? It's surely better to talk face to face than coldly email each other. And not just more congenial, issues are resolved much more rapidly this way too.

6. Empathetic health and care services

This starts with focusing on the principle of patient-centred care. In many places this is happening but in others it's merely having lip-service paid to it. And it's much easier said than done in a system that will remain underfunded and under strain. But, as the charity National Voices says: 'Make people the priority, not the system.' Good care planning involves acknowledging the expertise of doctors but also patients' priorities in a process of shared decision-making.

If we succeed in linking health and care services more closely, then reform of both will be easier. In his *Five Year Forward View*, published in 2014, NHS England's Chief Executive Simon Stevens committed to patients gaining far greater control over their own care, as well as to investment to help join health and social care services together. He accepts that resources are finite and says that prevention – the promotion of well-being – will be critical now and in the future. As we've seen, the empathy instinct has an important role to play both in the delivery of critical medicine and in well-being, particularly in relation to mental health.

The redrawing of medical training is already under way so as to emphasise the importance of cognitive and emotional empathy, in the right balance. Improvements in continuity of care, the encouragement of active listening, innovations like Schwartz Rounds – all these have the potential to transform the quality of care patients receive.

There is an argument for the screening of all those in the front line of patient care. This would require the development of new emotional intelligence and empathy tests. (Simon Baron-Cohen, who created one of the existing tests, feels they'll need to be developed further.[6]) This could help guide junior doctors along an appropriate career path, with those low in EQ more suited, for instance, to becoming pathologists or high-tech surgeons. And in the case of care workers, it could determine how much and what sort of training they need.

7. A justice system dedicated to rehabilitation

It's gradually dawning on even the most disciplinarian among us that our prisons are a disaster. Surely the most important thing is the protection of society. Continuing high levels of recidivism mean that currently we're witnessing the abject failure of the system. Incarceration is necessary only where the convicted are a danger to fellow citizens. Such prisoners should be given quality education in literacy and numeracy. And the provision of art, drama and music courses should also be made a core part of the Offenders' Learning and Skills Service arrangements. For everyone else, we have to re-establish a personal connection via humane probation services. The additional funding necessary will be more than compensated for by a smaller prison service.

We explored a range of other beneficial ideas: judges, with more sentencing latitude, following the progress of those they've convicted; widespread institution of restorative justice; the proper application of rehabilitative therapies such as arts activities. The changes needed are radical and fly in the face of the retributive moralism that has dominated our justice system for two centuries. But the scientific basis for them is becoming more compelling all the time.

8. Curbing prejudice and encouraging integration

While studies show that human beings tend to be inherently biased against people who look different to them, this attitude can be defeated through education and positive experience. The first members of *Homo sapiens* to travel out of Africa did so 100,000 years ago, and by 10,000 years ago they had reached the far corners of the world. During this time our ancestors evolved certain characteristics to help them in their environment – for instance, skin colours to suit differing intensities of sun, or a tolerance to milk in societies that reared cattle.

By contrast none of the traits that really bind us together as humans – language capacity, cognitive ability, creativity, empathy – changed one jot. Knowledge of this fundamental truth, a bond of brotherhood and sisterhood, should be continually instilled in people – at home, at school and in the workplace. The twenty-year-old Show Racism the Red Card campaign in football has demonstrably changed the culture in our football grounds. And the government now has a plan for tackling hate crime called Action against Hate. But the task requires constant vigilance and a profound understanding of human nature, to enable us to reach out beyond our natural tribes.

Measures to ensure that this happens should include anti-racism lessons like Jane Elliott's blue-eyed/brown-eyed one, and the viewing and reading of films and books which sympathise with instead of marginalise ethnic groups. Religion has the power to bring people closer but also to divide them. We believe in religious tolerance and thus in schools inspired by particular faiths. But we should apply the law properly: no school in the UK should have pupils exclusively of a single faith. Nor should their religious education focus solely on one faith. People need to leave school with at least a basic grasp of how other religions and cultures operate. This will promote understanding and tolerance. It happens at many but not all schools today.

Activities which make meaningful contact between different groups and slices of society should be pursued more actively. To this end, the excellent National Citizen Service could be expanded so that many more teenagers benefit from it. Peace-building initiatives have much to offer areas of protracted conflict, but they need to be more thoroughly evaluated so that only the most effective strategies are employed.

I've written many critical words about the digital era in this book. But here there's a huge opportunity to develop and distribute pro-social materials to bring 'tribes' together, as well as to counter the growing climate of racism online.

9. Pro-social arts and popular culture

There's a school of thought which argues that public funding of culture in the abundant era of YouTube, a system of regulated, public service broadcasting in a multi-channel universe, and a concentration on arts subjects in schools in an instrumental age of science and technology, are all otiose. But the opposite is true. All of these traditional forms are profoundly pro-social and are more needed in our digital dystopia than ever before. So the maintenance of public funding of the arts, from national and local government, from the National Lottery, from trusts and foundations, from business and from philanthropic individuals is far more important than most recognise. And the responsibilities which the BBC, ITV, Channel 4 and Channel 5 have to create public service programmes should be sustained.

Throughout this book we've shown that the shrewd deployment of the empathetic arts – in the home, in schools, in medical schools, in care homes, in prisons, in arenas of conflict

– are extraordinarily effective and are the essence of what it is to be human. As we've seen, they tend to prevent as well as cure, and thus are socially, culturally and economically positive. But in our schools the liberal arts are being squeezed out by concentration on STEM subjects. Art and music rooms are closing and theatre studies are disappearing. The narrower new syllabus, known as the EBACC, excludes these pro-social subjects. This is a mistake. Every child deserves to have the creative spark lit within them, something that connects them to their fellow pupils.

10. Artificial intelligence and the human spirit

We're beginning to think seriously about what AI will mean for us. Not merely in terms of its undoubted utility, but also what it will mean for our sense of humanity. When Stephen Hawking, Steve Wozniak and Noam Chomsky petition the UN for the prohibition of autonomous weapons we should sit up and take notice. Their sense of the dangers of AI, represented by the aggressive drone and its technological successors, has driven them to argue for a ban similar to those for biological and chemical weapons.

Conversely, Elon Musk has recently set up the not-for-profit research company OpenAI 'to advance digital intelligence in a way that is most likely to benefit humanity as whole'. As with the carefully developed field of ethics in medical science, agreement on a universally accepted code of ethics governing AI is urgently needed.

Nick Bostrom, author of *Superintelligence*, proposes a number of principles. He argues that we must put as much strategic analysis into what is *desirable* as into what is *possible*.

AI researchers need to declare a commitment to safety and 'a common goal'. And funders of AI – governments, private investors and philanthropists – must also define the positive outcomes they require. This has been described as a race between the growing power of technology and the wisdom with which we manage it. As Bostrom puts it: 'The challenge we face is, in part, to hold on to our humanity.'[7]

As applications of AI take root and spread rapidly this century, the empathy instinct becomes more critical than ever. We'll need to create university degrees in empathy, embed socio-emotional skills into job descriptions, and seek leaders with empathetic skills and understanding (they're more likely to be women).

Even if we manage to perfect the science of empathy, apply its power in the family, schools and the workplace, reform healthcare and our criminal justice system, unleash the pro-social power of arts and popular culture – in other words, even if we succeed in applying our Charter for Empathy, AI has the potential to negate it all.

• • •

If you stop someone in the street and ask them what they make of empathy, the chances are they'll tell you it's a fluffy, sentimental idea. There are plenty of academics, too, who are suspicious of the growing interest in the empathy instinct, distrusting such an apparently emotional construct. But what we've seen is that the empathy instinct is based on hard science, that it's an extraordinary resource and a powerful human force. We're developing the knowledge to apply the empathy instinct in revolutionary ways – at home, in education, at work, in the public sphere, wherever conflicts rage – and it really is an idea whose time has come. Now we need the public policies to drive it forward. By understanding and deploying the empathy instinct we really can create a more civil society.

ACKNOWLEDGEMENTS

First, my grateful thanks to Ned Pennant-Rea, who researched this book and applied his acute subeditorial skills to my writings – a valuable 'critical friend'. I'm also indebted to Roland Philipps and Becky Walsh of John Murray who judiciously gave me a 'helicopter view' of *The Empathy Instinct* at several important points, and to Caroline Westmore who led the editing. Thank you, too, to Alex Hickman and Kate Barker at Chartwell Speakers who championed this project. And to Diane Banks, latterly my agent. Finally, I'd like to express my gratitude to my wife, Hilary Newiss, who put up with my radio silence over many weekends of writing.

The following gave us valuable assistance with our researches: Jon Adams; Professor Simon Baron-Cohen, Cambridge University; Professor David Best, Sheffield Hallam University; Emile Bruneau, MIT; Ross Burnett; Peter Clarke, Chief Inspector of Prisons; Dr Hilary Cremin, Cambridge University; Jane Davis, The Reader; Bella Eacott, Clod Ensemble; Leslie Garrett, Abbeyfield; Professor Sir Denis Pereira Gray; David Greenberg; Sacha Grimes; Darren Henley, Chief Executive, Arts Council England; Steve Hodgkins, Jobs Friends Houses; Darrick Jolliffe; Roman Krznaric; Ian Livingstone; Miranda McKearney, the EmpathyLab; the staff of the National Holocaust Centre,

Nottinghamshire; Hilary Newiss, Chair, National Voices; Nicky Padfield, Master of Fitzwilliam College, Cambridge; Dr Daniel Reisel; Professor Sir Mike Richards; Sir Ken Robinson; Nick Ross; Indhu Rubasingham, Tricycle Theatre; Liam Sabec; Rae Snape; Nathalie Taman, Holocaust Memorial Foundation; Kenneth Tharp, the Place; Deanna Van Buren; Matt Waldman, Center for Empathy in International Affairs; John Whiston, ITV.

Limited; used by permission of Doubleday, a division of Random House, Inc., a division of Penguin Random House LLC. Extracts from *The Better Angels of Our Nature: A History of Violence and Humanity* by Steven Pinker (Allen Lane, 2011). Copyright © Steven Pinker, 2011. Reproduced by permission of Penguin Books Ltd; used by permission of Viking Books, an imprint of Penguin Publishing Group, a division of Penguin Random House LLC.

NOTES

Introduction

1. Early history of MRI: http://www.economist.com/node/2246166, accessed 18 March 2016. http://science.howstuffworks.com/fmri2.htm, accessed 18 March 2016.

2. https://www.youtube.com/watch?v=4md_A059JRc, accessed 19 September 2016.

3. My definition of 'sympathy' is an abbreviation of sense 3c in the Oxford English Dictionary: 'The quality or state of being thus affected by the suffering or sorrow of another; a feeling of compassion or commiseration.' http://www.oed.com/view/Entry/196271?rskey=fl7bJg&result=1#eid, accessed 21 September 2016.

4. My definition of 'empathy' is an adaptation of sense 2b in the Oxford English Dictionary: 'The ability to understand and appreciate another person's feelings, experience, etc.' http://www.oed.com/view/Entry/61284?redirectedFrom=empathy#eid, accessed 21 September 2016.

5. Definition of instinct from several dictionaries, chiefly http://dictionary.cambridge.org and http://www.merriam-webster.com.

Chapter 1: Societies without Empathy

1. De Waal, 'The Evolution of Empathy', in Keltner et al. (eds), *The Compassionate Instinct*, p. 23. Also available at http://greatergood.berkeley.edu/article/item/the_evolution_of_empathy, accessed 5 January 2016.

2. Hitler, *Mein Kampf*, p. 324.

3. Goldhagen, *Worse Than War*. Cited in Pinker, *The Better Angels of Our Nature*, p. 394.

4. Pinker, *The Better Angels of Our Nature*, p. 390.

5. http://www.welt.de/geschichte/himmler/article124223862/Insight-into-the-orderly-world-of-a-mass-murderer.html, accessed 20 March 2016.

6. Longerich, *Holocaust*, p. 123.

7. Binet, *HHhH*, ch. 108.

8. Blum, *V Was for Victory*, p. 71.

9. Gilbert, *The Righteous*, p. 144.

10. Ibid., pp. 184–5.

11. Ibid., p. 524.

12. https://www.gov.uk/government/uploads/system/uploads/attachment_data/file/398645/Holocaust_Commission_Report_Britains_promise_to_remember.pdf, accessed 25 March 2016.

13. Video testimony given to the Holocaust Memorial Foundation in 2016. Not publicly available.

14. Baron-Cohen, *Zero Degrees of Empathy*, pp. 198–9.

15. Pinker, *The Better Angels of Our Nature*, p. 398.

16. Sebag Montefiore, *Stalin*, Chapter 20.

17. Hughes, *The Holocaust and the Revival of Psychological History*, p. 16.

18. Pinker, *The Better Angels of Our Nature*, p. 672.

19. For examples, see ibid., pp. 1–26.

20. My main source for the following account of the Armenian genocide was Chapter 7 of Rogan, *The Fall of the Ottomans.*

21. Grigoris Balakian, *Armenian Golgotha.*

22. Peter Balakian, *The Burning Tigress*, p. 282.

23. Chabot et al., *Mass Media and the Genocide of the Armenians*, p. 150.

24. Marchand and Perrier, *Turkey and the Armenian Ghost* (trans. Blythe), p. 194.

25. Pinker, *The Better Angels of Our Nature*, pp. 702–6; D. Batson, 'Is Empathic Emotion a Source of Altruistic Motivation?', *Journal of Personality and Social Psychology* 40(2), 1981, pp. 290–302. doi: 10.1037/0022-3514.40.2.290.

26. https://m.youtube.com/watch?v=74yn2srU5G4, accessed 23 March 2016.

27. McGilchrist, *The Master and His Emissary*, p. 147.

28. Oliner and Oliner, *The Altruistic Personality.*

29. Gasore, *My Day to Die*, p. 32.

30. http://research.calvin.edu/german-propaganda-archive/goeb56.htm, accessed 10 July 2016.

31. http://www.rwandafile.com/rtlm/rtlm0002.html, accessed 26 March 2016.

32. De Waal, *The Age of Empathy*, p. 21.

33. Ibid., p. 8.

34. Quoted in J. Decety and J. Cowell, 'Empathy, Justice, and Moral Behavior', *AJOB Neuroscience* 6(3), 2015, pp. 3–14. doi: 10.1080/21507740.2015.1047055.

35. Ibid.

36. J. Decety et al., 'Love Hurts: An fMRI Study', *NeuroImage* 51(2), 2010, pp. 923–9. doi: 10.1016/j.neuroimage.2010.02.047.

37. Nussbaum, *Political Emotions*, p. 156.

38. Sen, *Identity and Violence*, p. 2.

39. http://www.newyorker.com/science/maria-konnikova/the-real-lesson-of-the-stanford-prison-experiment, accessed 19 March 2016.

40. R. Willer, K. Kuwabara and W. Macy, 'The False Enforcement of Unpopular Norms', *American Journal of Sociology* 115(2), 2009, pp. 451–90.

41. Browning, *Ordinary Men*, p. 36.

42. Pinker, *The Better Angels of Our Nature*, p. 694.

43. J. Decety and J. Cowell, 'Friends or Foes: Is Empathy Necessary for Moral Behavior?', *Perspectives on Psychological Science* 9(5), 2014, pp. 525–37. doi: 10.1177/1745691614545130.

44. http://www.nytimes.com/2015/03/22/magazine/the-brains-empathy-gap.html?_r=0, accessed 3 March 2016.

Chapter 2: The Science of Empathy

1. Baron-Cohen, *Zero Degrees of Empathy*, p. 103.

2. A. Sagi and M. Hoffman, 'Empathic Distress in the Newborn', *Developmental Psychology* 12(2), 1976, pp. 175–6. Cited in de Waal, *The Age of Empathy*, p. 67.

3. I. Norscia et al., '*She* More than *He*: Gender Bias Supports the Empathic Nature of Yawn Contagion in *Homo sapiens*', *Royal Society Open Science* 3, 2016, 150459. doi: 10.1098/rsos.150459.

4. P. Ferández-Berrocal et al., 'Gender Differences in Emotional Intelligence: The Mediating Effect of Age', *Behavioral Psychology* 20(1), 2012, pp. 77–89.

5. https://www.theguardian.com/business/2015/mar/06/johns-davids-and-ians-outnumber-female-chief-executives-in-ftse-100, accessed 18 July 2016.

6. Darwin, *The Expression of the Emotions in Man and Animals*, p. 306.

7. Darwin, *The Descent of Man and Selection in Relation to Sex*, p. 97.

8. Ridley, *The Origins of Virtue*, p. 249.

9. Townshend, *Darwin's Dogs*, p. 100.

10. He was Wolfgang Köhler. See de Waal, *The Age of Empathy*, p. 60.

11. Ibid., p. 75.

12. Ibid., p. 61.

13. Ibid., p. 62.

14. Ibid., p. 61.

15. Ibid., p. 62.

16. Ibid., pp. 133–5.

17. Ibid., pp. 121–2.

18. Ibid., p. 107.

19. Ibid., pp. 172–4.

20. Ibid., p. 187.

21. Ibid., pp. 208–9.

22. Ibid., pp. 140–2.

23. Ibid., p. 157.

24. https://www.technologyreview.com/s/421480/the-evolutionary-origin-of-laughter/, accessed 22 September 2016.

25. F. Marineli et al., 'Mary Mallon (1869–1938) and the History of Typhoid Fever', *Annals of Gastroenterology: Quarterly Publication of the Hellenic Society of Gastroenterology* 26(2), 2013, pp. 132–4.

26. Skloot, *The Immortal Life of Henrietta Lacks*.

27. Baron-Cohen, *Zero Degrees of Empathy*, pp. 21–2; Pinker, *The Better Angels of Our Nature*, pp. 605–9; http://www.smithsonianmag.com/history/phineas-gage-neurosciences-most-famous-patient-11390067/, accessed 6 May 2016.

28. Smith, *The Theory of Moral Sentiments*, p. 14.

29. De Waal, *The Age of Empathy*, pp. 65–7.

30. G. Rizzolatti and M. Fabbri-Destro, 'Mirror Neurons: From Discovery to Autism', *Experimental Brain Research* 200(3–4), 2010, pp. 223–37. doi: 10.1007/s00221-009-2002-3.

31. https:/psychologytoday.com/blog/brain-myths/201212/mirror-neurons-the-most-hyped-concept-in-neuroscience, accessed 20 August 2016. J. Kilner and R. Lemon, 'What We Know Currently about Mirror Neurons', *Current Biology* 23(23), 2013. doi: 10.1016/j.cub.2013.10.051; Rizzolatti, *Mirrors in the Brain*; Iacobini, *Mirroring People*; Hickok, *The Myth of Mirror Neurons*.

32. Rizzolatti, *Mirrors in the Brain*, p. xii.

33. Ibid.

34. McGilchrist, *The Master and His Emissary*, p. 58.

35. https://www.theguardian.com/science/2013/jan/04/barack-obama-empathy-deficit, accessed 29 March 2016.

36. https://www.mpg.de/research/supramarginal-gyrus-empathy, accessed 30 March 2016.

37. Baron-Cohen, *Zero Degrees of Empathy*, pp. 19–28.

38. Neat animated summary of the book: https://www.youtube.com/watch?v=dFs9WO2B8uI, accessed 18 July 2016.

39. Spindle neurons: de Waal, *The Age of Empathy*, p. 138; http://www.smithsonianmag.com/science-nature/brain-cells-for-socializing- 133855450/, accessed 2 May 2016.

40. Pinker, *The Better Angels of Our Nature*, p. 699.

41. Baron-Cohen, *Zero Degrees of Empathy*, p. 27.

42. T. Horikawa et al., 'Neural Decoding of Visual Imagery during Sleep', *Science* 340(6132), 2013, pp. 639–42. doi: 10.1126/science.1234330. Cited in http://www.theverge.com/2013/6/19/4445684/brain--scan-fmri-identify-emotion, accessed 3 April 2016; and in http://www.npr.org/sections/health-shots/2013/04/04/176224026/researchers-use-brain-scans-to-reveal-hidden-dreamscape, accessed 3 April 2016.

43. http://www.hss.cmu.edu/pressreleases/pressreleases/mindreading.html, accessed 3 April 2016.

44. K. Kassam et al., 'Identifying Emotions on the Basis of Neural Activation', *PLoS ONE* 8(6), 2013: e66032. doi: http://dx.doi.org/10.1371/journal.pone.0066032.

45. For more, see Ockelford, *In the Key of Genius*.

46. http://www.psychiatrictimes.com/autism/autism-and-schizophrenia, accessed 22 July 2016.

47. http://www.hscic.gov.uk/catalogue/PUB05061/esti-prev-auti-ext-07-psyc-morb-surv-rep.pdf, accessed 22 July 2016.

48. Interview with Baron-Cohen in Cambridge, 22 June 2016.

49. http://www.bbc.co.uk/news/magazine-35350880, accessed 24 July 2016.

50. A. Carré et al., 'The Basic Empathy Scale in Adults: Factor Structure of a Revised Form', *Psychological Assessment* 25(3), 2013, pp. 679–91. doi: 10.1037/a0032297.

51. H. Takahasi et al., 'When Your Gain Is My Pain and Your Pain Is My Gain: Neural Correlates of Envy and Schadenfreude', *Science* 323(5916), 2009, pp. 937–9. doi: 10.1126/science.1165604. Cited in Pinker, *The Better Angels of Our Nature*, pp. 663–4.

52. Baron-Cohen, *Zero Degrees of Empathy*, pp. 55–7.

53. A. Marsh, 'Empathy and Compassion: A Cognitive Neuroscience Perspective', in Decety (ed.), *Empathy*, p. 195; A. Marsh et al.,

'Accurate Identification of Fear Facial Expressions Predicts Prosocial Behavior', *Emotion* 7(1), 2007, pp. 239–51.

54. R. Blair, 'Neurobiological Basis of Psychopathy', *British Journal of Psychiatry* 182(1), 2003, pp. 5–7. doi:10.1192/bjp.182.1.5.

55. Shakespeare, *Othello*, Act 1, scene 1, lines 59–60. Greenblatt et al. (eds), *The Norton Shakespeare*, p. 2101.

56. For more, see http://quoteinvestigator.com/2010/05/21/death-statistic/, accessed 19 July 2016.

57. Pinker, *The Better Angels of Our Nature*, p. 714.

58. Goodman, *Consequences of Compassion*. Cited in https://boston-review.net/forum/paul-bloom-against-empathy, accessed 2 March 2016.

59. Mill, 'The Utility of Religion', *Three Essays on Religion.*

60. Quoted in Boyd, *On the Origin of Stories*, p. 134.

61. 'Song of Myself', https://www.poetryfoundation.org/poems-and-poets/poems/detail/45477, accessed 5 August 2016.

62. Smith, *The Theory of Moral Sentiments*, p. 14.

63. Ibid., p. 373.

64. Hume, *A Treatise of Human Nature*, p. 576.

65. Nussbaum, *Political Emotions*, p. 150.

66. Russell, *A History of Western Philosophy*, pp. 738–9.

67. G. Eliot, 'The Natural History of German Life', *Westminster Review*, July 1856.

68. The letter was to John Bray and is quoted in Willey, *Nineteenth-Century Studies*, p. 244.

69. Eliot, *Middlemarch*, p. 301.

70. Ibid., p. 10.

71. Ibid., p. 279.

72. Ibid., p. 194.

73. Keltner et al. (eds), *The Compassionate Instinct*, p. 15.

Chapter 3: The Nature and Nurture of Empathy

1. https://www.theguardian.com/commentisfree/2014/jun/03/how-i-discovered-i-have-the-brain-of-a-psychopath, accessed 4 May 2016.

2. The ballet was Agnes de Mille's *Fall River Legend*, which premiered in New York in 1948. The doggerel is cited in http://www.history.com/this-day-in-history/borden-parents-found-dead, accessed 19 September 2016.

3. https://www.theguardian.com/commentisfree/2014/jun/03/how-i-discovered-i-have-the-brain-of-a-psychopath, accessed 4 May 2016.

4. Cross and Livingstone (eds), *The Oxford Dictionary of the Christian Church*, 2005. 'Original sin', cited in https://en.wikipedia.org/wiki/Original_sin#cite_note-53, accessed 14 May 2016.

5. Tappert, *The Book of Concord*, p. 29. Cited in https://en.wikipedia.org/wiki/Original_sin#cite_note-53, accessed 14 May 2016.

6. Locke, *Some Thoughts Concerning Education*, Section 217. http://www.bartleby.com/37/1/22.html, accessed 13 May 2016.

7. http://www.bl.uk/romantics-and-victorians/articles/perceptions-of-childhood, accessed 21 July 2016.

8. Ridley, *Nature via Nurture*, Prologue.

9. Baron-Cohen, *Zero Degrees of Empathy*, pp. 102–3.

10. Pinker, *The Better Angels of Our Nature*, p. 534.

11. T. Polderman et al., 'Meta-Analysis of the Heritability of Human Traits Based on Fifty Years of Twin Studies', *Nature Genetics* 47, 2015, pp. 702–9. doi: 10.1038/ng.3285.

12. Music, *Nurturing Natures*, Chapter 19.

13. Shakespeare, *Julius Caesar*, Act 1, scene 2, lines 140–1. Greenblatt et al. (eds), *The Norton Shakespeare*, p. 1538.

14. Twin studies: Pinker, *The Better Angels of Our Nature*, pp. 742–4; http://www.ted.com/talks/steven_pinker_chalks_it_up_to_the_blank_slate?language=en#t-287271, accessed 20 July 2016.

15. MAOA gene: Baron-Cohen, *Zero Degrees of Empathy*, pp. 89–91; Ridley, *Nature via Nurture*, pp. 267–9; Pinker, *The Better Angels of Our Nature*, pp. 746–9.

16. Baron-Cohen, *Zero Degrees of Empathy*, p. 88.

17. Ibid., p. 97; and S. Baron-Cohen et al., 'Genetic Variation in GABRB3 is Associated with Asperger Syndrome and Multiple Endophenotypes Relevant to Autism', *Molecular Autism* 4(48), 2013. doi: 10.1186/2040-2392-4-48.

18. http://www.cam.ac.uk/research/news/study-confirms-a-gene-linked-to-asperger-syndrome-and-empathy, accessed 19 July 2016.

19. Baron-Cohen, *Zero Degrees of Empathy*, p. 93.

20. S. Lutchmaya et al., 'Foetal Testosterone and Eye Contact in 12-Month-Old Infants', *Infant Behavior and Development* 25, 2002, pp. 327–35. doi: 10.1186/2040-2392-1-11. S. Lutchmaya and S. Baron-Cohen, 'Foetal Testosterone and Vocabulary Size in 18- and 24-Month-Old Infants', *Infant Behavior and Development* 24, 2002, pp. 418–24. doi: 10.1186/2040-2392-1-11.

21. http://graphics.wsj.com/image-grid/what-to-expect-in-2016/1666/steven-pinker-on-new-advances-in-behavioral-genetics, accessed 20 July 2016.

22. Ridley, *Nature via Nurture*, p. 168.

23. Ibid., p. 180.

24. Ibid.; and de Waal, *The Age of Empathy*, pp. 11–13.

25. Dawkins, *The Oxford Book of Modern Science Writing*, p. 26.

26. Eagleman, *The Brain*, Chapter 1; also see Nelson, *Romania's Abandoned Children*.

27. Ridley, *Nature via Nurture*, pp. 182–3.

28. Ibid., pp. 189–90.

29. Ibid., pp. 192–4.

30. Eagleman, *The Brain*, Chapter 1.

31. McGilchrist, *The Master and His Emissary*, pp. 87–8.

32. Baron-Cohen, *Zero Degrees of Empathy*, pp. 48–50.

33. https://www.ucl.ac.uk/news/news-articles/1112/111205-maltreated-children-fMRI-study, accessed 20 July 2016.

34. Baron-Cohen, *Zero Degrees of Empathy*, pp. 48–50.

35. Mukherjee, *The Gene*, p. 459.

36. G. H. Brody et al., 'Prevention Effects Moderate the Association of 5-HTTLPR and Youth Risk Behavior Initiation: Gene × Environment Hypotheses Tested via a Randomized Prevention Design', *Child Development* 80(3), 2009, pp. 645–61. doi: 10.1017/S0954579414001266. And G. H. Brody et al, 'Differential Susceptibility to Prevention: GABAergic, dopaminergic, and multilocus effects', *Journal of Child Psychology and Psychiatry* 54(8), 2013, pp. 863–71.

37. https://thepsychologist.bps.org.uk/volume-27/edition-2/interview-marinus-van-ijzendoorn, accessed 19 September 2016.

38. S. Light and C. Zahn-Waxler, 'Nature and Forms of Empathy in the First Years of Life', in Decety (ed.), *Empathy*, p. 109.

39. Hoffman, *Empathy and Moral Development*, pp. 64–86.

40. Leach, *Your Baby and Child from Birth to Age Five*; Faber and Mazlish, *How to Talk So Kids Will Listen and Listen So Kids Will Talk*; Tess Hilton, *The Great Ormond Street New Baby and*

Childcare Book; Gopnik, Meltzoff and Kuhl, *How Babies Think*; Murray and Andrews, *The Social Baby*; Gerhardt, *Why Love Matters*; Sunderland, *The Science of Parenting*; Fernyhough, *The Baby in the Mirror*; Halsey, *Baby Development*; Janis-Norton, *Calmer Easier Happier Parenting*; Lathey, *Small Talk*; Murray, *The Psychology of Babies*; Clegg, *The Blissful Toddler Expert*; Callahan, *The Science of Mom*; Christakis, *The Importance of Being Little*.

41. http://developingchild.harvard.edu/science/deep-dives/lifelong-health/, accessed 25 July 2016.

42. http://developingchild.harvard.edu/science/key-concepts/serve-and-return/, accessed 25 July 2016.

43. Janis-Norton, *Calmer Easier Happier Parenting*, Chapter 5.

44. http://developingchild.harvard.edu/science/key-concepts/toxic-stress/, accessed 25 July 2016.

45. Baron-Cohen, *Zero Degrees of Empathy*, p. 51.

46. Schweinhart et al., *Lifetime Effects: The High/Scope Perry Preschool Study through Age 40*.

47. M. Fort, A. Ichino et al., 'Cognitive and Non-Cognitive Costs of Daycare 0–2 for Girls', 2016. Available online at http://ftp.iza.org/dp9756.pdf, accessed 19 September 2016.

48. https://www.google.co.uk/url?sa=t&rct=j&q=&esrc=s&source=web&cd=1&ved=0ahUKEwioqJup3I7OAhUrIcAKHYlJB7cQFggcMAA&url=http%3A%2F%2Fresearchbriefings.files.parliament.uk%2Fdocuments%2FCBP-7257%2FCBP-7257.pdf&usg=AFQjCNEJkeg3Faz1M4diUwSvIdwFNfEpow&sig2=-3fj5r9XE6iUHO3lW5molw&bvm=bv.127984354,d.ZGg, accessed 25 July 2016.

49. https://www.theguardian.com/society/2015/nov/11/troubled-family-programme-government-success-council-figures, accessed 25 July 2016.

50. http://www.bbc.co.uk/news/uk-politics-37010486, accessed 9 August 2016.

51. https://www.gov.uk/government/speeches/prime-ministers-speech-on-life-chances, accessed 25 July 2016.

52. Finnish education: Christakis, *The Importance of Being Little*, pp. 102–6; http://www.nytimes.com/2011/12/13/education/from-finland-an-intriguing-school-reform-model.html, accessed 25 July 2016.

53. http://babylaughter.net/, accessed 25 July 2016.

54. Hilton, *More Human*, Chapter 6.

55. https://www.gov.uk/government/speeches/prime-ministers-speech-on-life-chances, accessed 25 July 2016.

Chapter 4: The Digital Dystopia

1. https://techcrunch.com/2015/09/15/the-sorry-button/, accessed 28 June, 2016.

2. https://research.facebook.com/publications/once-more-with-feeling-supportive-responses-to-social-sharing-on-facebook, accessed 14 July 2016.

3. http://www.bbc.co.uk/news/technology-36321169, accessed 11 July 2016.

4. http://www.nytimes.com/2014/09/11/fashion/steve-jobs-apple-was-a-low-tech-parent.html?_r=0), accessed 16 July 2015.

5. Christakis, *The Importance of Being Little*, p. 174.

6. Borba draws on V. Rideout et al., *Generation M2: Media in the Lives of 8- to 18-Year-Olds*, 2010. Available online at http://files.eric.ed.gov/fulltext/ED527859.pdf, accessed 20 September 2016.

7. Borba, *UnSelfie*, Chapter 1.

8. https://www2.highlights.com/newsroom/national-survey-reveals-62-kids-think-parents-are-too-distracted-listen, accessed 25 July 2016.

9. J. Radesky et al., 'Patterns of Mobile Device Use by Caregivers and Children during Meals in Fast Food Restaurants', *Pediatrics* 133, 2014, e843–9. doi: 10.1542/peds.2013-3703. Cited in http://well.blogs.nytimes.com/2014/03/10/parents-wired-to-distraction, accessed 25 July 2016.

10. http://www.telegraph.co.uk/news/worldnews/asia/southkorea/10138403/Surge-in-digital-dementia.html, accessed 20 July 2016.

11. Ibid.

12. http://www.pewinternet.org/2014/10/22/online-harassment/, accessed 15 June 2016.

13. https://www.theguardian.com/commentisfree/2016/apr/11/the-guardian-view-on-online-abuse-building-the-web-we-want, accessed 12 July 2016; https://www.theguardian.com/technology/2016/apr/12/the-dark-side-of-guardian-comments, accessed 12 July 2016.

14. https://www.theguardian.com/technology/2016/jun/18/vile-online-abuse-against-women-mps-needs-to-be-challenged-now, accessed 21 June 2016.

15. http://www.bbc.co.uk/news/uk-36042718, accessed 21 June 2016.

16. http://edition.cnn.com/2010/LIVING/10/07/hope.witsells.story/, accessed 20 June 2016.

17. https://www.theguardian.com/world/2010/sep/30/tyler-clementi-gay-student-suicide, accessed 28 June 2016.

18. http://www.bbc.co.uk/news/uk-36746763, accessed 12 July 2016.

19. http://www.bbc.co.uk/news/uk-36042718, accessed 21 June 2016.

20. https://www.theguardian.com/technology/2016/may/08/they-I-know-they-were-victims-revenge-porn-helpline-sees-alarming-rise?CMP=Share_iOSApp_Other, accessed 21 June 2016.

21. http://www.nbcsandiego.com/news/local/Kevin-Bollaert-Revenge-Porn-Sentencing-San-Diego-298603981.html, accessed 17 June 2016.

22. https://www.theguardian.com/uk-news/2016/jun/11/revenge-porn-threats-crime-england-wales?CMP=Share_iOSApp_Other, accessed 14 July 2016.

23. https://www.quilliamfoundation.org/wp/wp-content/uploads/publications/free/white-paper-youth-led-pathways-from-extremism.pdf, accessed 2 June 2016.

24. https://www.theguardian.com/education/2016/jan/19/nicky-morgan-islamist-extremists-grooming-tactics-paedophiles, accessed 13 July 2016.

25. http://www.independent.co.uk/life-style/gadgets-and-tech/news/porn-site-age-verification-laws-could-force-users-to-register-credit-cards-a7035666.html, accessed 8 July 2016.

26. http://www.childrenscommissioner.gov.uk/sites/default/files/publications/MDX%20NSPCC%20OCC%20pornography%20report%20June%202016.pdf, accessed 5 July 2016; http://www.childrenscommissioner.gov.uk/news/children-may-become-%E2%80%98desensitised%E2%80%99-damaging-impact-online-porn, accessed 18 July 2016.

27. https://www.barnardos.org.uk/now_i_know_it_was_wrong.pdf, accessed 20 July 2916.

28. http://www.ibtimes.co.uk/online-porn-leads-increase-child-sex-abuse-by-children-1569862, accessed 25 July 2016.

29. M. Klaassen and J. Peter, 'Gender (In)equality in Internet Pornography: A Content Analysis of Popular Pornographic Internet Videos', *Journal of Sex Research* 52(7), 2015, pp. 721–35. doi: 10.1080/00224499.2014.976781.

30. McDermid, *Forensics*, pp. 210–14.

31. http://www.theguardian.com/lifeandstyle/2010/jul/02/gail-dines-pornography, accessed 2 July 2016.

32. https://www.psychologytoday.com/blog/women-who-stray/201402/common-sense-about-the-effects-pornography, accessed 2 July 2016.

33. S. Kühn and J. Gallinat, 'Brain Structure and Functional Connectivity Associated with Pornography Consumption', *JAMA Psychiatry*, 71(7), 2014, pp. 827–34.

34. V. Voon et al., 'Neural Correlates of Sexual Cue Reactivity in Individuals with and without Compulsive Sexual Behaviours', *PLoS ONE* 9(7), 2014, e102419. doi: 10.1371/journal.pone.0102419. S. Kühn and J. Gallinat, 'Brain Structure and Functional Connectivity Associated with Pornography Consumption: The Brain on Porn', *JAMA Psychiatry* 71(7), 2014, pp. 827–34. doi: 10.1001/jamapsychiatry.2014.93.

35. http://www.childrenscommissioner.gov.uk/sites/default/files/publications/Basically_porn_is_everywhere_cyp_version.pdf, accessed 1 June 2016.

36. https://www.b-eat.co.uk/about-beat/media-centre/information-and-statistics-about-eating-disorders, accessed 4 June 2016.

37. https://www.theguardian.com/society/2015/jun/25/eating-disorders-rise-children-blamed-celebrity-bodies-advertising, accessed 4 June 2016.

38. S. Livingstone et al., 'Risks and Safety on the Internet: The

Perspective of European Children', 2011. doi: http://eprints.lse.ac.uk/33731/. Cited in Bartlett, *The Dark Net*, p. 193.

39. http://www.ucs.ac.uk/Faculties-and-Centres/Faculty-of-Arts,-Business-and-Applied-Social-Science/Department-of-Children,-Young-People-and-Education/Virtually%20Anorexic.pdf, accessed 6 June 2016.

40. Baron-Cohen, *Zero Degrees of Empathy*, p. 106.

41. https://www.washingtonpost.com/news/wonk/wp/2016/06/13/the-four-cryptic-words-donald-trump-cant-stop-saying/, accessed 27 July 2016.

42. https://www.ted.com/talks/chris_milk_how_virtual_reality_can_create_the_ultimate_empathy_machine?language=en, accessed 9 July 2016.

43. Ibid.

44. Hilton, *More Human*, Chapter 10.

45. https://www.theguardian.com/uk-news/2016/jun/11/revenge-porn-threats-crime-england-wales?CMP=Share_iOSApp_Other, accessed 15 July 2016.

46. http://www.bbc.co.uk/news/uk-36042718, accessed 15 July 2016.

47. https://www.theguardian.com/uk-news/2016/mar/04/online-abuse-existing-laws-too-fragmented-and-I-serve-victims-says-police-chief, accessed 15 July 2016.

48. https://app.ft.com/cms/s/1a392244-055e-11e6-9b51-0fb5e65703ce.html?sectionid=companies, accessed 16 July 2016.

49. http://www.nytimes.com/2015/12/24/technology/personaltech/for-parental-controls-iphones-beat-androids.html?_r=0, accessed 17 July 2016.

50. http://www.wired.co.uk/article/porn-websites-age-verification-queens-speech, accessed 17 July 2016.

51. https://www.gov.uk/government/publications/child-safety-online-a-practical-guide-for-providers-of-social-media-and-interactive-services/child-safety-online-a-practical-guide-for-providers-of-social-media-and-interactive-services, accessed 18 July 2016.

52. http://webarchive.nationalarchives.gov.uk/+/http:/www.homeoffice.gov.uk/documents/sexualisation-of-young-people.pdf, accessed 18 July 2016.

53. http://www.huffingtonpost.com/cris-rowan/10-reasons-why-handheld-devices-should-be-banned_b_4899218.html, accessed 19 July 2016.

54. K. Schonert-Reichl et al., 'Promoting Children's Prosocial Behaviors in School: Impact of the "Roots of Empathy" Program on the Social and Emotional Competence of School-Aged Children', *School Mental Health* 4(1), 2012, pp. 1–21. doi: 10.1007/s12310-011-9064-7.

55. http://www.rootsofempathy.org/about-us/, accessed 8 July 2016.

56. Borba, *UnSelfie*, Epilogue.

57. https://www.cs.kent.ac.uk/events/2015/AISB2015/proceedings/hri/15-Becker-embodimentemotionand.pdf, accessed 6 July 2016. https://www.researchgate.net/publication/228848453_iCat_the_affective_chess_player, accessed 6 July 2016.

58. N. Luke and R. Banerjee, 'Differentiated Associations between Childhood Maltreatment Experiences and Social Understanding: A Meta-Analysis and Systematic Review', *Developmental Review* 33(1), 2013, pp. 1–28.

59. Bombèr and Hughes, *Settling Troubled Pupils to Learn*, Chapter 6.

60. Telephone conversation with educational psychologist Sacha Grimes, 26 February 2016.

61. Visit to Netley Marsh, 25 April 2016.

62. Visit to Beck, 3 May 2016.

63. http://www.independent.co.uk/news/uk/politics/teenage-volunteers-show-true-grit-at-the-national-citizen-service-8793020.html, accessed 7 July 2016.

64. Different from the Head Start which Lyndon Johnson founded in 1965. Its website is http://www.the-challenge.org/our-programmes/headstart, accessed 20 September 2016.

65. http://www.theatlantic.com/business/archive/2014/09/should-the-laborer-fear-machines/380476/, accessed 8 July 2016.

66. http://www.ft.com/cms/s/0/46d12e7c-4948-11e6-b387-64ab0a67014c.html, accessed 20 July 2016.

67. http://www.theatlantic.com/magazine/archive/2015/07/world-without-work/395294/, accessed 25 July 2016.

68. http://www.pewinternet.org/2014/08/06/future-of-jobs/, accessed 27 July 2016.

69. https://www.theguardian.com/society/2015/nov/29/five-ways-work-will-change-future-of-workplace-ai-cloud-retirement-remote, accessed 27 July 2016.

70. http://www.theaustralian.com.au/business/in-depth/perpetual/work-may-change-but-empathy-jobs-will-endure/news-story/f70b6d729e5136357af45f952ab80886, accessed 27 July 2016.

71. http://www.theatlantic.com/magazine/archive/2015/07/world-without-work/395294/, accessed 26 July 2016.

72. https://www.theguardian.com/technology/2016/mar/15/killer-robots-driverless-cars-alphago-and-the-social-impact-artificial-intelligence, accessed 27 July 2016.

73. http://www.pewinternet.org/2014/08/06/future-of-jobs/, accessed 27 July 2016.

74. http://www.ft.com/cms/s/0/46d12e7c-4948-11e6-b387-64ab0a67014c.html, accessed 27 July 2016.

Chapter 5: Crime and Punishment

1. http://www.campbellcollaboration.org/artman2/uploads/1/Parent_training_programs_3P_UK_User_Abstract.pdf, accessed 12 June 2016.
2. Ross, *Crime*, Chapter 17.
3. D. Jolliffe and D. Farrington, 'Empathy and Offending: A Systematic Review and Meta-Analysis', *Aggression and Violent Behavior* 9(5), 2003, pp. 441–76.
4. M. van Langen et al., 'The Relation between Empathy and Offending: A Meta-Analysis', *Aggression and Violent Behavior* 19(2), 2014, pp. 179–89.
5. D. Vachon et al., 'The (Non)Relation between Empathy and Aggression: Surprising Results from a Meta-Analysis', *Psychological Bulletin* 140(3), 2013, pp. 751–3. doi: 10.1037/a0035236.
6. Conversation with Darrick Jolliffe, 21 March 2016.
7. Ibid.
8. *Inside: Artists and Writers in Reading Prison*, curated by Artangel, October–November 2016.
9. Hari, *Chasing the Scream*, Chapter 18; Alexander, *The Globalization of Addiction*.
10. http://www.centreforsocialjustice.org.uk/UserStorage/pdf/Pdf%20reports/CSJJ3090_Drugs_in_Prison.pdf, accessed 10 June 2016.
11. https://www.theguardian.com/society/2016/may/01/synthetic-

cannabis-having-a-devastating-impact-in-uk-prisons, accessed 9 June 2016.

12. Email exchange, 26 July 2016.

13. http://www.york.ac.uk/media/healthsciences/images/research/mharg/projects/scoping%20and%20feasibility%20report%20with%20full%20appendices%2031.3.14.pdf, accessed 11 May 2016.

14. This and the previous four stats are from David Cameron's speech on prison reform, 8 February 2016. https://www.gov.uk/government/speeches/prison-reform-prime-ministers-speech, accessed 13 May 2016.

15. https://www.gov.uk/government/uploads/system/uploads/attachment_data/file/543284/safety-in-custody-bulletin.pdf, accessed 18 July 2016.

16. http://www.centreforsocialjustice.org.uk/UserStorage/pdf/Pdf%20reports/CSJJ3090_Drugs_in_Prison.pdf, accessed 15 May 2016.

17. Ibid.

18. Von Hirsch et al., *Criminal Deterrence and Sentence Severity*.

19. http://www.ncsc.org/~/media/Microsites/Files/CSI/Additional%20Learning%20Materials/Handout%20P3%20Judicial%20Paper.ashx, accessed 2 August 2016.

20. Norwegian prisons: http://www.theguardian.com/society/2013/feb/25/norwegian-prison-inmates-treated-like-people, accessed 3 May 2016; http://uk.businessinsider.com/why-norways-prison-system-is-so-successful-2014-12?r=US&IR=T, accessed 3 May 2016.

21. https://www.theguardian.com/commentisfree/2014/dec/08/ban-books-prisoners-ministry-of-justice-mark-haddon, accessed 24 July 2016.

22. https://www.gov.uk/government/uploads/system/uploads/attachment_data/file/524013/education-review-report.pdf, accessed 22 July 2016.

23. https://www.gov.uk/government/speeches/prison-reform-prime-ministers-speech, accessed 18 May 2016.

24. https://www.gov.uk/government/uploads/system/uploads/attachment_data/file/448854/portland-fmi.pdf, accessed 4 June 2016.

25. https://www.ted.com/talks/daniel_reisel_the_neuroscience_of_restorative_justice?language=en, accessed 3 June 2016.

26. Interview with Reisel, 22 April 2016; and see Reisel, 'Towards a Neuroscience of Morality', in Gavrielides (ed.), *The Psychology of Restorative Justice*, pp. 59–60.

27. https://www.bostonglobe.com/lifestyle/2016/04/18/tracking-risks-and-rewards-transcranial-magnetic-stimulation/VrMoJhIpWgMPDXe2sbyFpI/story.html, accessed 19 May 2016.

28. http://www.telegraph.co.uk/news/uknews/law-and-order/11455089/What-happens-when-victims-of-crime-meet-their-tormentors.html, accessed 22 May 2016.

29. http://hopehawaii.net/assets/state-of-the-art-of-hope-probation-w-c.pdf, accessed 10 May 2016

30. http://www.nuffieldfoundation.org/sites/default/files/files/FDAC_May2014_FinalReport_V2.pdf, accessed 9 May 2016. Cited in http://www.economist.com/news/britain/21692920-government-once-again-tries-make-courts-more-caring-smart-justice, accessed 7 May 2016.

31. http://www.economist.com/news/britain/21692920-government-once-again-tries-make-courts-more-caring-smart-justice, accessed 7 May 2016.

32. B. Hölzel et al., 'Mindfulness Practice Leads to Increases in Regional Brain Gray Matter Density', *Psychiatry Research* 191(1), 2011, pp. 36–43. doi: 10.1016/j.pscychresns. 2010.08.006.

33. Ross, *Crime*, Chapter 18.

34. https://www.theguardian.com/commentisfree/2015/dec/17/ mental-health-prison-segregation-units-prisoners, accessed 10 May 2016.

35. James, *Redeemable*, p. 340.

36. Ibid., p. 298.

37. http://www.ahrc.ac.uk/documents/publications/cultural-value- project-final-report/, accessed 14 May 2016.

38. https://www.gov.uk/government/uploads/system/uploads/ attachment_data/file/524013/education-review-report.pdf, accessed 27 July 2016.

39. https://irenetaylortrust.com/changing-lives/evaluations/, accessed 29 May 2016.

40. Email correspondence with Jane Davis, Director, 13 June 2016.

41. http://www.cresc.ac.uk/sites/default/files/The%20Academy%20 a%20Report%20on%20Outcomes%20for%20Participants.pdf, accessed 27 May 2016.

42. M. van Poortvliet et al., 'Trial and Error: Children and young people in trouble with the law: A guide for charities and funders', New Philanthropy Capital, 2010. Available online at http://www.thinknpc.org/publications/trial-and-error/trial-and- error-2/?post-parent=5204, accessed 20 September 2016.

43. L. Cheliotis and A. Jordanoska, 'The Arts of Desistance: Assessing the Role of Arts-Based Programmes in Reducing Reoffending', *Howard Journal of Crime and Justice* 55, 2016, pp. 25–41. doi: 10.1111/hojo.12154.

44. https://www.artsincriminaljustice.org.uk/leading-world-arts-and-criminal-justice-international-context, accessed 27 May 2016.

45. P. C. Giordano et al., 'Gender, Crime, and Desistance: Toward a Theory of Cognitive Transformation', *American Journal of Sociology*, 107(4), 2002, pp. 990–1064.

46. Cited in http://www.artsevidence.org.uk/media/uploads/evaluation-downloads/mc-inspiring-change-april-2011.pdf, accessed 24 May 2016.

47. http://www.bbc.co.uk/news/uk-34571936, accessed 22 May 2016.

48. http://www.telegraph.co.uk/news/uknews/law-and-order/11455089/What-happens-when-victims-of-crime-meet-their-tormentors.html, accessed 22 May 2016.

49. Ibid.

50. Ibid.

51. http://www.bbc.co.uk/news/uk-england-bristol-22024927, accessed 23 May 2016.

52. http://www.telegraph.co.uk/news/uknews/law-and-order/11455089/What-happens-when-victims-of-crime-meet-their-tormentors.html, accessed 22 May 2016.

53. https://www.theguardian.com/society/2014/sep/17/restorative-justice-young-offenders-crime, accessed 22 May 2016.

54. Ibid.

55. https://www.restorativejustice.org.uk/sites/default/files/files/Briefing.pdf, accessed 21 May 2016.

56. https://www.restorativejustice.org.uk/standards-and-quality, accessed 22 May 2016.

57. http://jobsfriendshouses.org.uk/wp-content/uploads/2016/05/JobsFriendsHouses_ExecSummary_FirstYearEvaluation.pdf,

accessed 11 May 2016. http://jobsfriendshouses.org.uk/our-mission/, accessed 11 May 2016.

58. http://www.scopic.ac.uk/StudiesSPooCS.html#spoocs_desistance, accessed 13 May 2016.

59. Skype conversation with Krznaric, 21 April 2016.

Chapter 6: In Sickness and in Health

1. http://www.cqc.org.uk/sites/default/files/20160608_ip15_statistical_release.pdf, accessed 2 August 2016.

2. http://www.telegraph.co.uk/news/health/heal-our-hospitals/9782537/Stafford-Hospital-scandal-the-battle-by-campaigner-to-shine-light-on-failings.html, accessed 5 June 2016; http://www.bbc.co.uk/news/health-21252393, accessed 20 May 2016.

3. https://www.gov.uk/government/uploads/system/uploads/attachment_data/file/279124/0947.pdf, accessed 4 May 2016.

4. Email correspondence with Gray, 5 May 2016.

5. Interview with Richards, 7 April 2016.

6. B. Lown et al., 'An Agenda for Improving Compassionate Care: A Survey Shows About Half of Patients Say Such Care Is Missing', *Health Affairs* 30(9), 2011, pp. 1772–8. doi: 10.1377/hlthaff.2011.0539. Cited in http://greatergood.berkeley.edu/article/item/should_we_train_doctors_for_empathy, accessed 6 April 2016.

7. K. Pollak et al., 'Oncologist Communication about Emotion during Visits with Patients with Advanced Cancer', *American Society of Clinical Oncology* 25(36), 2007, pp. 5748–52. doi: 10.1200/JCO.2007.12.4180. Cited in http://greatergood.

berkeley.edu/article/item/should_we_train_doctors_for_
empathy, accessed 6 April 2016.

8. M. Neumann et al., 'Empathy Decline and Its Reasons: A
    Systematic Review of Studies with Medical Students and
    Residents', *Academic Medicine* 86(8), 2011, pp. 996–1009. doi:
    10.1097/ACM.0b013e318221e615.

9. M. Hojat et al., 'The Devil Is in the Third Year: A Longitudinal
    Study of Erosion of Empathy in Medical School', *Academic Medicine*
    84(9), 2009, pp. 1182–91. doi: 10.1097/ACM.0b013e3181b17e55.

10. http://greatergood.berkeley.edu/article/item/should_we_train_
    doctors_for_empathy, accessed 6 April 2016.

11. Steve Hilton, *More Human*, Chapter 3.

12. http://www.thetimes.co.uk/article/ill-fed-unwashed-abandoned-
    and-they-call-it-carehidden-cameras-expose-poor-home-care-
    for-elderly-396q9pzgz, accessed 20 May 2016.

13. http://www.barnet-today.co.uk/article.cfm?id=110400&headline=
    Haringey%20home%20care%20scandal:council%20axes%20
    firm%27s%20contract&sectionIs=news&searchyear=2016,
    accessed 13 May 2016.

14. Steve Hilton, *More Human*, Chapter 3.

15. http://www.cqc.org.uk/sites/default/files/20151013_cqc_state_
    of_care_summary_web.pdf, accessed 7 April 2016.

16. http://www.ombudsman.org.uk/__data/assets/pdf_
    file/0005/36698/A_report_of_investigations_into_unsafe_
    discharge_from_hospital.pdf, accessed 8 June 2016.

17. http://greatergood.berkeley.edu/article/item/should_we_train_
    doctors_for_empathy, accessed 6 April 2016.

18. M. Hojat et al., 'Physicians' Empathy and Clinical Outcomes
    for Diabetic Patients', *Academic Medicine* 86(3), 2011, pp.
    359–64. doi: 10.1097/ACM.0b013e3182086fe1.

19. H. Reiss, 'Empathy in Medicine: A Neurobiological Perspective', *Journal of the American Medical Association* 304(14), 2010, pp. 1604–5. doi: 10.1001/jama.2010.1455.

20. S. Kim and S. Kaplowitz, 'The Effects of Physician Empathy on Patient Satisfaction and Compliance', *Evaluation and the Health Professions* 27(3), 2004, pp. 237–51. Cited in http://greatergood.berkeley.edu/article/item/should_we_train_doctors_for_empathy, accessed 6 April 2016.

21. D. Rakel et al., 'Perception of Empathy in the Therapeutic Encounter: Effects on the Common Cold', *Patient Education and Counseling* 85(3), 2011, pp. 390–7. doi: 10.1016/j.pec.2011.01.009. Cited in http://greatergood.berkeley.edu/article/item/should_we_train_doctors_for_empathy, accessed 6 April 2016.

22. S. Steinhausen et al., 'Physician Empathy and Subjective Evaluation of Medical Treatment Outcome in Trauma Surgery Patients', *Patient Education and Counseling* 95(1), 2014, pp. 53–60.

23. S. Del Canale et al., 'The Relationship between Physician Empathy and Disease Complications: An Empirical Study of Primary Care Physicians and Their Diabetic Patients in Parma, Italy', *Academic Medicine* 87(9), 2012, pp. 1243–9.

24. F. Derksen et al., 'Effectiveness of Empathy in General Practice: A Systematic Review', *British Journal of General Practice* 63(606), 2013, e76–e84. doi: 0.3399/bjgp13X660814.

25. D. P. Gray et al., 'Towards a Theory of Continuity of Care', *Journal of the Royal Society of Medicine* 96(4), 2003, pp. 160–6.

26. Email correspondence with Gray, 5 May 2016.

27. E. Gleichgerrcht and J. Decety, 'Empathy in Clinical Practice: How Individual Dispositions, Gender, and Experience Moderate

Empathic Concern, Burnout, and Emotional Distress in Physicians', *PLoS One* 8(4), 2013, e61526. doi: 10.1371/journal. pone.0061526. Cited in http://greatergood.berkeley.edu/article/item/should_we_train_doctors_for_empathy, accessed 6 April 2016.

28. http://greatergood.berkeley.edu/article/item/should_we_train_doctors_for_empathy, accessed 6 April 2016.

29. M. Hojat et al., 'The Devil Is in the Third Year: A Longitudinal Study of Erosion of Empathy in Medical School', *Academic Medicine* 84(9), 2009, pp. 1182–91. doi: 10.1097/ACM.0b013e3181b17e55. Cited in http://greatergood.berkeley.edu/article/item/should_we_train_doctors_for_empathy, accessed 6 April 2016.

30. Ibid.

31. Ibid.

32. Ballatt and Campling, *Intelligent Kindness*, Chapter 4.

33. http://greatergood.berkeley.edu/article/item/should_we_train_doctors_for_empathy, accessed 6 April 2016.

34. H. Riess and J. Kelley, 'Empathy Training for Resident Physicians: A Randomized Controlled Trial of a Neuroscience-Informed Curriculum', *Journal of General International Medicine* 27(10), 2012, pp. 1280–6. doi: 10.1007/s11606-012-2063-z. Cited in http://greatergood.berkeley.edu/article/item/should_we_train_doctors_for_empathy, accessed 6 April 2016.

35. Circle of Care: launch event in London, 17 May 2016; meeting with Bella Eacott of Clod Ensemble, 3 June 2016.

36. https://www.pointofcarefoundation.org.uk/wp-content/uploads/2014/01/POCF_FINAL-inc-references.pdf, accessed 10 April 2016.

37. Ballatt and Campling, *Intelligent Kindness*, Chapter 3.

38. Interview with Richards, 7 April 2016.

39. S. Bernstein and G. D'Onofrio, 'A Promising Approach for Emergency Departments to Care for Patients with Substance Use and Behavioral Disorders', *Health Affairs* 32(12), 2013, pp. 2122–8. doi: 10.1377/hlthaff.2013.0664.

40. https://www.pointofcarefoundation.org.uk/wp-content/uploads/2014/01/POCF_FINAL-inc-references.pdf, accessed 10 April 2016.

41. D. Hirsh et al., 'Into the Future: Patient-Centredness Endures in Longitudinal Integrated Clerkship Graduates', *Medical Education* 48(6), 2014, pp. 572–82.

42. Ballatt and Campling, *Intelligent Kindness*, Chapter 3.

43. http://www.institute.nhs.uk/quality_and_value/productivity_series/productive_ward.html, accessed 8 April 2016.

44. https://www.rcn.org.uk/-/media/royal-college-of-nursing/documents/policies-and-briefings/scotland/publications/sco-a-positive-choice.pdf, accessed 6 April 2016.

45. https://www.gov.uk/government/uploads/system/uploads/attachment_data/file/236212/Cavendish_Review.pdf, accessed 9 April 2016.

46. http://www.skillsforcare.org.uk/Documents/Learning-and-development/Care-Certificate/The-Care-Certificate-Standards.pdf, accessed 10 April 2016.

47. https://www.nice.org.uk/guidance/ng21/resources/home-care-delivering-personal-care-and-practical-support-to-older-people-living-in-their-own-homes-1837326858181, accessed 9 April 2016.

48. Telephone interview with Lesley Garrett, 17 June 2016.

Chapter 7: Race, Religion and Conflict Resolution

1. http://news.npcc.police.uk/releases/sara-thornton-blog-unity-and-respect-needed-not-hate-crime-30-june-2016, accessed 20 July 2016.

2. http://www.demos.co.uk/wp-content/uploads/2016/07/From-Brussels-to-Brexit_-Islamophobia-Xenophobia-Racism-and-Reports-of-Hateful-Incidents-on-Twitter-Research-Prepared-for-Channel-4-Dispatches-%E2%80%98Racist-Britain%E2%80%99-.pdf, accessed 20 July 2016.

3. http://www.demos.co.uk/files/DEMOS_Anti-social_Media.pdf?1391774638, accessed 20 July 2016.

4. De Waal, *The Age of Empathy*, p. 44.

5. Jane Elliott: http://www.smithsonianmag.com/history/lesson-of-a-lifetime-72754306/?page=2, accessed 20 July 2016; https://en.wikipedia.org/wiki/Jane_Elliott, accessed 20 July 2016.

6. Srebrenica: Malcolm, *Bosnia*; http://www.icty.org/x/cases/krstic/tjug/en/010802_Krstic_summary_en.pdf, accessed 11 May 2016; https://www.theguardian.com/world/2016/mar/24/radovan-karadzic-criminally-responsible-for-genocide-at-srebenica, accessed 3 April 2016.

7. D. M. Kahan et al., 'They Saw a Protest: Cognitive Illiberalism and the Speech-Conduct Distinction', *Stanford Law Review* 64, 2012, p. 851. Cited in Greene, *Moral Tribes*, p. 90.

8. Greene, *Moral Tribes*, p.148.

9. Pinker, *The Better Angels of Our Nature*, pp. 7–21.

10. http://www.channel4.com/info/press/news/c4-survey-and-documentary-reveals-what-british-muslims-really-think, accessed 15 June 2016.

11. Homosexuality: Pinker, *The Better Angels of Our Nature*, pp. 534–48.

12. Ibid., p. xxiv.

13. Fink, *War Hospital*, pp. 74–9.

14. Glover, *Humanity*, p.151.

15. Ibid., p. 150.

16. Allport, *The Nature of Prejudice*; H. Tajfel et al., 'Social Categorization and Intergroup Behaviour', *European Journal of Social Psychology* 1(2), 1971, pp. 149–78. doi: 10.1002/ejsp.2420010202; Pinker, *The Better Angels of Our Nature*, pp. 630–1; http://www.theguardian.com/news/2015/nov/05/integrated-school-waterford-academy-oldham, accessed 4 May 2016.

17. http://www.bbc.co.uk/culture/story/20140822-music-uniting-arabs-and-israelis, accessed 16 June 2016.

18. https://www.theguardian.com/news/2015/nov/05/integrated-school-waterford-academy-oldham, accessed 4 May 2016.

19. http://europe.newsweek.com/israeli-palestinian-teens-lead-example-peaceful-dialogue-263312, accessed 8 May 2016.

20. R. Feldman, 'Attenuated Brain Response to Pain of the Other in Israeli and Palestinian Youth', talk at the conference 'Empathy Neuroscience: Relevance to Conflict Resolution', British Academy, London, March 2016.

21. J. Decety and J. Cowell, 'Friends or Foes: Is Empathy Necessary for Moral Behavior?', *Perspectives on Psychological Science* 9(5), 2014, pp. 525–37. doi: 10.1177/1745691614545130.

22. D. Malhotra and S. Liyanaga, 'Long-Term Effects of Peace Workshops in Protracted Conflicts', *Journal of Conflict Resolution* 49, 2005, pp. 908–24. doi: 10.1177/0022002705281153.

23. http://www.huffingtonpost.com/2012/06/11/perspective-taking-sympathy-conflict_n_1587447.html, accessed 14 June 2016.

24. T. Pettigrew and L. Tropp, 'How Does Intergroup Contact Reduce Prejudice? Meta-Analytic Tests of Three Mediators', *European Journal of Social Psychology* 38(6), 2008, pp. 922–34.

25. http://www.ft.com/cms/s/0/5a3b661c-fc45-11e5-b5f5-070dca6 doaod.html, accessed 8 July 2016.

26. http://www.centerforempathy.org/wp-content/uploads/2016/06/ CEIA-Empathy-in-Conflict-Resolution.pdf, accessed 10 July 2016.

27. J. Duffy, 'Empathy, Neutrality and Emotional Intelligence: A Balancing Act for the Emotional Einstein', *Queensland University of Technology Law and Justice Journal* 10(1), 2010, pp. 44–61.

28. Ibid., and Skype conversation with Waldman, 22 April 2016.

29. Quoted in Pinker, *The Better Angels of Our Nature*, pp. 708–10.

30. https://www.theguardian.com/news/2015/nov/05/integrated-school-waterford-academy-oldham, accessed 21 September 2016.

31. Ibid., accessed 4 May 2016.

32. https://www.theguardian.com/commentisfree/2015/dec/06/ faith-british-schools-hope, accessed 8 May 2016.

33. Ibid., and http://accordcoalition.org.uk/2012/11/12/nearly-three-quarters-of-the-british-public-disagrees-with-religious-selection-in-admissions-at-state-funded-schools/, accessed 8 May 2016.

34. http://www.telegraph.co.uk/education/2016/03/14/primary-school-tables-faith-schools-dominating-rankings/, accessed 8 May 2016.

35. http://www.bbc.co.uk/news/uk-27273053, accessed 8 May 2016.

36. http://www.spectator.co.uk/2014/03/sorry-campaining-mums-its-faith-that-makes-faith-schools-work/, accessed 10 May 2016.

37. https://www.theguardian.com/education/2016/jan/26/end-favours-faith-schools-religion-communities, accessed 10 May 2016.

38. Emile Bruneau, Skype conversation, 3 February 2016; and http://www.nytimes.com/2015/03/22/magazine/the-brains-empathy-gap.html?_r=0, accessed 5 April 2016.

39. E. Bruneau et al., 'The Benefits of Being Heard: Perspective-Taking and "Perspective-Giving" in the Context of Intergroup Conflict', *Journal of Experimental Social Psychology* 48, 2012, pp. 855–66.

40. R. B. van Baaren et al., 'Mimicry and Prosocial Behavior', *Psychological Science* 15(1), 2004, pp. 71–4.

41. Skype conversation with Bruneau, 3 February 2016.

42. Powell, *Talking to Terrorists*, p. 1.

43. Ibid., p. 224.

44. Glover, *Humanity*, p. 150.

Chapter 8: The Art of Empathy

1. Haddon, *The Curious Incident of the Dog in the Night-Time*, Chapter 163.

2. Telephone interview with Jon Adams, 28 April 2016.

3. http://www.penguinrandomhouse.com/books/73405/the-curious-incident-of-the-dog-in-the-night-time-by-mark-haddon/9781101911617/, accessed 3 August 2016.

4. Quoted in Booth, *The Company We Keep*.

5. http://www.standard.co.uk/goingout/theatre/minefield-theatre-review-work-of-extraordinary-compassion-makes-courageous-statement-a3264491.html, accessed 13 June 2016.

6. Plato, *The Republic*, Book 3 (400d). https://tavaana.org/sites/default/files/Burnyeat99.pdf, accessed 1 August 2016.

7. Shelley, *A Defence of Poetry*, p. 34.

8. Krznaric, *Empathy*, p. 138.

9. Baron-Cohen, *The Essential Difference*, p. 2.

10. Gottschall, *The Storytelling Animal*, p. 67.

11. Borba, *UnSelfie*, Chapter 4.

12. Email correspondence with Jane Davis, 13 June 2016.

13. Ibid.

14. Oatley, *Such Stuff as Dreams*, p. 1.

15. https://www.youtube.com/watch?v=T2FsnPzgZJw, accessed 3 August 2016.

16. Shakespeare, *Richard III*, Act 5, scene 6, line 49. Greenblatt et al. (eds), *The Norton Shakespeare*, p. 593.

17. https://www.youtube.com/watch?v=mWIpo7xi6MI, accessed 10 June 2016.

18. Williams, *Culture and Society 1780–1950*, p. 119.

19. Keltner et al. (eds), *The Compassionate Instinct*, p. 23.

20. Interview with Rubasingham, August 2016.

21. Ibid.

22. https://en.wikipedia.org/wiki/Thomas_Aikenhead, accessed 20 July 2016.

23. K. Oatley et al., 'On Being Moved by Art: How Reading Fiction Transforms the Self', *Creativity Research Journal* 21(1), 2009, pp. 24–9. doi: http://dx.doi.org/10.1080/10400410802633392.

24. http://greatergood.berkeley.edu/article/item/a_feeling_for_fiction, accessed 1 Jun 2016.

25. G. Weston, 'The Art of Medicine: Developing Judgement, Not Being Judgemental,' *Lancet*, 10 January 2015, p. 385.